THE LANGUAGE AND LOGIC OF THE BIBLE: THE ROAD TO REFORMATION

THE LANGUAGE AND LOGIC OF THE BIBLE: THE ROAD TO REFORMATION

G. R. EVANS
Fitzwilliam College, Cambridge

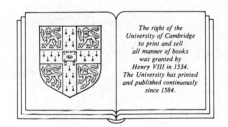

The right of the
University of Cambridge
to print and sell
all manner of books
was granted by
Henry VIII in 1534.
The University has printed
and published continuously
since 1584.

CAMBRIDGE UNIVERSITY PRESS

Cambridge
London   New York   New Rochelle
Melbourne   Sydney

Published by the Press Syndicate of the University of Cambridge
The Pitt Building, Trumpington Street, Cambridge CB2 1RP
32 East 57th Street, New York, NY 10022, USA
10 Stamford Road, Oakleigh, Melbourne 3166, Australia

First published 1985

Printed in Great Britain at
the University Press, Cambridge

Library of Congress catalogue card number: 85–4740

British Library cataloguing in publication data
Evans, G. R.
The language and logic of the Bible: the
road to reformation.
1. Bible – Hermeneutics
I. Title
220.6   BS476
ISBN 0 521 30548 9

T.D.

CONTENTS

Contents

III   Practical interpretation

ABBREVIATIONS

AHDLMA — *Archives d'histoire doctrinale et littéraire du moyen âge*

Aquinas — Commentary on Romans, Commentary on Galatians, Commentary on Thessalonians, in *Lecturae super Epistolas S. Pauli*, ed. P. Raphael, Rome, 1953

Arch. Frat. Pred. — *Archivum Fratrum Predicatorum*

Bellarmine — *De Verbo Dei*, Book I of *De Controversiis Christianae Fidei adversus huius temporis Haereticos*, Venice, 1587

Cahiers — *Cahiers de l'Institut Grec et Latin du Moyen Age*, Copenhagen

Cambridge History Bible — *Cambridge History of the Bible*, ed. G.W.H. Lampe, Cambridge, 1963–70

Cambridge History LMP — *Cambridge History of Later Mediaeval Philosophy*, ed. N. Kretzmann, A. Kenny, J. Pinborg, Cambridge, 1982

CCSL — *Corpus Christianorum Series Latina*

Coll. Franc. — *Collectanea Franciscana*

Fasciculi Zizaniorum — *Fasciculi Zizaniorum*, ed. W. W. Shirley, Rolls Series, 5, London, 1858

Language and Logic I — G. R. Evans, *The Language and Logic of the Bible: The Earlier Middle Ages*, Cambridge, 1984

Luther, *Table Talk* — Luther, *Table Talk*, ed. and tr. T. G. Tappert, Philadelphia, 1967

Luther, WA — *Martin Luthers Werke*, Weimar, 1906–80

Luther's *Works* — Luther, *Works*, tr. J. Pelikan et al., St Louis, 1960– , 55 vols.

PG — *Patrologia Graeca*

PL — *Patrologia Latina*

RTAM — *Recherches de théologie ancienne et médiévale*

Smalley, *Friars*	B. Smalley, *English Friars and Antiquity in the Early Fourteenth Century*, Oxford, 1960
Smalley, *Studies*	B. Smalley, *Studies in Mediaeval Thought and Learning*, Oxford, 1979
SSL	*Spicilegium Sacrum Lovaniense*
Wyclif, *Sermones* I–IV	Wyclif, *Sermones*, ed. J. Loserth, 1887–9 4 vols.

SOURCES

Abelard, Peter, Gloss on *De Interpretatione*, ed. M. dal Pra, in *Pietro Abelardo: Scritti di Logica*, Rome, 1969
Dialectica, ed. L. M. de Rijk, Assen, 1970
Adelard of Bath, *Quaestiones Naturales*, ed. M. Müller, *Beiträge zur Geschichte der Philosophie*, 31, 2, 1934
Albertus Magnus, *Postilla super Isaiam*, ed. F. Siepmann, Aschendorff, 1952
Alexander of Hales, *Glossa in Quatuor Libros Sententiarum Petri Lombardi*, Quaracchi, Florence, 1951
Anselm, *Opera Omnia*, ed. F. S. Schmitt, Rome, Edinburgh, 1938–69
Aquinas, Thomas, *Quaestiones Disputatae*, ed. R. Spiazzi, Rome, Turin, 1928
Catena Aurea, ed. P. Angelici Guarentini, Rome, 1953
Lecturae super Epistolas S. Pauli, ed. P. Raphael, Rome, 1953
Summa Theologiae, ed. P. Caramello, Turin, 1962–3, 3 vols.
Augustine, *Soliloquies*, PL 32
Bacon, Roger, *Opus Maius*, ed. J. H. Bridges, Oxford, 1897
Bellarmine, Robert, *De Verbo Dei*, Book I of *De Controversiis Christianae Fidei adversus huius Temporis Haereticos*, Venice, 1587, 3 vols.
The Use and Great Moment of the Notes of the Church, London, 1687
Liber de Locis Communibus, ed. S. Tromp, Rome, 1935
Biel, Gabriel, *Defensorium Obedientiae Apostolicae et alia Documenta*, ed. and tr. H. A. Oberman, D. E. Zerfoss and W. J. Courtenay, Cambridge, Mass., 1968
Collectorium circa Quattuor Libros Sententiarum, ed. W. Werbeck and U. Hofmann, Tübingen, 1973
Boethius, *De Hebdomadibus*, in *Theological Tractates*, ed. H. F. Stewart, E. K. Rand and S. J. Tester, London, 1973

Bonaventure, *Opera Omnia*, Quaracchi, Florence, 1882–1902, 11 vols.

Collationes in Hexameron, ed. R. P. F. Delorme, *Biblioteca Franciscana Scholastica Medii Aevi*, 8, Florence, 1934

Bradwardine, Thomas, *Treatise on Incipit and Desinit*, ed. O. L. Nielsen, *Cahiers*, 42, 1982, 1–83

Brevicoxa, *Tractatus de Fide et Ecclesia, Romano Pontifice et Concilio Generali*, in J. Gerson, *Opera Omnia*, ed. L. E. du Pin, Antwerp, 1706, I.805–904 and tr. H. A. Oberman, *Forerunners of the Reformation*, Eng. tr., London, 1967

Brito, Radulphus, *Quaestiones super Priscianum Minorem*, ed. H. W. Enders and J. Pinborg, Stuttgart, 1980

Bucer, Martin, *Commonplaces*, tr. D. F. Wright, Abingdon, 1972

Bull, George, *Harmonia Apostolica*, 1670, 2nd ed. Oxford, 1844

Buridan, John, *Quaestiones Longe super Librum Periermeneias*, ed. R. van der Lecq, *Artistarium*, Nijmegen, 1983

Burleigh, Walter, *De Puritate Artis Logicae*, ed. P. Boehner, New York, 1955

Quaestiones in Librum Perihermeneias, ed. S. F. Brown, *Franciscan Studies*, 34, 1974

Cajetan, Thomas de Vio, *Opera Omnia*, Lyons, 1639, 5 vols.

Calvin, John, *Opera Omnia*, ed. G. Baum *et al.*, *Corpus Reformatorum*, Berlin, 1863–1900, vols. 29–87, London, 1958

A Harmony of the Gospels, tr. A. W. Morrison, Edinburgh, 1972

Cassiodorus, *Opera*, CCSL, 96–8, Turnhout, 1958–73

Cicero, *Topics*, ed. H. M. Hubbell, London, 1968

Colet, John, *An Exposition of St. Paul's Epistle to the Romans*, ed. and tr. J. H. Lupton, London, 1873

Coverdale, M., *Remains*, ed. G. Pearson, Cambridge, 1846

Cranmer, *Remains*, ed. H. Jenkins, Oxford, 1833

Duns Scotus, *Commentaria Oxoniensia ad IV Libros Magistri Sententiarum*, ed. P. Marianus and P. M. F. Garcia, Florence, 1912, 2 vols.

Opera Omnia, ed. C. Balić *et al.*, Vatican, 1960–73, 17 vols.

Durand de Huesca, *Liber contra Manicheos*, ed. C. Thouzellier, SSL, 32, 1964

Eck, Johann, *Johann Ecks Predigttätigkeit*, ed. A. Brandt, Münster, 1914

Eckhardt, Meister, *Opus Tripartitum*, ed. K. Weisse, *Der Lateinischen Werke*, Stuttgart, 1964, vol. I

Parisian Questions and Prologues, tr. A. A. Maurer, Toronto, 1974

Erasmus, *Opus Epistolarum*, ed. P. S. Allen, H. M. Allen and H. W. Garrod, Oxford, 1906–58, 12 vols.

Erasmus and his Age, Selected Letters, ed. H. J. Hillerbrand and M. A. Haworth, New York, 1970

Fisher, John, *Opera Omnia*, Würzburg, 1697, facsimile, 1967

Fulke, William, *Defence of the English Translation of the Holy Scriptures*, ed. C. H. Hartshorne, Cambridge, 1843

Gagny, Jean, *Clarissima et Facillima in Quatuor Sacra Iesu Christi Evangelia necnon in Actus Apostolicos Scholia*, Paris, 1552

Gerson, Jean, *Six Sermons*, ed. L. Mourin, Paris, 1946

Oeuvres Complètes, ed. P. Glorieux, Paris, 1963, vol. V

Gilbert of Poitiers, *Commentaries on Boethius*, ed. N. M. Häring, Toronto, 1966

Godfrey of Fontaine, *Abridgement of Boethius of Dacia's 'Modi Significanti' sive 'Quaestiones super Priscianum Maiorem'*, ed. A. C. Senape McDermott, *Studies in the History of Linguistics*, 22, Amsterdam, 1980

Grosseteste, Robert, *De Libero Arbitrio*, ed. L. Baur, Aschendorff, 1919

Hexameron, ed. R. C. Dales and S. Gieben, London, 1983

Hildegard, *Analecta Sanctae Hildegardis*, ed. J. B. Pitra, *Spicilegium Solesmensis*, 1880, and M. Böckeler, Salzburg, 1975

Humbert of Romans, *Opera de Vita Regulari*, ed. N. J. Berthier, Rome, 1888–9

Treatise on the Formation of preachers, in S. Tugwell, *Early Dominicans*, London, 1982

Hus, John, *Super IV Sententiarum*, ed. W. J. Flajšhans and M. Komínková, *Opera Omnia*, 2, Prague, 1903

Jacobus Faber Stapulensis, *Commentarii in Epistolas Pauli*, Cologne, 1531

Jerome, *In Galatians*, PL 26

John of Ragusa, Oration at the Council of Basle, N. *Coleti, Concilia*, 17, Venice, 1781

Jordan of Saxony, *Liber Vitasfratrum*, ed. R. Arbesmann and W. Hümpfner, New York, 1943

Luther, Martin, *Vorlesung über den Hebräerbrief*, 1517–18, ed. J. Ficker, Leipzig, 1929

Vorlesung über den Hebräerbrief nach der vatikanischen Handschrift, ed. E. Hirsch and H. Rückert, Berlin, 1929

Werke, ed. E. Vogelsang *et al.*, Berlin, 1955

Briefwechsel, ed. E. L. Enders, Stuttgart, 1884ff

Werke, Kritische Gesamtausgabe, Weimar, 1906–80

Table Talk, ed. and tr. T. G. Tappert, *Works*, 54, Philadelphia, 1967

Marsilio Ficino, *Opera*, Basle, 1561

The Philebus Commentary, ed. and tr. J. B. Allen, California, 1975

Marsilius of Inghen (d. 1396), *Treatises on the Properties of Terms*, ed. and tr. E. P. Bos, Dordrecht, 1983

Marsilius of Padua, *Defensor Pacis*, ed. C. W. Prévité-Orton, Cambridge, 1928

Martin of Alnwick, *De Veritate et Falsitate Propositionis*, in L. M. de Rijk, 'Some Fourteenth Century Tracts on the *Probationes Terminorum*', *Artistarium*, 3, 1982

Mathesius, Johann, *Ausgewählte Werke*, ed. G. Losche, Prague, 1906, vol. 3

Matthew of Janova, *Regulae Veteris et Novi Testamenti*, ed. V. Kybal and O. Odložilik, Innsbruck and Prague, 1908–26, 5 vols.

Melanchthon, Philip, *Opera Omnia*, *Corpus Reformatorum*, Brunswick, 1834–59, vols. 1–27

Werke, ed. H. Engelland, Tübingen, 1952, 1952 and R. Nürnberger, Tübingen, 1961

Loci Communes, ed. and tr. C. L. Manschreck, Oxford, 1965

Neckham, Alexander, *Correctiones super Genesim*, British Library, London, MS Harley 6

Nicholas of Dresden, 'Master Nicholas of Dresden, the Old Colour and the New', ed. H. Kaminsky, D. L. Bilderbach, I. Boba and P. N. Rosenberg, *Transactions of the American Philosophical Society*, 55, 1965, 5–93

Nicholas of Lyra, *Biblia cum Glossa Ordinaria et Expositione Litterali et Morali necnon Additionibus ac Replicis*, Basle, 1498, 6 vols.

Origen, *Werke*, ed. P. Koetschau *et al.*, Leipzig, 1899, vol. 1– .

Paul of Venice, *Logica Magna: De Suppositionibus*, ed. A. R. Perreiah, New York, 1971

Peter Aureoli, *Compendium Sensus Litteralis Totius Divinae Scripturae*, ed. P. Seeboeck, Florence, 1896

Peter Lombard, *Sententiae*, Florence, 1971–81, 4 vols.

Peter of Rheims, *Sermon on the Evangelists*, in S. Tugwell, *Early Dominicans*, London, 1982

Peter of Spain, *Tractatus Syncategorematum*, tr. J. P. Mullaly, Milwaukee, 1964

Pico della Mirandola, *Opera Omnia*, 1557–73, ed. C. Vasoli, Hildesheim, 1969

Conclusiones, ed. B. Kieszkowski, Geneva, 1973

Poole, Matthew, *A Commentary on the Holy Bible*, 1685, repr. London, 1963, 3 vols.

On Revelation, reprinted London, 1963

Quidort, John, *De Potestate Regia et Papali*, ed. F. Bleienstein, Stuttgart, 1969

Raymonde of Sabunde, *Theologia Naturalis*, 1502

Reuchlin, Johannes, *Lexicon Hebraicum*, Basle, 1537

Sacconi, Raynerius, *Summa de Catharis, Arch. Frat. pred.*, 44, 1974, 31–60

Staphylus, Frederick, *Apologiae*, Antwerp, 1565

Stapleton, Thomas, *Promptuarium*, Antwerp, 1583

Relectio Scholastica, in *Opera*, Paris, 1620, I.507–838

A Fortress of the Faith first Planted among us Englishmen, St Omer, 1625

Stillingfleet, William, *The Council of Trent Examin'd and Disproved by Catholic Tradition*, 2nd ed., *corrected with an Appendix concerning the Prohibiting of Scripture in Vulgar Languages*, London, 1688

Thomas of Erfurt, *Grammatica Speculativa*, ed. and tr., G. L. Bursill-Hall, London, 1972

Thomas of Sutton, *Quodlibeta*, ed. M. Schmaus and M. González-Haba, Munich, 1969

Quaestiones Ordinarie, ed. J. Schneider, Munich, 1977

Tyndale, William, *Works*, ed. H. Walter, Cambridge, 1848–50

Whitaker, William, *A Disputation on Holy Scripture*, ed. W. Fitzgerald, Cambridge, 1849

William of Ockham, *Tractatus contra Benedictum*, ed. H. S. Offler, *Guillielmi de Ockham, Opera Politica*, 3, Manchester, 1956

De Praedestinatione, ed. P. Boehner and S. Brown, Franciscan Institute, 1978

Quodlibeta Septem, ed. J. C. Wey, New York, 1980

William of Sherwood, *Introductiones in Logicam*, ed. M. Grabmann, Munich, 1937, tr. N. Kretzmann, Minneapolis, 1966

Syncategoremata, ed. J. R. O'Donnell, *Mediaeval Studies*, 3, 1941, 46–93

Wilson, Thomas, *The Arte of Rhetorique*, 1553, facsimile with introduction, R. H. Bowers, Florida, 1962

Wyclif, John, *Polemical Works*, ed. R. Buddensieg, London, 1883, 2 vols.

Sermones, ed. J. Loserth, London, 1887–9, 4 vols.

Logica, ed. M. H. Dziewicki, London, 1893–9, 3 vols.

Opus Evangelicum, ed. J. Loserth, London, 1895
De Mandatis Divinis, ed. F. D. Matthew, London, 1896
De Veritate Sacrae Scripturae, ed. R. Buddensieg, London, 1905
De Statu Innocentiae, ed. J. Loserth and F. D. Matthew, London, 1922
De Trinitate, ed. A. du Pont Brech, Colorado, 1972
Summa Insolubilium, ed. P. V. Spade and G. A. Wilson, forthcoming
Zwingli, Ulrich, *Opera Omnia, Corpus Reformatorum*, Berlin, Zurich, 1901–1959, vols. 88–101
Of the Clarity and Certainty of the Word of God, tr. G. W. Bromiley, London, 1953

Anonymous

Accessus ad Auctores, ed. R. B. C. Huygens, Leiden, 1970
'Anonymi Bodleiani in Sophisticos Elenchos Aristotelis Commentarii Fragmentum', ed. S. Ebbesen, *Cahiers*, 8, 1972, 3–32
Fasciculi Zizaniorum, ed. W. W. Shirley, *Rolls Series*, 5, London, 1858
Four English Political Tracts of the Later Middle Ages, ed. J. P. Genet, London, 1977
Heresy Trials in the Diocese of Norwich, 1428–31, ed. N. P. Tanner, London, 1977
Incertorum Auctorum Quaestiones super Sophisticos Elenchos, ed. S. Ebbesen, Copenhagen, 1977
Logica Modernorum, ed. L. M. de Rijk, Assen, 1967
Monumenta historica S. Dominici, ed. M. H. Laurent, *Monumenta Ordinis Fratrum Praedicatorum Historica*, 15, Paris, 1933
Selections from English Wycliffite Writings, ed. A. Hudson, Cambridge, 1978
English Wycliffite Sermons, ed. A. Hudson, Oxford, 1983

BIOGRAPHICAL NOTES ON SOME OF THE MASTERS AND SCHOLARS MENTIONED IN THE TEXT

ALEXANDER OF HALES, (c. 1186–1245). He was educated and taught at Paris. In 1236 he joined the relatively new Franciscan Order and continued, now as one of the leading mendicant academics, to hold a Chair at Paris. He was one of the Masters who seems to have been influential in encouraging the use of Peter Lombard's *Sentences* as the basic textbook for theology students, after the Bible. (On Peter Lombard's *Sentences*, see pp. 101ff.).

AQUINAS, THOMAS, (c. 1225–74). He was educated first at the Benedictine house at Monte Cassino, then at the University of Naples. In 1244 he became a Dominican and was sent to study at Paris, under Albertus Magnus. In 1248 he accompanied Albert to Cologne, where he went to teach at the Dominican *studium generale*. Aquinas returned to Paris four years later to become lecturer at the Dominican house at St Jacques. He continued to lecture for the Order at Paris and in Italy. He was valuable to the Dominicans in several ways, but notably (for our purposes) as the compiler of a syllabus and textbooks of systematic theology which complemented the study of the Bible. He was a commentator, too, and his *Catena Aurea* brought together a 'chain' of patristic material for use in the study of Scripture.

BACON, ROGER, (c. 1214–92). He began his studies at Oxford. By 1236, if not before, he was in Paris, where he lectured on Aristotle's scientific works. About 1247 he gave up his chair to concentrate on scientific work, including some experimentation. About 1251 he returned to England and it is probably about then that he joined the Franciscan Order. In the later 1250s he was back in France. In the mid-60s Pope Clement IV asked him for an account of his teaching and Bacon set about writing his *Opus Maius* and his *Opus Minus* and other pieces, which he sent to the Pope. They reached him too late; he died in 1268, and Bacon was not only denied papal recognition but also condemned by many who found his views novel and his temper unpleasant. Bacon questioned many established ideas. Although he was not primarily a Biblical scholar, he argued for the importance of the study of Greek and Hebrew as a basis for exegesis, and took a fresh look at problems of textual criticism.

BELLARMINE, ROBERT, (1542–1621). An Italian Jesuit, he became Professor of Theology at Louvain in 1570. In 1576 he went to Rome, where he became Professor of Controversial Theology at the newly-founded Collegium Romanum. He brought to his work there a knowledge of the theological work of the reformers which he had gained at Louvain. He was made a cardinal in 1599. He was a prominent controversialist, whose *Disputationes de Controversiis Christianae Fidei* (printed in three volumes, 1586–93) set out clearly and systematically the arguments for the Roman Catholic position against that of various reforming schools of thought. He included a substantial section on the Bible.

BIEL, GABRIEL, (c. 1420–95). He was educated at Heidelberg and Erfurt and later joined the Brethren of the Common Life at Butzbach. He was responsible, with Count Eberhard of Würtemberg, for founding the University of Tübingen, and was Professor of Theology there. He was a follower of William of Ockham and one of the last major scholastic thinkers. He was also eclectic and forward-looking in his commentaries, of which the most notable is perhaps his commentary on the *Sentences* of Peter Lombard (see pp. 101ff.).

BONAVENTURE, (1221–74). He was born John of Fidenza and studied at Paris under Alexander of Hales. He taught at Paris from 1248 until 1255 and again from 1257. He preferred to keep clear of the new Aristotelianism as far as possible and to keep to the Fathers, although he was well-grounded in logic and familiar with much of the new learning. He attempted to bring together the analytical and academic study of theology with the spiritual and aspiring in a way which is more characteristic of the twelfth century than of his own. His commentaries on the Bible show strong marks of the new learning, although they are substantially traditional.

BRADWARDINE, THOMAS, (c. 1290–1349). He studied at Oxford. Bradwardine was respected as a theologian and mathematician and he acted in various diplomatic capacities on behalf of the king, as well as pursuing a career in ecclesiastical adminis-

tration. He was consecrated Archbishop of Canterbury shortly
before his death. He supported the doctrine of the necessity and
irresistibility of divine grace against a group of contemporary
'Pelagians', and it is in this connection that he appears in this
study.

BUCER, MARTIN, (1491–1551). He became a Dominican in 1506. In
1518 he began to correspond with Luther. In 1521 he received
a papal dispensation from his monastic vows and soon after he
married. He became a leader of reform in Switzerland especially
after the death of Zwingli in 1531 and in Germany. He took part
in unsuccessful conferences between Protestants and Roman
Catholics at Hagenau (1540), Worms (1540) and Ratisbon
(1541), and tried unsuccessfully to introduce reformed doctrines at Cologne. In 1549 he went to England in disillusion,
where he was welcomed by Edward VI and Cranmer. In the
same year he became Regius Professor of Divinity at
Cambridge. He had some influence on Cranmer.

CALVIN, JOHN, (1509–64). His parents intended him for an ecclesiastical career, but after some years of study at Paris (1523–8) he
seems to have doubted his vocation. He went on to study law at
Orléans and then at Bourges. There he came under the influence
of a group of protestant thinkers. He wanted to settle in Basle as
a scholar, and there he wrote the first edition of the *Institutes*,
published early in 1536. But in 1536 he felt it his duty to join
Farel in organising the reforming changes which were under
way at Geneva. He was appointed preacher and Professor of
Theology there. After an interlude at Strasbourg, where he
became a close friend of Martin Bucer (1538–41) and completed a fresh edition of his *Institutes* and a commentary on
Romans, he returned to Geneva. Before his death his influence
as a controversialist and theologian spread widely beyond
Geneva. He is the author of a massive series of commentaries on
the Bible.

COLET, JOHN, (1466?–1519). He studied at Oxford, and later at the
University of Paris, and in Italy, where he was able to learn
Greek. His humanist sympathies and the Neoplatonic ideas he
picked up in Italy helped form a strong bond of friendship
between Colet and Erasmus of Rotterdam. He was also a friend
of Sir Thomas More. He delivered a series of lectures at Oxford
on the Pauline Epistles in 1497. From 1505 he was Dean of St
Paul's, and when, on his father's death, he inherited a fortune,

he founded St Paul's School, where Greek was taught as well as Latin (to boys of every nationality).

ECK, JOHANN, (1486–1543). From 1510 he was Professor of Theology at Ingolstadt. He was influenced by humanists with whom he came into contact to write anti-scholastic commentaries on Aristotle and Peter of Spain. Friendly with Luther until he quarrelled with him in 1519, he became a leader of Catholic opposition to German protestantism and took the Catholic side at Augsburg in 1530, when the Lutheran confession of faith was presented to the Emperor Charles V for his approval. He himself published a German version of the Bible for Roman Catholic use in 1537. He is an example of a humanist who was not in the end attracted to the reforming position.

ERASMUS, DESIDERIUS, (c. 1466–1536). He was educated by a humanist Master at the school of the Brethren of the Common Life. In 1486 he became an Augustinian canon and in 1492 he was ordained priest. In 1495 he studied at Paris, and in 1499 travelled to England with his pupil William Blount. He made a friend of John Colet and, on a later visit to England, of Thomas More. He continued to lead a wandering life, settling at Basle from 1521 to 1529 and then at Freiburg until 1535. He produced a Greek New Testament with a new translation into classical Latin and editions of a number of works of the Fathers, as well as writing on matters of theological controversy.

FULKE, WILLIAM, (1538–89). He was educated at St John's College, Cambridge. He became a fellow in 1564, and in 1578 was elected Master of Pembroke Hall. He took a prominent part in controversy, supporting the puritan position against the Jesuit Edmund Campion. His influence was mainly confined to England.

GERSON, JEAN, (1363–1429). He studied and taught at Paris, working for reform of the Church on the side of the Conciliarists, but without wanting to deny papal primacy. A major author of spiritual writings, including commentaries on the Magnificat and the Song of Songs, his mystical teaching was influential on Martin Luther in his youth and on a number of Counter-Reformation figures, notably Robert Bellarmine. He was also the author of a body of sermons, some in the vernacular, which he used as a vehicle for commentary, too.

GROSSETESTE, ROBERT, (d. 1253). He studied at Oxford, where he became Chancellor and the first instructor of the Franciscans there. He taught himself Greek and made translations of the new logical and scientific works of Aristotle now available in the schools. He wrote a number of Biblical commentaries, notably that on the Hexameron, where he marshalled his scientific learning to some effect. From 1235 he was Bishop of Lincoln.

HOLCOT, ROBERT, (d. c. 1349). The author of a commentary on the *Sentences*, which was finished c. 1332–6, he held the Dominican Chair at Oxford until 1333–4. He may have been Regent at Cambridge later. He was one of the 'Pelagians' attacked by Thomas Bradwardine. His commentary on Wisdom was popular. He was also the author of commentaries on Ecclesiasticus and the twelve minor prophets.

HUS, JOHN, (c. 1369–1415). He taught at the University of Prague. Influenced by Wycliffite writings, he was condemned for similar opinions, for which he was martyred in 1415. Hus was especially drawn to Wyclif's political ideas (that property-owning was wrong and that society ought not to be organised in a way which kept some people forever as underdogs). He denounced corruption among the clergy, as Wyclif did, and disliked the Church's abuse of the system of Indulgences.

JOHN OF RAGUSA, (d. c. 1443). He entered the Dominican Order at an early age and in 1420 became Master of Theology at Paris. In 1422 he attended the Council of Pavia as Legate of the University. He preached the opening sermon at the Council of Basle of 1431.

LUTHER, MARTIN, (1483–1546). Educated at the cathedral school at Magdeburg and at the University of Erfurt, he became an Augustinian hermit. He was ordained priest in 1507 and sent to Wittenberg to study and lecture. He continued as professor there from 1511 until his death. Between 1515 and 1520 his thinking came to move along reforming lines. There were disputations, with Johann Eck and Martin Bucer among others. He was summoned before the Diet of Worms in 1521 and refused to alter his views. During the period which followed, when he broke with his Order and with the Church, he translated the Bible into German, and his teaching began to become influential. He is the author of a substantial corpus of Scriptural commentaries. On certain books of the Bible – the Psalms for example – he lectured more than once, and there is a clear development of thought and method between the earlier and the later versions. He was one of the most significant single figures in setting the Reformation in motion.

MARSILIUS OF PADUA, (c. 1275–1342). He studied at Padua and Paris and was the author of the *Defensor Pacis* (1324), an immensely controversial work in its own day. It presents a challenging and original view of the relationship of Church and State and it provided material for later thinkers who wanted to question the claims to power made by the Church in their own day. Wyclif is perhaps the most important of these in the use he made of these ideas in interpreting the Bible.

MELANCHTHON, PHILIP, (1497–1560). He studied at Heidelberg and Tübingen and in 1518 he became Professor of Greek at Wittenberg. A friend of Luther, his *Loci Communes* (1521) set out the doctrines of the reformers. He was present at several of the Diets and Colloquies which met on Reformation matters during the 1520s and at the Diet of Augsburg (1530), where he was mainly responsible for the framing of the Lutheran statement, the Augsburg Confession, which was presented to the Emperor Charles V. He was a man of stronger humanist leanings than many of the reformers. He was the author of a number of Biblical commentaries, in which he emphasised the need for a historian's approach to interpretation, but which also show the marks of scholastic method.

NICHOLAS OF LYRE, (c. 1270–1340). He was a Franciscan and was Regent Master at Paris from 1308. He was a Hebrew scholar and familiar with Jewish commentaries, although he did not know Greek. He set out to establish the literal sense of Scripture and to concentrate on it rather than the allegorical interpretations others preferred. The foundations he laid made him a standard author well into the sixteenth century, and his *Postillae* became the first Biblical commentary to be printed.

REUCHLIN, JOHANNES, (1455–1522). He studied Latin and Greek at Freiburg, Paris and Basle, studied law and became a diplomat. About 1485 he began to study Hebrew and became interested in cabbalistic teaching. He wrote plays. He became involved in controversies over the destruction of Hebrew books in Cologne; Reuchlin fought for their preservation. He was a great uncle of Melanchthon; he was anxious to separate him from Luther and was himself a Catholic until his death. His principal influence (for our purposes) was on the study of Hebrew. In 1506 he published a Hebrew grammar and lexicon (*De Rudibus Hebraicis*) and in 1512 an edition of the seven penitential Psalms in Hebrew with a Latin translation. In 1518 he published a treatise on Hebrew accents. His work encouraged contemporaries to add work on the Hebrew text of the Bible to the flourishing new endeavour concerned with the Greek.

TYNDALE, WILLIAM, (c. 1494–1536). He studied at Oxford and then at Cambridge. He began to plan a translation of the Bible about 1522, but the Bishop of London opposed the scheme. Tyndale went to Germany and never returned to England. His translation was printed at Cologne (where the local magistrates stopped it) and at Worms in 1525. Tyndale lived out his life mostly in the English House at Antwerp, working on the text of the New Testament and writing. He emphasised the authority of Scripture. He wrote some commentary (notably on Romans) and a number of controversial and theological works, among them *The Obedience of a Christian Man*.

WYCLIF, JOHN, (c. 1329–84). He studied and taught at Oxford until 1374. Late in his career he became involved in theological and political controversy. His followers led the Lollard movement. He developed the view that lordship depends on grace (*De Dominio Divino* and *De Civili Dominio*). He argued that the present corruption of the Church was an indication that it could not be in a state of grace, and therefore its property was forfeit. Conversely, since grace confers lordship, even the poor and humble have true lordship if they are in a state of grace. The only test of the acts of the Church was, said Wyclif, whether or not they conformed with Scripture. He denounced the worship of saints, and a number of other abuses. He wanted people to be able to read the Bible for themselves, and he began the translation into English which was continued by Nicholas of Hereford and Purvey.

ZWINGLI, ULRICH, (1484–1531). He studied at Berne, Vienna and Basle, and was an admirer of Erasmus; he learned Greek. He became leader of the Reformation in Switzerland, lecturing on the New Testament in 1519. He was not, it seems, much indebted to Luther's work. Nevertheless, he taught similar reforming doctrines: that all the apparatus of the Church was unnecessary; only the Gospel contained truth and in it was to be found all truth necessary to salvation. His main difference of opinion with Luther was over the doctrine of the Eucharist, which he developed in the 1520s. He believed that it was purely symbolic. Zwingli upheld his opinions in more than one public disputation, and his movement divided Switzerland between his reforming party and its opponents. His influence extended beyond Switzerland through his writings.

INTRODUCTION

The Protestant sixteenth century saw changes in the study of the Bible which had huge consequences. A new textual criticism, an acceptance of translations into the vernacular, new theological pre-occupations, brought elements in the Bible's teaching which had not been so apparent before to a lasting prominence. It was felt that a necessary break was being made with the traditions of the late Middle Ages, that there was much which had to be rejected in the scholasticism of previous generations. Erasmus of Rotterdam wrote to his friend Martin Dorp in May, 1515:

What connection is there, I ask, between Christ and Aristotle? Between the petty fallacies of logic and the mysteries of eternal Wisdom? What is the purpose of this maze of disputations? How much of it is deadening and destructive by the very fact that it breeds contention and disagreement! Some problems, of course, should be investigated and others definitely settled . . . But on the other hand, there are many problems which it would be better to pass over than to examine.[1]

The reformers and the pioneers of the new criticism were not by any means always in agreement. Erasmus accuses Luther of a lack of the 'courtesy' of Christ himself: that 'evangelical spirit' which 'has its own prudence, . . . its own courtesy and gentleness'. 'What has been accomplished,' he asks, 'by so many harsh little books, by so much foolish talk, by so many formidable threats, and by so much bombast, save that what was previously debated in the universities as probable opinion may be hereafter an article of faith, and that then indeed it may be scarcely safe to teach the Gospel, while everything is seized and misrepresented because all have been exasperated?'[2] Controversy breeds hard opinions and extreme views. One result was an artificial crystallising of the picture sixteenth century reformers had of the scholastics and their opinions. In certain respects, these opinions were brought into sharp focus; a good deal else was obscured.

The temper of Erasmus's own mind was more moderate and more subtle in its selection of helps from the past. He was heir to a long

1

tradition of Italian humanism which had run quite comfortably
beside scholastic endeavour for a century or two. He sees no objection to using 'certain comparisons between the divine and the
human', for did not the 'parables have something in common with
the fables of the ancients? Evangelical truth sinks in more pleasingly
and takes a firmer hold in souls when dressed up in these little entice-
ments than if it is simply stated as naked truth, an effect Augustine
certainly strives for in his work on Christian doctrine.'[3] That in the
end marked the character of the change: something was taken and
something left. Matthew Poole, writing in the seventeenth century,
approaches Romans with the same preliminary questions as Aquinas
had asked – why Paul was given his name; where Romans comes in
the sequence of the Pauline Epistles – and with some of his answers
drawn from the same tradition.[4]

This study seeks to show something of the direction of endeavour
of the last mediaeval centuries in work on the Bible, and to point
towards some of its results in the debates of the sixteenth century.
There was, undoubtedly, much in the outcome that was new and
revolutionary and a sense of making a fresh start. But the extent to
which mediaeval scholarship led the way has often been underesti-
mated, and the condemnation of the scholastics has tended to sink
with them a proper recognition of what they achieved as students of
the Bible. Sixteenth century writers were themselves not always quite
clear what it was they were putting behind them. They were less clear
still perhaps how much they were taking with them.

I have tried to tell the story up to the end of the twelfth century in
an earlier volume.[5] This is its sequel. It can be no more than an
interim study. A vast quantity of commentary material remains in
manuscript. We are particularly ill-informed about the fifteenth century. But the main lines of development seem clear enough, and
perhaps there is something to be said for setting them out as the skel-
eton of that bridge which must be made from the Middle Ages into
the sixteenth century if we are to understand the nature of Reformation and Counter-Reformation thinking about the Bible.

Certain influential aspects of the late mediaeval study of the Bible
have had to be neglected in order to bring the problems raised by the
Bible's language to the forefront: the liturgical use of the Bible; the
way the Bible was used to support new political movements; the
relationship between Bible study and canon law; the mystics'
approach to the Bible; the influence of the new Platonism. (In the
areas of technical discussion with which this study is chiefly con-

cerned Aristotle is dominant.) These aspects can only be touched on here. I hope in due course to continue the story in a study of the sixteenth century and its immediate environs in which the work of the humanists on the original languages and the great questions of reform can be given greater space and weight. On the road to Reformation certain features can be seen ahead. They remain glimpses until we can come up to them and see them at close quarters, but it is important to understand the lie of the land first. This book attempts to provide a map of the later mediaeval scene and a pointer to what lay ahead, as questions of logic gave way to questions of language.

PART I

SCRIPTURE'S DIVINE WARRANT

1

'SCRIPTURE HATH FOR ITS AUTHOR GOD HIMSELF'

1

During the sixteenth century the Church in the West ceased to be a single body of the faithful. The Protestant reformers brought about a division in which lay many further divisions. Thomas Stapleton (1535–98), the English Catholic polemicist, sneers at the multiplicity and confusion of protestant beliefs:

Now, so ye be no priest, ye may be a Sacramentary, an Anabaptist, or a Lutheran; and then a Civil, a Zealous or a Disordered Lutheran, among all which ye may choose of what sort in each branch ye list to be; whether ye allow two sacraments with the Zealous Lutherans, three with the Leipsians or four with the Wittenbergers; whether ye will be an Osiandrin, a half-Osiandrin or an Antiosiandrin.[1]

In the web of politics, social and economic change and religious and theological developments which brought about this fragmentation one continuous thread is visible from at least the beginning of the fourteenth century. Those scholars and preachers and demagogues (Marsilius of Padua, Wyclif and the Lollards, the Hussites, for example) who challenged the authority of the Church as it was then institutionally constituted, held up the authority of the Bible in its place and argued that the interpretation of Scripture was no matter for the Church to regulate if by the Church was meant the Pope and his cardinals. Instead, the individual must read for himself under the guidance of the Holy Spirit.

The study of the Bible had always formed the basis of Christian theological endeavour; so much so that it was not until the twelfth or thirteenth century that the word 'theology' came into use in the schools of the West alongside 'the study of the Sacred Page'. The changes of the late Middle Ages in the way the Bible was interpreted did not altogether supersede the old approach but they altered the emphasis and threw new light on the whole enterprise. Their importance in the events of the sixteenth century is perhaps best understood if we take the work of late mediaeval Bible study as a whole, old and new together, and try to get a picture of what it was that the reformers thought they had discovered.

Discovery it seemed to be. His first encounter with a copy of the Bible, which he had – like most mediaeval students – met before only in pieces, had a powerful impact on Luther:

On one occasion he came across a Latin Bible such as he had never seen. Greatly astonished, he observed that it contained far more passages, epistles and gospels than were customarily expounded in the postils and from the pulpits. Since all was so new to him he began to desire earnestly that God would sometime give him a copy of this book.[2]

Biblical study in this spirit of discovering a new world focussed and brought together otherwise disparate elements, many of which were far from new,[3] in the discontent of the reformers. It made sense of much that was being said. For Luther, its force and power was the greater because he was deeply offended by what he saw as a young man in Rome: the cynicism of those celebrating Mass, for example.

But for all its directness and air of cutting through a muddle of accretions to the truth, Bible reading was still a matter of close, detailed study. Luther again: he was troubled by the word 'righteousness' in the first chapter of Romans, because he was haunted by a sense of sin, even though he led a life as a monk which he could not see how to make better. Then it seemed to become clear to him that the word has a 'passive' sense in this passage, that is, that it refers not to God's punishment of the sinner but to his justification of the sinner by his mercy. Luther was filled with joy at this discovery. 'My mind ran through the Scriptures,' he says, 'as far as I was able to recollect them, seeking analogies in other phrases, such as the work of God, by which he makes *us* strong, the wisdom of God by which he makes *us* wise', and so on.[4] To his friend and superior Staupitz he wrote in a letter of 1518, 'This your word fixed itself in me like a sharp arrow of the mighty. At once I began to compare it with the Scripture texts on repentance. And behold, I had a most pleasant surprise! Statements from all sides began to stand forth in harmony, and, plainly smiling, to gather round this dictum, so that the word "repentance", which had been the most bitter term in the whole Bible to me, . . . now became to me the most sweet and pleasant-sounding word of all.' He did not stop at comparing texts. He looked into the Greek and 'discovered that the original meaning of this Greek word *metanoia*, from *meta* and *nous*, which mean "afterwards" and "mind", is "coming to one's right mind again" . . . Next I saw, as I made progress, that *metanoia* can also be derived from "over again" and signify a change of mind and affection, indicating, it seems, not only the fact, but also the method of the change, that is, the grace of God.'[5]

2

Scripture hath for its author God himself; from whom it first proceeded and came forth. Therefore, the authority of Scripture may be proved from the author himself, since the authority of God himself shines forth in it.[6]

The English Calvinist and contentious Cambridge academic William Whitaker (1547–95) takes a position which had come to be central to the thought of the reformers: that God not only provides the only sure witness to the truth of the Bible, but that he does so exclusively in what he says in the Bible itself.

The first of these ideas, that God is his own authority, is one thing, and by and large caused no difficulties in the Middle Ages.

The fifteenth century advent of the new Platonism, although it threatened to turn the theory of knowledge on its head, did not disturb this picture. Rather, it reinforced it. Aristotle's epistemology tends to draw knowledge from sensation, Plato's from the inward teaching of God.[7] Marsilio Ficino (1433–99) describes the authoritative divine illumination like this in an aside on Scripture in his commentary on the *Philebus*:

It is not without great mystery that Paul attributes all the acts of a living being to the divine word, making it penetrate the spirit and the soul and the body, making it distinguish between affections and thoughts and see and hear all. It's as if God himself were there in his words even when they're represented through the prophets.[8]

The second notion in Whitaker, the principle of *sola scriptura*, is another and more controversial matter. To assert that God authorises for belief only what he says in the Bible and that he does so directly to the individual reader, is to challenge the Church both as official interpreter of the Bible and as having authority to decide questions of doctrine. These implications gave a coloration to the debates of the sixteenth century protestants so strong that it sometimes obscures other elements in the mediaeval discussion of Scripture's authority which went into the forming of the reformers' ideas. Of these old and deep threads the clearest and most continuous with mediaeval work, and with the patristic tradition to which fresh direct reference was now being made, was the principle that God 'authorises' his own Scriptures, and we must begin from that.

3 The image of God

The Trinity, says the thirteenth century Franciscan Alexander of Hales, is revealed in three ways: by teaching (*doctrina*), as through authoritative writings (*ut per auctoritatem*); by means of created things, which are the works of the Trinity; by the inspiration of faith (*inspiratione fidei*). In the last, God works directly. The others may involve human agents.[9] Behind those human agents stands God, authenticating what he chooses to teach through men. The doctrine that God bears witness to himself like this[10] is a commonplace of early mediaeval exegesis. On it rests the mediaeval notion of Biblical authority. Still in the thirteenth century, the Dominican Thomas Aquinas has in mind the first two methods when he explains that Paul's preaching was authenticated not only by the arguments he used (*doctrina*) but also by signs which confirmed that God was speaking through him.[11]

This account of authority was not unchallenged. English Wycliffite writings protest about the tendency for 'images' to become objects of worship in themselves, as the 'rude wittis of many' forget that all wonders are God's work and attribute them to statues or pictures.[12] Some of the Lollards themselves were not free from confusion: one Margery Baxter, tried for heresy at Norwich in the third decade of the fourteenth century, believed that the honouring of images was wrong because they contained devils, who fell with Lucifer and entered into the *ymagines* which stand in churches and dwell there.[13] Margery Baxter's notion reflects the long tradition of heretical dualist teaching going back to the Gnostics, which was interfused with Lollardy at a number of points; it represents the view that no material thing can body forth a God who is all spirit, and that only spiritual beings in whom something has gone fearsomely wrong can manifest themselves in ways the senses can perceive. What the senses show us is likely to mislead us in the search for God. In the earlier instance, the 'rude wittis' of simple men are led astray in this way, so that they fail to see God because the image itself strikes their imaginations so forcibly that they do not look beyond it. This questioning of the divine use of images runs as a counter-current in patristic and mediaeval thought in both East and West. But the usual view was that of Alexander of Hales: that God speaks in words in his

Scriptures and provides evidence for what he says in what can be observed in the natural world, in events and objects of various sorts; he confirms the truth of what he says by giving men an inner certainty, the gift of faith.

Raymonde of Sabunde describes the 'two books given us by God', the Book of Nature and the Book of Holy Scripture. The first was given to man at the creation of the world, and is available to everyone, a book which cannot be altered, into which no mistakes can creep. The second only the literate can read and it can be corrupted and misinterpreted. The two ought to be in perfect agreement, and so they are to the man who is *naturaliter rationalis*, and open to instruction (*Theologia Naturalis*, printed 1502, Prologue).

The idea that God teaches and confirms his teaching by signs still seemed sound to Melanchthon and Zwingli in the sixteenth century. Melanchthon explains that from the very beginning God set up external signs pointing to his Word. Adam, Abel, Seth and Noah sacrificed lambs by divine revelation to signify the Saviour to come, whom God himself would sacrifice for mankind. God himself told the Jews to circumcise their children to remind them of the sacrifices the patriarchs had made. In our own time he gives signs and pledges of divine grace in the sacraments.[14] His intention is to make it possible for those he calls to be sure that he calls them; he is demonstrating the authority of his Scriptures. In a sermon given to the Dominican nuns of the Oetenbach convent in 1522, Zwingli asks what is meant by saying that man is made in God's image. He looks at the way in which 'eyes, ears, a mouth, a face, hands and feet are all ascribed to God in Scripture'. This does not tell us that God has a body like ours. In terms much like those used by Gregory the Great in the sixth century to explain the same principle, Zwingli shows how these members are mentioned to help us understand in familiar terms the works of God: we see with our eyes, and so Scripture ascribes eyes to God to indicate his perfect knowledge and perception of all things. It ascribes ears to God because he 'hears' all our prayers, a mouth, because he reveals his will by his Word, a face because he gives and withholds grace like someone looking towards or away from us. It is apparent from these metaphorical references to the outward signs of the soul's operation in man that man's resemblance to God, the point at which he can be said to be made in his image, lies not in his body but in the soul, which acts, in its creaturely way, like the divine spirit. It is 'in respect of the mind or soul that we are made in the image of God' (and here Zwingli mentions Augustine's account of the 'trinity' of memory, will and understanding in the mind of man). Thus God speaks to us in the Word of Scripture, confirms what he says by using metaphors and images and things familiar to our bodily senses, and enlightens the mind of man inwardly by 'shining' on his understanding. Like Melanchthon, Zwingli is sure that this demonstrates God's wish to make what he says clear to men and to give them reason to accept its authority: God wanted to give his message to man in a gentle and attractive way, for it is the nature of that which is presented in parables and proverbs and riddles to appeal to men's understanding and bring them to knowledge. Images are helpful to human understanding and reassuring.[15]

'The Lord of mercy . . . has raised everywhere, in all places and in all things, his ensigns and emblems, under blazons so clear and intelligible that no-one can pretend ignorance in not knowing such a sovereign Lord; . . . who has, in all parts of the world, in heaven and on earth, written and as it were engraved the glory of his power, goodness, wisdom and eternity. St. Paul has therefore said quite rightly that the Lord has never left himself without a witness; even among those to whom he has never sent any knowledge of his word.'[16]

The mutual testimony borne to one another by the words of Scripture and the signs and miracles which witness to their truth (and are knit together by God in men's minds by faith) is nowhere more characteristically exemplified in Scripture than by the working out of prophecy's fulfilment.

The most popular and influential teaching in this area was undoubtedly that of Joachim of Fiore (c. 1132–1202). He looked at the Bible as a history of God's work, stretching not only back to the beginning but also to the end of the world, by prefiguring what was to come. He saw patterns of numbers and events repeated and he postulated that when they occurred again they would signify the imminence of the end of the world. But his popularity owed a great deal to the fact that he touched a chord in politically-minded interpreters, and he falls outside our immediate concern with the Bible's language.

In two further areas the subject of prophecy carried over from mediaeval to Reformation thinking as a topic of lively debate. Successful prophecy implies that the Holy Spirit has spoken through the prophet and that the will of God inescapably brings about what it wills; the sign is proved true in the event. The discussion of contin-

gent and necessary futurity much occupied late mediaeval scholastics, and we shall come to their work later (II.3.vi). The debate
reawakened the Pelagian controversy.[17] Reformation scholars
inherited an awareness of predestination as a burning issue. The connection with prophecy remained clear in Calvin's mind, but for him
the unfolding of God's purposes in history is bound up with a personal doctrine of predestination.[18] He concentrates not on reconcil-
ing free will and divine foreknowledge, but on the importance of a
conscious renunciation of the individual's free will, so that he leans
upon God and gives himself up to God's will for him.[19]

The second area of continuing debate in which the working out of
past signs in future realities was discussed involved the relationship
of the Old Testament to the New. This had consistently been an
important issue in Christian thought since the first Christian centuries. John Chrysostom took the view that the Old Testament points
forward to the New, providing additional evidence for the *excel-
lentia Christi* (PG 63.14). The difference between the two, for him as
for Aquinas and for Nicholas of Lyre, lies in the 'comparative excellence' of the New Testament. Christ is *superior* to the High Priests of
the Old Testament, but for the comparison to be made at all there
must be similarities as well as differences (PG 63.291). The Old
Testament is not merely a foreshadowing of the New, although it *is*
such a foreshadowing. In some sense it contains the New within it, by
prophecy and by describing persons and events which are 'types' of
what is to come. As William of Auxerre puts it in his thirteenth century account of Ezekiel's 'wheel within a wheel', 'the New Testament
is in the Old according to prefiguration and the Old in the New
according to exposition'.[20] There is equality of authority.

The general principle was entirely congenial to Melanchthon, who
held that the Christian faith is identical in all ages, that the faith given
to Adam was complete; that the Church of the two Testaments is the
same, its message the same. The New Covenant is, as it were, the
mirror-image of the Old. What was then in the future is now in the
past. The Apostles said nothing new; indeed they appealed to the Old
Testament for authority.[21] Tyndale says that 'the New Testament
was ever, even from the beginning of the world. For there were
always promises of Christ to come, by faith in which promises the
elect were then justified inwardly before God and outwardly before
the world by keeping of the law and ceremonies.'[22] Alexander of
Hales's pattern of divine teaching through Scripture, supported by
signs which prove to be reliable and confirmed inwardly by a God-

given faith, still provides the main elements in Tyndale's account, together with that awareness of the movement from past to future under an irresistible divine governance which was also strongly marked in mediaeval writers.[23]

This underlying structure of mutual authentication holds even for thinkers who would put the Old Testament somewhat lower than the New in certain respects. For Aquinas, the Old Testament derives its value from the *dignitas* of the witnesses, 'when it speaks through the prophets, to whom they were revealed before, the things which were to be fulfilled concerning the Incarnate Word'.[24] The guarantee of the *testimonium authenticum*[25] lies in the internal harmony by which the Bible speaks truly of itself and of what comes about in history and is related in its pages. In the seventeenth century we still find Matthew Poole commenting on the harmony of Revelation with 'Daniel's prophecy in the Old Testament, and with the types made use of by the holy prophets' and exclaiming at 'such an agreement of the doctrine contained within it with the doctrine of the Old and New Testament'.[26]

The emphasis of the reformers was upon the third of Alexander of Hales's proofs, the *inspiratio fidei*, but always in intimate connection with the words of Scripture which guide faith and which are endorsed by the experience of faith. Yet signs have, as we see, a place in their thinking, too; there remains a certain 'trinity' of authority supporting Scripture behind the claim that Christian doctrine is to be derived authoritatively from Scripture alone, *sola scriptura*.

2

THE HUMAN AUTHORS OF SCRIPTURE

'Canonical Scripture, both Testaments, that is, is believed to have been written by the Holy Spirit dictating and inspiring it (*dictante et inspirante*)',[1] says Gabriel Biel a century before the Reformation.

The words of the Bible were written down by human authors. Did they do so with a full understanding of what they were writing? Did the inspiration of the Holy Spirit extend to every letter they wrote or only to a general indication of what they were to say? Did the Holy Spirit intend every part of Scripture to be received in the same way, or are there levels of importance in the various parts of the Bible? Did the Holy Spirit supervise the transmission of the text at every stage, including its subsequent translation? Does he still do so? These questions arose in the Middle Ages with some force, but with an urgency masked to some extent by an overriding concern with the divine authorship of God himself and the implications of that divine authority for what the Bible says.

Following Augustine and Gregory, mediaeval authors had usually striven to see discrepancies in the text as evidences that God adapts himself to men in their limited and confused understanding. The notion that its oddities might be the result of human error uncorrected by the Holy Spirit was slow to take hold, although, as we shall see, there were some traces of it in later mediaeval discussions. Perhaps the single most important change in the principles of hermeneutics to be brought about by the sixteenth century humanists and reformers was this more general acknowledgement that there were not only copyists' errors of recent date, of which some mediaeval scholars had already tried to purge the text,[2] but long-standing errors and faults left in it by its human authors.

That concession went, perhaps ironically, with a renewed sense of the central importance of Scripture, as the only source of teaching the Christian ought to look to.

Even in the thirteenth century there was some awareness of the factor of human fallibility. The Franciscan Duns Scotus (c. 1264–1308) considers various possibilities: that the human authors of Scripture may have lied deliberately, or been deceived; he asks whether they could conceivably have been bribed to speak falsely, and so on.[3] Perhaps the question of most interest to thirteenth century scholars – possibly because it was prompted by Gregory the Great's widely-used account of prophets and prophecy in his Homilies on Ezekiel – was whether a true prophet always knows the meaning of what he is saying. Not all the Fathers thought so, but Hugh of St Cher, Master of Theology at the Dominican house in Paris, argues that there can be no prophecy without knowledge, and by implication that the human authors of Scripture wrote with understanding and in intelligent control of what they were saying. He marshals a series of texts to prove his assertion: for instance Daniel 10, and Job 13.1: 'My eye has seen all this and my ear has heard and I have understood.'[4]

Hugh of St Cher breaks down the prophetic experience into stages. God impresses the message on the prophet's mind; then God tells him what it means (*significationis revelatio*); and then the prophet announces it (*denonciatio*).[5] This account would seem to have been somewhat controversial among his contemporaries; examining various points in Cassiodorus's definition (as restated in the twelfth century by Peter Lombard) Hugh queries the statement that *revelatio* or *inspiratio* is *divina*. Unless the word 'divine' is redundant, that would seem to imply that some 'inspiration' is not divine. Hugh's view is that when knowledge (*cognitio*) comes from nothing (*ex nihilo*) and is made and formed by the Spirit, with nothing beforehand to suggest the image thus given (*nulla praeexistente similitudine*), it must be of God alone (*solius Dei est*).[6] The emphasis is upon prophecy as knowledge (*scientia*), (*cognitio*).

There are residual difficulties. We must suppose that 'inspiration' when it comes from demons or angels does not confer knowledge, but only an illusion of knowledge.[7] There is the problem of Jonah's unfulfilled prophecy. If we say that Jonah told a lie knowingly, we run into difficulties; if we say that he spoke the truth *secundum intentionem suam*, in intention and as far as he understood it, we run into another set of difficulties, especially the implication that he was a prophet who did not enjoy divine instruction about what he was saying. It seems, as Gregory the Great believed, that even true prophets sometimes do not prophesy by the Holy Spirit and cannot always tell the difference between a message given them by the Holy Spirit and a message which originates with themselves.[8] The only test of true prophecy is the good life of the prophet and the outcome of his prophecy.[9] These difficulties are not successfully resolved by Hugh, and his discussions clearly reflect a considerable body of contemporary debate. The question of inspiration remained a vexed one, in which it was unclear whether the human authors of Scripture in general, and the prophets in particular, spoke and wrote with a knowledge both that what they said was God's Word and of its meaning.

Hugh's contemporary Albertus Magnus considers some of these matters in the Prologue to his *Postilla super Isaiam*, as he looks at Isaiah's claim to be a prophet and the authority of what he says. He sums up the grounds on which his testimony is to be accepted. His very name is significant, the way his subject-matter fits with his name, the authority of the revelation, the quality of the vision, the holiness of his purpose, the value of the work, the faithfulness of his words (*a nominis cum materia congruitate, a revelationis auctoritate, a visionis qualitate, ab intentionis pietate, (ab) operis utilitate, a dictorum fidelitate*).[10]

The same issues were still current in the fourteenth century. Discussing Matthew 9.9–10: 'I say to you that he is a prophet and more than a prophet' in a sermon, Wyclif is led from his resolution of the apparent contradiction in the statement to a consideration of the nature of prophecy. Prophecy may concern past, present or future. Moses prophesied about the past when he wrote the account in Genesis about the creation of the world; Elisabeth prophesied about the present when the Mother of the Lord came to her; prophecies about the future are common. Tenses do not matter; there is no more than a formal difference (*differentia formalis*) between the statements 'Christ will be incarnate' and 'Christ was incarnate'. As to the prophet himself: he is a rational creature, having the spirit of prophecy, and so the prophet is as likely to be an angel as a man. He may understand what he prophesies (Christ himself was the *propheta maximus*) or he may not. A prophet ought to speak the truth.[11]

These mediaeval authors were worrying at the difficulty of assessing the human against the divine contribution to the text of the Sacred Page which lay before them. In the human author's failure to understand and to reproduce perfectly what the Word told him to write lay the best hope for the future of salvaging the absolute authority of Scripture while making it possible to acknowledge that there were errors in it; thus in some sense inspiration, while sure and reliable, was also fallible in its outworking in human writers.

Paradoxically, perhaps, a comparative diminishing of the standards of accuracy and consistency expected of the authors of Scripture was accompanied by a recognition of their humanity which
brought them to life. On the one hand we find Calvin saying that 'we
need not make a great fuss' over the identity of the writers of the
Gospel story; 'it has little significance for us, once we realise that he
was a witness of standing and of divine appointment, publishing
nothing except by the previous dictation of the Holy Spirit'.[12] In con-
trast, we have Luther in his table-talk entering into the mind of the
author of the book of Job as well as he is able. 'Job didn't speak the
way it is written, but he thought those things. One doesn't speak that
way under temptation. Nevertheless, the things reported actually
happened. They are like the plot of a story which a writer like
Terence adopts and to which he adds characters and circumstances.
The author wished to paint a picture of patience. It's possible that
Solomon himself wrote this book, for the style is not very different
from his. At the time of Solomon the story which he undertook to
write was old and well known. It was as if I today were to take up the
stories of Joseph or Rebekah. The Hebrew Poet, whoever he was,
saw and wrote about those temptations as Virgil described
Aeneas.'[13] In a similar spirit he tried to put himself in the place of the
characters described. 'It must have been very painful to Adam to
drive out his firstborn son . . . "Go away," he must have said, "and
don't let me ever see you again!" . . . Adam must have preached Cain
an earnest sermon.'[14] When his wife asked him about a passage in
Psalm 18 (20, 24) Luther answered, 'David is speaking even as I can
now speak to you.'[15]

Thus Luther could maintain on the one hand that no iota of the
Bible, no syllable, is in vain, and at the same time find no difficulty in
Matthew's making a mistake in referring to Jeremiah instead of
Zechariah (Matthew 27.9). 'Such points do not bother me particularly'. Calvin saw the human authors of Scripture as *authentici
amanuenses*, secretaries of the Holy Ghost, but he, too, could allow
for errors of detail.[16]

There remain some questions posed neatly late in the sixteenth
century by the English Counter-Reformation polemicist Thomas
Stapleton: 'The question is, from whom ought we to receive the
Scripture and through whom ought we to understand it?'[17] In short,
what of tradition (both in its broad sense of 'handing on' and in its
narrower sense of the oral as distinct from the written transmission

of the faith) and of the first Christian scholars and interpreters, the Fathers? A full treatment of the sixteenth century debate on Scripture and tradition must wait for a future volume, but the background has a place here.

3

HANDING ON AND EXPLANATIONS

1 The Fathers

In the late sixteenth century William Fulke gives a picture of the protestant position on the Fathers which, with a nice irony, both puts them in their secondary place and, at the same time, defers to their judgement. There is, he says, no intention on the part of the reformers 'to discredit the ... expositions of the Fathers'; the plan is 'to fetch the truth, upon which the hope of our salvation is grounded, out of the first fountains and springs', the Hebrew text of the Old Testament and the Greek text of the new, 'rather than out of any streams that are derived from them'. 'And this we do,' he adds, 'agreeable to the ancient Fathers' judgements.' The Fathers are not the 'first fountains and springs'. But they have authority, as 'derived' from the sources.[1] This idea that the Fathers derive an authority from a source behind them, and that their authority flows in a stream onward to others after them, is a standard picture. The Counter-Reformation polemicist Thomas Stapleton also finds it helpful in the sixteenth century; he employs the image in his *Praefatio ad Lectorem* in his *Promptuarium* on the Sunday Gospels (Antwerp, 1593).

Marsilius of Padua sets out to show in the early fourteenth century what power and authority Christ wanted to grant to the apostles and their successors. He argues a point 'in accordance with the mind of the Master of the *Sentences*', Peter Lombard, 'or rather of the Scripture and of the saints by whose authority he speaks'; and also in accordance with the opinion of Richard of St Victor. 'From these authorities of the saints, the Master and Richard, it is thus clear ... '[2] Despite all that he has to say that is new, the structure of authority for Marsilius remains a conventional one. He takes it as 'self-evident to all Christians' not only that 'the Holy Scripture must be firmly believed and acknowledged to be true', but that the same firm belief must be given to the 'interpretations of the Fathers', for it is evident that 'it must be piously held that these interpretations were revealed

20

to us by the same Spirit as the Scriptures'. This, he asserts, can be proved by Scripture and by a secure argument grounded on it, for Christ would not have handed down the law of eternal salvation to the faithful without revealing what it meant.[3] The streams which flow out from the springs are part of the divine revelation, a means of further explication of the teaching given in Scripture itself. Jean Gerson (1363–1429) describes how the literal sense of Scripture was first revealed by Christ and the apostles, its truth attested by miracles and by the blood of the martyrs who died for it, and brought out by the 'holy doctors'.[4]

The Fathers in fact constituted the bedrock of mediaeval exegesis, but in an increasingly selected and extracted form in the later Middle Ages. Certain Fathers – notably Chrysostom and Augustine – dominate the selections.[5] The use of handbooks of extracts (of which Peter Lombard's *Sentences* is perhaps the most notable although it is very much more than a *florilegium*) goes back to the earliest Middle Ages. It encouraged a lack of historical sense in treating the Fathers; later authors are cited alongside the Fathers, often without distinction and out of order: Gelasius comes after Bernard of Clairvaux, for example, in Gabriel Biel's account of the grounds of papal authority.[6] Luther, too, was ready to bracket Bernard of Clairvaux with Jerome and Gregory.[7]

An author might become a focus of great loyalty in the course of controversy, as happened to Augustine because he furnished so much material of use in the debates on predestination which were stirred up by Thomas Bradwardine and others.[8] Indeed it might be said that Augustine divided Reformation scholars more fiercely than any other single author.

The habit of looking to the Fathers was not broken in the changes of the Reformation. On the contrary, it seemed to many of the reformers that it was only since the patristic age that things had begun to go wrong, and that it was therefore necessary to go back to the Fathers for help in interpretation. Melanchthon thought that the trouble began with Gregory the Great, who had initiated papal claims which he had tried to make binding on all Christians. Among the Greek Fathers he criticised Origen for his allegorical method, which he believed had led the reader away from Scripture's real meaning into fantasy.[9] In the reformers' view, this misapplication and misunderstanding had become a serious problem in the course of the Middle Ages. It therefore made sense to go back to the first formulations of the early Church and the Fathers, Greek as well as

Latin, now that that was possible with the more widespread knowledge of Greek.[10] That did not mean that mediaeval authorities were not read: Luther uses the *Glossa Ordinaria*, Aquinas, Nicholas of Lyre and others.[11] But it threw the emphasis of scholarship back upon the earliest interpreters of the Bible.

Yet, paradoxically, it altered the nature of the respect in which they were held. Once the line between *sacra scriptura* (meaning the Bible itself) and those 'holy writings' which were by the Fathers had been far from sharp. Now the experience of reading the Bible afresh diminished the Fathers to the level of fellow-readers: readers with the advantage of closeness to the source, but men like modern scholars and equally fallible and limited. If we let Luther talk he will paint us a lively picture. He compares Augustine's temperament with Jerome's and with his own as though they were all on a level as 'doctors' of theology: 'St. Jerome, like the rest of us – Dr. Jonas, Pomeranus and me – we are all much more inclined to angry outbursts. Nor do I know which of our doctors today has Augustine's temperament except Brenz and Justus Menius.'[12] The truth is, he says, that he has found the Fathers unsatisfactory ever since he came to understand the Bible itself more deeply. 'At first I devoured . . . Augustine. But when the door was opened for me in Paul, so that I understood what justification by faith is, it was all over with Augustine. There are only two notable assertions in all of Augustine. The first is that when sin is forgiven it does not cease to exist, but ceases to damn and control us. The second is that the law is kept when that is forgiven which does not happen. The books of his Confessions teach nothing; they only incite the reader; they are made up merely of examples, but do not instruct.'[13] He often took advantage of the opportunity to sneer at the Fathers in his talk. On one occasion there was a discussion about the writings of the Fathers on the Bible and how they left the reader uncertain what to think. Luther remarked tartly, 'I'm not allowed to make judgements about them because they are writers of recognised authority and I am compelled to be an apostate. But let him who wishes read them, and Chrysostom in particular. He was the supreme orator, but how he digressed from the thing at hand to other matters! While I was lecturing on the letter to the Hebrews and consulted Chrysostom, [I found that] he wrote nothing about the contents of the letter . . . It ought to be the primary and principal function of a preacher to reflect upon the substance, contents and sum total of the matter and instruct his hearer accordingly.'[14]

He particularly disliked Jerome: 'If he were now living Augustine would enjoy reading this book, . . . St. Jerome, if he were alive, would probably write against the book like any other [sic] barefoot friar.'[15] 'Jerome can be read for the sake of history, but he has nothing at all to say about faith and the teaching of true religion. I have no use for Chrysostom either, for he is only a gossip. Basil doesn't amount to anything; he was a monk after all, and I wouldn't give a penny for him. Philip's Apology [Melanchthon's Augsburg Confession of 1530] is superior to all the doctors of the Church, even to Augustine himself. Hilary and Theophylact are good, and so is Ambrose. The last sometimes treats excellently of the forgiveness of sins, which is the chief article, namely, that the divine majesty pardons by grace.'[16] 'I think Jerome has somehow been saved by his faith in Christ. But God forgive him for the harm he has done through his teaching. I know very well that he has done me much harm . . . I know no doctor whom I hate so much, although I once loved him ardently, and read him voraciously. Surely there's more learning in Aesop than in all of Jerome.'[17] The reasons for Luther's dislike are clear enough. He has reacted strongly against authors whom he once found deeply satisfying; he has done so because they have nothing to say about what has come to seem to him the essence of the matter; the Bible has become all in all to him.

The greatest theologians, such as Augustine and Bernard, and . . . their predecessors, Cyprian, Tertullian, and the like, . . . when questions are set before them, . . . seldom remain on the right track but take something away from Scripture, give in to the particular case or the person, and do violence to the words of God. Observe them in what they write, as they did against Arius, or Jerome against Jovinians, or Augustine against the Manichees, or Bernard against free will; and you will see that I speak truly.[18]

2 Traditions

Much was at stake. The fourteenth century scholar Brevicoxa (d. 1367) emphasises that 'any pilgrim', any Christian in this life who is of sound mind (nothing is required of children and the insane) and has been sufficiently instructed, is required to believe certain truths as a condition of his salvation. If only truths found in the Bible can fall into this category, then salvation is to be had *sola scriptura*. But some say that further truths not found in Scripture are equally necessary for salvation.[19]

What are these further truths? The Church taught certain things which are not to be found stated in the Bible but which were held to be based on an oral tradition going back to the apostles. This tradition derived its authority from the agreement of the early Church, by a process of general acceptance on the part of the faithful, or by the decrees of assemblies (councils and synods), behind all of which the Holy Spirit was held to be standing as a guide who would ensure that nothing went wrong. This guardian role of the Holy Spirit was emphasised by the Fathers who, broadly speaking, saw the decisions of councils as denying errors rather than as adding new truths of faith to the list. As the papacy emerged in a position of supremacy in the mediaeval West and defined its plenitude of power, the decree of Peter's successor was held to carry a peculiar authority in the process of reception, in defining both the nature and the content of tradition.

Robert Bellarmine gives a clear account of the state of the debate at the end of the sixteenth century. (He comments that there is much discussion of tradition among his contemporaries, or at least those whose work he has seen.)

First there is disagreement about what 'tradition' means. In general, it is *doctrina* which is communicated by one to another, whether written or unwritten. In theological usage it is more strictly confined to 'oral' tradition.[20] This seemed to the protestant William Fulke an abuse of the term 'tradition' which, he says, 'signifieth properly a delivery or a thing delivered' but which 'the papists' describe as something 'delivered only by word of mouth, and so received from hand to hand, that it is never put into writing, but hath this credit without the holy scriptures of God'.

Secondly, the objection of the reformers was to the notion that anything so transmitted, and therefore not available for the Christian to study for himself in a reliable and canonical text, could be of such importance that no-one could be saved without it. If that were possible, the Church held the keys to salvation, and no-one could come to God directly by himself. So Fulke protests 'that the Church at this day, or ever since the New Testament was written, had any tradition by word of mouth of any matter necessary to salvation which was not contained in the Old or New Testament, we will never grant, neither', he asserts, 'shall you ever be able out of . . . any text in the Bible to prove it'.[21]

Bellarmine meets this objection with vigorous assertions of the absolute necessity of tradition and its ultimate derivation from divine authority. He insists that the 'authors' of oral tradition include Christ himself: in his institution of the Eucharist he established more details, Bellarmine believes, than are recorded in the New Testament, and these have come down to us. There are also apostolic traditions and traditions of the Church, those *consuetudines antiquae* which, whether begun by priests or people, have by the silent consent of the people come to have the force of law. Certain of these oral traditions of the apostles and the Church have the same force (*vis*) as what is written in the Gospels.[22]

Bellarmine insists that tradition is a necessary addition to Scripture.[23] This he seeks to demonstrate from Scripture itself (John 16.12, for example: 'I have many things to say to you but you are not able to bear them now'), and by positive and negative arguments. 'If Scripture did not contain everything which was necessary, it would be necessary for there to be a tradition, or God would not have provided for the Church.' But there is such a tradition. The heretics of old (Arians, Donatists and others) 'were always urging the Scriptures'; their opposition to tradition surely demonstrates that it is necessary.[24]

Thirdly, there is the question of the continuance of the process of handing on in the church. Aquinas sees a parallel between the way in which the prophets taught the people in Old Testament times after the giving of the Law and the way in which the apostles taught the people in New Testament times after the giving of the Gospels. 'The apostles,' he says, 'handed on to the faithful what they had heard from the Lord: *ea quae a Domino audierunt, tradiderunt fidelibus.*'[25] That handing-on by the apostles could be seen as continuing in the Church. Stillingfleet in the seventeenth century lays down 'some reasonable *postulata*' on tradition: '1. That a Catholic Tradition must be universally received among the sound Members of the Catholic Church. 2. That the force of Tradition lies in the Certainty of Conveyance of Matters of Faith from the Apostolical Times.'[26] His *postulata* were acceptable to a variety of both protestant and Catholic authors well into the seventeenth century. Matthew Poole, writing as a Protestant, was able to regard it as a warrant of 'the divine authority of this mysterious piece of holy writ' (he is speaking of the book of Revelation), that it has had a 'general reception by the Church as such in all late ages', although some said that the more recent the testimony the less its authority.[27] Gabriel Biel, two centuries before, argues as Bellarmine was to do that what the Church accepts ought to be received with the same reverence as if it were written in the Bible itself. That is the case, he argues, precisely because the Church is apostolic, founded in the faith of the apostles and thus sharing in the same authority as the Bible at a human level.[28] Even the Protestant Whitaker uses the same rule in reverse to show that the apocryphal books are not canonical: 'The apostles never cite testimonies from these books, nor can anything be adduced to show that any authority was attributed to them by the apostles ... it is clear from the testimonies of councils, Fathers and writers, that these books deserve no place in the true canon of Scripture.'[29]

The mediaeval Church argued that there can be no conflict between Scripture and tradition. The Pope cannot issue definitions and precepts against canonical Scripture which are binding, although his decrees are binding if they do not conflict with Scripture,[30] and can therefore be regarded as enlarging upon it in some way. In this sense, and only in this sense, is there a limit on the power of the Church to interpret, just as there was a limit on the pronouncements of the early councils of the church in their capacity to expand or add to the truths of faith. Scripture and tradition are intertwined in their authority.

Aquinas says that nothing is to be taught except what is contained either implicitly or explicitly, in 'the Gospels and Epistles and Sacred Scripture'.[31] But in his view that allows additions which are in the spirit of the text of the Bible. 'The Word of the Lord is taken to mean that you shall not add anything contrary or alien to the words which I shall speak. But to add certain things not contrary was lawful, for example, certain solemn days and the like, as was done in the time of Mordecai and of Judith, in memory of the blessings they received from God.'[32]

If the principle that something other than Scripture may be authoritative is once admitted, the question of the divine guarantee becomes more complex. To give a single instance, we can distinguish between 'possible', 'probable' and 'true' interpretations. Erasmus, too, considers probability as the way to judge 'wherever the inviolate authority of Scripture and the decrees of the Church allow', but he will submit his own interpretation (*sensus*) to the Church, 'whether I grasp what it prescribes or whether I do not grasp it'.[33]

How, then, do we know what is a true tradition? Bellarmine has five *regulae* for us.[34] A tradition is to be relied on when the universal Church embraces something as a dogma of faith, which is not found in the Bible; when the Church preserves something which no one but God could have instituted, and is not found in the Bible; when something has been preserved throughout the ages by the Church, even if it could have been instituted by the Church it is to be taken as apostolic in origin; when all the doctors of the Church teach something with common consent; when there is a continuous succession from the apostles; all these indicate that there is truth in a tradition.

For our purposes the most important implication of these debates is the placing of the Church beside Scripture as an authority to which Christians can and must turn to find what is necessary for their salvation. When they looked at the undoubted corruptions in the Church of their day, reformers from Wyclif onwards were inclined to reject everything it stood for and to turn to the Bible as sole authority. Scripture and tradition began to seem not colleagues but rivals.

3 Gospel before Church

Hostility was focussed on the institutional Church of the later Middle Ages and especially upon the Pope as its head. In one dispute we meet the assertion that the Christian faith *is* Holy Scripture: *fides ... Christiana est Scriptura Sacra*. The Pope, it is suggested, claims 'to be able to take any book out of the canon of Scripture and to insert a new one; *per consequens* he can make the whole Bible anew, and *per consequens* he can make the whole Scripture heretical and opposed to the catholic faith'.[35] We are not told in this account of a Lollard debate that *per consequens* it follows that he has done so, but that was an assumption of much Lollard and early Protestant thought. William Tyndale describes the Church's leaders as having engaged in a conspiracy. 'They have feigned false books and put them forth.' They have deliberately attacked 'the right sense' of Scripture 'for their lucre sake' – for their own financial gain. 'Even so would they have destroyed it also, if they could, rather than the people should have come to a right understanding of it ... For as they have destroyed the right sense of it with their leaven; and as they destroy daily the true preachers of it; and as they keep it from the lay people, that they should not see how they juggle with it; even so would they destroy it also, could they bring it about, rather than that we should come by the true understanding of it.'[36]

If that was the case, the established Church, with the Pope at its head, could not, it seems, be the true Church. What 'power and authority' had Christ really given Peter and the apostles to exercise in the world?[37] Marsilius of Padua, writing in the early fourteenth century, had his own political reasons for questioning the scope of that authority. He wanted to show that the papal claims to ultimate supremacy in secular as well as spiritual matters which had been put forward since the end of the eleventh century went beyond the divine commission entrusted to Peter, in order to make out a case for a new society in which the ecclesiastical hierarchy had a subordinate place and the secular government was supreme.

He set out to show that Christ gave only a spiritual jurisdiction to the apostles. He helped to give currency among the leaders of thought who influenced the Lollards and other reforming movements in Europe to the general notion that 'the Roman bishops and their accomplices' are the enemy, actively fighting for power and for the possession of temporal goods, and deliberately misleading the faithful for their own ends. They abuse the power of binding and loosing and threaten the faithful with damnation to bring them to heel. They do not behave as Christ intended his apostles and successors to do. They are not true followers of Christ. These all-embracing criticisms include strong objections to the Church's claims to authority in the establishment and interpretation of Scripture.[38]

Marsilius's authority for his contentions is the Bible itself. He uses the Scripture on which the 'Roman bishops and their accomplices' base their claims to support arguments against them. He challenges their right to sole authority in its interpretation. He adduces the authority of Scripture himself, 'with the expositions of the holy interpreters', against the 'fictitious and foreign interpretations of them by certain men, whereby it might seem possible to prove that to the Roman bishop rightfully belongs the highest of all coercive jurisdictions or rulerships'.[39]

The double challenge – to the authenticity of the Church and to the unique authority it claims to interpret Scripture – continued to be associated in later writers who pursued Marsilius's line of thought on the political aspects of the papal position. It was maintained equally by those whose first concern was with the interpretation of the Bible, and who were obliged by their view of the Church's explanations to question whether it was indeed the Church at all.

Marsilius distinguishes several meanings of the word 'church' along established lines. It may refer to the temple or house in which believers worship together, or to all the priests or bishops, deacons and others who minister in the temple or church (and among the 'moderns', he says, this is taken especially to imply those who preside over the metropolitan Church). Its last and most 'fitting' meaning is, for Marsilius, its first 'imposition', in accordance with the intention of those who first used it, which is its original meaning. 'According to this signification, the "church" means the whole body of the faithful who believe in and invoke the name of Christ, and all the parts of this whole body in any community, even the household.' This is the way the word was used among the apostles.[40] Marsilius employs technical terms of logic ('imposition', 'intention') which we shall meet again, to underline the superiority and primacy of this last signification.

Two centuries later William Tyndale's *Answer to Sir Thomas More's Dialogue* contains the same list, prefaced by the same challenge: 'Judge, therefore, reader, whether the Pope with his be the church; whether their authority be above the scripture; whether all they teach without scripture be equal with the scripture; whether they have erred, and not only whether they can.'[41] Tyndale's meanings of the word 'church' are these:

1 'It signifieth a place or house; whither christian people were wont in the old times to resort at times convenient for to hear the word of doctrine, the law of God, and the faith of our saviour Jesus Christ . . . For the officer, thereto appointed, preached the pure word of God only, and prayed in a tongue that all men understood.'
2 'In another signification, it is abused and mistaken for a multitude of shaven, shorn, and oiled; which we now call the spirituality and clergy.'
3 'It hath yet, or should have, another signification, little known among the common people now-a-days. That is to wit, it signifieth a congregation; a multitude or company gathered together in one, of all degrees of people . . . And in this third signification is the church of God, or Christ, taken in the Scripture; even for the whole multitude of all of them that receive the name of Christ to believe in him, and not for the clergy only.'[42]

Tyndale explains that it is in order to bring out and emphasise this meaning that he has translated 'church' as 'congregation'.

Much follows from the adoption of this last definition of the Church, in ways beyond what Marsilius can have envisaged. Marsilius was sure that it was necessary to have authoritative 'determination' of doubtful meanings of Scripture, 'especially with regard to articles of the faith, commands and prohibitions'.[43] No scholastically trained author of the day could have thought differently; the Master's determination in disputations was of the essence of the question-solving process in the schools, an outgrowth of the lecture and as fundamental to speculative theology or to the study of philosophical texts as to the study of the Bible. Marsilius argues that such determinations could be made authoritatively at the level of the Church itself only by general councils. The Pope cannot do it, either alone or with his college of cardinals. Such councils, he holds, may include 'non-priests', 'who will properly participate in the deliberations of the council together with the priests and help formulate its decrees'.[44] Marsilius had other reasons than Tyndale for insisting on lay right here. But the role of the laity was upheld and enlarged even further in the Church as conceived of by the reformers. 'The church, then,' says Tyndale, 'is the multitude of all them that believe in Christ for the remission of sin,' and so on. 'This is the church that cannot err damnably, nor any long time', nor all its members at once, for 'as soon as any question ariseth, the truth of God's promise stirreth up one or other to teach them the truth of every thing needful to salvation out of God's word'. That 'lighteneth the hearts of the other true members, to see the same, and to consent thereto'.[45] The Church's members act as a check and balance upon one another and the whole community is kept on the right course in that way. Thus all Christians are apostles and true preachers.

In response to this challenge the Roman Catholic Church put an emphasis on the 'notes' or distinguishing marks of the Church. The reformers say that a Church is nothing else but a society of believers. The Counter-Reformation scholars argue that it is much more than that. It is universal (Catholic), ancient, and it endures perpetually, outlasting all earthly empires and kingdoms. It is a great multitude, not a small sect, 'answerable to the dignity and majesty' of Christ its Lord. There must be a clear apostolic succession, and the consent of the faithful in the earliest Christian times. There must be intimate unity with Christ as the Church's Head and of the members with one another. There must be holiness of doctrine, effectiveness in preaching against unbelievers, the holiness of the Fathers, the glory of miracles, the gift of prophecy, and the signs too of conversion of the Church's enemies.[46] The individual's witness to what the Holy Spirit tells him can do no more than confirm the Church's teaching; if it seems to do anything else it must be considered false witness.

It is not hard to see how these two positions drew further apart until they appeared irreconcilable. Tyndale poses the Reformation question squarely as it relates to the study of the Bible: whether 'the church or congregation be before the gospel, or the gospel before the church'.[47]

4

SOLA SCRIPTURA

The appeal to Scripture alone was in part an appeal to origins, in part
– and inseparably – an appeal directly to Christ. 'If we abide in the
old doctrine which the apostles taught, and hearken to no new learning', says Tyndale, 'then abide we in the Son (for upon the Son build
they us), and in the Father through confidence in the Son; and are
heirs of everlasting life.'[1] Calvin explains that Christ says that Scripture itself is his witness: 'Search the Scriptures . . . they are they which
testify of me' (John 5.39).[3] 'Without [the Gospel] we should be ignorant of the great blessings and promises which Jesus Christ has given
us . . . This is what we should in short seek in the whole of Scripture:
truly to know Jesus Christ, and the infinite riches that are comprised
in him.'[3] William Whitaker lists three 'witnesses to himself' used by
Christ: 'First, the works which he performed; secondly his Father
who sent him; thirdly the holy Scriptures themselves, which he calls
his witnesses.'[4]

There is, however, a logical difficulty here. Can Scripture
authorise its own authority? William Whitaker quotes Thomas
Stapleton's answer to this problem: 'Scripture (says he) cannot be
proved by Scripture: therefore it must be proved by the Church; and
consequently the authority of the Church is greater than that of
Scripture.' Whitaker's answer is one which goes back to Origen at
least: that the Bible is not attesting itself; there is another witness
between the Bible and its readers, authenticating the first to the
second. The Holy Spirit is this witness; it is he who 'makes the Scripture canonical and authentic in itself', and it is he who 'makes it also
to appear such to us'.[5]

This picture clarified and simplified, at least in principle, much
that had appeared complex and even confusing to mediaeval
scholars. Duns Scotus discusses in his commentary on Peter
Lombard's *Sentences* whether men of Old Testament times who did
not have the whole of the Bible as it now stands lacked anything
which was *necessaria* and *sufficiens* to their own salvation. If they

31

did not, it seems that the New Testament cannot be a necessary part of Scripture. Again: do the Scriptures contain an account of what is to be believed only, or also of what is to be hoped for and what is to be done by Christians? Again: is *sola scriptura* to be thought of as including the Bible alone, or can *scriptura*, as in the usage of earlier Christian centuries, include material other than that contained in the canon – even patristic writings?[6]

For the reformers the important principle is that the Bible is not only its own witness through the Holy Spirit, but also its own interpreter, proving, judging, illuminating itself.[7] Luther insists that Scripture itself is clearer than all the commentaries of the Fathers. William Fulke says that 'the scriptures are plain and easy to be understood, of them that use the ordinary means to come to it, for all doctrine necessary to be known, and sufficient to determine every matter'. Ironically, he brings the Fathers to bear witness to this statement, alongside Scripture itself. 'The Holy Ghost doth testify (II Timothy 3.16), and some of the ancient Fathers also do bear witness. As Augustine . . . Chrysostom.'[8] Indeed Fulke has no objection to the use of the old interpreters, so long as their status of mere helps is understood: 'We will not refuse the arbitrement and judgement of the ancient Fathers, of general Councils, of universal custom and places in the Catholic Church.'[9] There is a world of difference between Fulke's position and Bellarmine's contention that the Church's interpretation is indispensable.[10] 'Controversies cannot be ended from Scripture alone'; private judgement leads to chaos because not everyone has the true inner illumination 'which is necessary for the right understanding of Scripture'; a judge ought to have coercive authority; private individuals have no such authority; he points out that even with their mastery of many languages the Lutherans and the Zwinglians cannot agree on the meaning of *hoc est corpus meum*.[11]

The principle of *sola scriptura* was formally stated at Leipzig in 1519 and at Worms in 1521–2; Zwingli took a stand on it at Zurich in 1523. The Thirty-Nine Articles of the Church of England state that one 'Holy Scripture containeth all things necessary to salvation, so that whatsoever is not read therein, nor may be proved thereby, is not to be required of any man'.[12]

5

TOWARDS PRIVATE JUDGEMENT: 'THE CHILDREN OF GOD SPY OUT THEIR FATHER'[1]

It had been a matter of only moderate concern to the scholars of the earlier Middle Ages how the laity were to go on in the faith with only a limited knowledge of it. In the mid-twelfth century Simon of Tournai thought it enough that they should look on what they could not understand with reverence and awe, in the assurance that they were being brought to salvation.[2]

Behind that confidence that the outcome was securely in God's hands lay long tradition that the Holy Spirit is the educator of men's hearts. The visions of the saintly abbess Hildegard of the same period came to an uneducated mind, she says; but they came in the form of Biblical imagery and she was enabled to write about them with impressive fluency and – in time – with learning.[3] The simple laity were not granted the same understanding, but they were kept on the right road of the soul by the Holy Spirit just as Hildegard and the other holy women of the later Middle Ages were.

The movement to translate the Bible into the vernacular and to put it into the hands of the laity was to extend that principle to apply to all Christians. As Calvin puts it: 'The same Spirit who made Moses and the prophets certain of their calling, has now testified to our own hearts.'[4]

Robert Bellarmine points to a danger: 'Is only that which the Holy Spirit says privately to each in his heart to be received as the Word of God?' He sees human judgement of what is thus taught it as 'often deceptive and always uncertain'.[5]

Even guided by others, private judgement may be at sea if it is not certain which teachers are to be relied on, as Luther points out:

If we are to believe neither the pope nor the fathers nor Luther nor anyone else unless they teach us the pure Word of God, whom are we to believe? Who will give our consciences sure information about which party is teaching us the pure Word of God, we or our opponents? For they, too, claim to have and to teach the pure Word of God . . . What is to be done here? Is every fanatic to have the right to teach whatever he pleases?[6]

33

Calvin, too, acknowledges the danger: 'If everyone has a right to be a judge and arbiter in this matter, nothing can be set down as certain; and our whole religion will be full of uncertainty.'[7] The answer, he thinks, is to apply a two-fold test, 'private and public'. 'By private testing each one establishes his own faith, and accepts only the teaching he knows to be from God. Public testing of doctrine has to do with the common consent and polity of the church.'[8] That is one option, and it was acceptable to the reformers if the Church was thought of as the communion of all faithful people rather than as the institutional edifice headed by the Bishop of Rome which they had come to conceive as a monster of Antichrist. 'The papists are foolish,' says Calvin, 'when they conclude that no private interpretation by an individual is valid.' They abuse the words of Peter (II Peter 1.20: 'Knowing this first, that no prophecy of Scripture is of any private interpretation'). Certainly we are not 'to set up our own acumen as capable of understanding Scripture'; but we are 'to submit to the authority of the Holy Spirit' and then we shall be guided to understanding. Peter means that it is not right for individuals 'to come out with something out of their own heads', that is, which is not revealed to them by the Spirit. Believers, 'illumined inwardly by the Holy Spirit, know as true only what God says by his word'. The papists argue falsely when they want to give their councils alone the right to interpret Scripture. 'Anyone . . . who opens his eyes with the obedience of faith shall know by experience that Scripture has not been called "light" in vain.'[9]

This emphasis upon an inward and individual judgement taught by the Holy Scripture is already there in Tyndale, with the same resort to the body of the faithful in the background to provide a 'public' judgement acceptable to reformed thinking. Tyndale thought it of the first importance that the Christian should be taught 'the profession of his baptism', so that he will have an understanding of what he believes, with special emphasis upon the 'knowledge of the law of God' interpreted as Christ interprets it ('love the Lord God with all thy heart', and so on) and upon the 'promises of mercy which are in our Saviour Christ'. The underlying idea is that just as 'he who knoweth his letters well and can spell perfectly, cannot but read if he be diligent . . . even so whosoever hath the profession of baptism written in his heart, cannot but understand the Scripture, if he exercise himself therein, and compare one place to another, and mark the manner of speech, and ask here and there the meaning of a sentence of them that be better exercised . . .[10] No man, that hath the profession of his baptism written in his heart, can stumble in the Scripture, and fall into heresies, or become a maker of division and sects, and a defender of wild and vain opinions.'[11] It is not simply the possession of a knowledge of the elements of the faith but the experience of their meaning which will keep the Christian from misinterpretation; his mind is guided by the Holy Spirit, not in blind faith but in understanding. Nevertheless, Tyndale will not have every man 'a common preacher', able to 'preach everywhere by his own authority'. 'Every man ought to preach in word and deed unto his household, and to them that are under his governance', but only those 'called and chosen thereto by the common ordinance of the congregation' are to preach generally. There is a protection in some public judgement of a man's opinions, where that public judgement is made by the body of the faithful.[12] A similar cautious resort to a backdrop of authority is noticeable elsewhere, and not always in terms entirely foreign to the Church's position during preceding centuries. Cranmer instructed all clergy to read aloud this declaration to their flocks on the publication of the Bible in English in 1538:

If at any time by reading, any doubt shall come upon any of you, touching the sense and meaning of any part thereof; that then, not giving too much to your own minds, fantasies and opinions, nor having thereof any open reasoning in your open taverns or alehouses, ye shall have recourse to such learned men as be or shall be authorised to preach and declare the same. So that avoiding all contentions and disputations in such alehouses, and other places unmeet for such conferences, and submitting your opinions to the judgements of such learned men as shall be appointed . . . you use this benefit quietly and charitably every one of you, to the edifying of himself, his wife and family.[13]

Cranmer goes a long way towards setting up the Church as authority in this passage, although he would perhaps have wished to avoid a direct comparison with earlier practice.

But the main thrust of his words is the encouragement to every Christian to read the Bible for himself and think about it for himself, exercising his own judgement as far as he can. Martin Bucer recommended each man to 'examine his own faith under the direction of the Scriptures and by the aid of the Spirit, that all may enjoy fullness of conviction and remain faithful to the Gospel and to the confession of Christ'.[14] Far from being a procedure rather doubtful and to be entered on with caution, it is every man's duty to study the Bible daily. 'This passage' (Jeremiah 26.4–5), says Calvin, 'teaches that all those who reject the daily exercise of learning the Scriptures are godless men and quench, so far as is in their power, the grace of the

Spirit.'[15] The Word of God is an active teacher and gives its own guidance: 'To those who meditate on the Law the very rock of Scripture gushes forth abundant streams and flowing waters of knowledge and wisdom, and grace and sweetness besides . . . ; the experienced person knows that one who meditates on the Law of the Lord is taught many things in a short time and suddenly, and a deluge of insights rushes in with "the voice of his cataracts" (Psalm 42.7).'[16] So we come full circle to the idea that God himself is the educator of men's hearts, but now with a new picture of the method by which he does it. For the reformers the general notion that God would somehow look after the needs of the ignorant was not adequate. They looked for detailed instruction by the Book, and that brought them up against a multitude of practical and theoretical difficulties inseparable from mass education, difficulties of which there had been no more than a hint when the movement to translate the Bible into the vernacular began.

This, then, is the background of thought and debate about the principles and purpose of Bible study against which methods of exegesis were developed and practical Bible study went on in the late Middle Ages and the sixteenth century. The problems we have touched on briefly are of immense depth and complexity and it has not been possible to do more than point to them. Some of their ramifications will become clear as we go on. Others must wait for a future volume. For our immediate purposes the most important thing is perhaps the strength of feeling and commitment they aroused in the partisans of opposing viewpoints. Although much of that feeling derived from political and ecclesiastical concerns beyond the immediate scope of the exegete's task, the Bible lay, as it were, always open on the table before the protagonists.

PART II

THE RULES OF INTERPRETATION

6

THE GROUND RULES

In 1433 at the Council of Basle John of Ragusa gave a series of rules for the interpretation of Scripture: the whole of Scripture may be taken to be inspired by the Holy Spirit. Nothing it asserts definitely or explicitly (*positum, expressum*) can deceive or mislead. The teaching of Scripture is in accordance with divine goodness. Scripture has many senses, of which the literal sense is the principal one, and contains within it the figurative sense. The literal sense is the sense the author intended. It is infallible. It contains everything necessary to salvation. When he is trying to understand a passage, the reader should look at what comes before it and after it. He should ask what kind of material the text contains. Difficulties in the text are useful and necessary. However, they make it necessary for Scripture to be expounded. Of earlier interpreters the Fathers (Jerome, Ambrose, Augustine, Gregory) are to be preferred to the moderns. Commentators should be compared and reduced to agreement if possible. If that cannot be done, the one closest to Scriptural truth is to be preferred. Heretics have interpreted Scripture falsely. The aim of all interpretation is to arrive at the truth.[1]

Juxtaposed in this list are principles which would have appeared in a list made by Augustine, or by Peter Lombard in the twelfth century, and principles which had come to be established only very recently, within the century and a half or two centuries before John of Ragusa's lifetime. That the Bible is wholly inspired, that its texts have many senses, that the difficulties of understanding it presents are put there by its wise Author for the benefit of its human readers – these had been the cardinal principles of earlier mediaeval exegesis in the West since they were set out by Augustine and Gregory the Great. The two last are profoundly connected. It is because of the confused state of human thinking since the Fall that it is necessary for God to put into the words of the Bible not only their obvious meaning but other, more or less hidden and figurative meanings, so that men in their various conditions may grasp what God is saying to them at

whatever level and in whatever way is appropriate to their understanding. Thus the difficulties the text presents are God's way of
coming to meet men's damaged minds.[2]

The first of the shifts of emphasis reflected in John of Ragusa's list
was already taking place in the twelfth century. A new interest in the
literal sense and a new respect for it altered an old balance in favour
of the 'spiritual' senses, the allegorical, tropological and anagogical,
which had led some of the Fathers to regard certain passages as
having no literal sense at all.[3] The literal sense began to look more
attractive when twelfth century developments in the study of grammar and logic made it possible to render intelligible much that was
puzzling; scholars felt that they were gaining a deeper insight into the
nature and functioning of the Bible's language. The intellectual challenge of speculative grammar and logic was exciting, and it partially
obscured other, and in the long term perhaps more important, work
on the Hebrew text,[4] which also encouraged a new seriousness in the
effort to arrive at the right literal sense. The triumph of the literal
sense was not without its detractors. The letter still seemed to some
to be a 'harlot' (*omnis quippe litera meretrix est*),[5] because it exposes
itself freely to everyone.

This twelfth century work upon the long-running task of reconcil-
ing the Bible's apparent contradictions led to the inclusion of metaphorical usages within the literal sense: for where a term is used
metaphorically in one statement but not in another, the contradiction vanishes. It is to this change – to which we shall return in due
course – that John of Ragusa refers when he says that the literal sense
can contain figurative usages.[6]

Other rules in John of Ragusa's list hint at the beginnings of an
approach to criticism which was to carry forward into the sixteenth
century: the habit of looking at a passage in context, of asking what
kind of writing is involved, what the purpose of the statement is, had
been inculcated earlier by the use of the *accessus* which taught the
reader to consider the purpose and content and authorship of a
book.[7] But it was becoming an altogether more sophisticated procedure.

There are indications of warfare in the schools: the battle against
heretical interpretation covered both the arguments of out-and-out
heretics, Cathars and Waldensians, and those of men within the
academic system who taught in opposition to currently fashionable
schools of thought. Out of the schools came challenges to the very
truth of Scripture, if we are to believe Wyclif, and certainly John of

Ragusa would seem to have something of the sort in mind in assert-
ing that Scripture cannot mislead when it asserts *positum* or
expressum.[8] And there is the promise that Scripture contains what is
necessary to salvation, which hints at the claims of the reformers that
it contains everything necessary to salvation.

John of Ragusa's list of rules for exegesis reflects obliquely and
sometimes by allusion the mixture of assumption and controversy
which was forming contemporary study of the Bible and pressing
further the changes which had begun to take place and which were to
lead to some of the debates of the Reformation. He provides us with
an account of, as it were, the mid-point of that development, and a
vantage-point from which to look both forward and back.

7

THE LITERAL SENSE

Littera gesta docet, quid credas allegoria,
Moralis quid agas, quid speres anagogia.[1]

The ancient mnemonic implicitly places the four senses of Scripture on the same level of authority. The literal, allegorical, tropological and anagogical senses are assumed to be there to teach, each in its own way, what the divine Author of Scripture intends the reader to learn from the passage in question. The emphasis, at least from the time of Gregory the Great, who put the four senses decisively into the mediaeval tradition, was upon the divine intention rather than upon any conscious intention of the human author. Any interpretation which could be put upon the text and was in keeping with the faith and edifying, had the warrant of God himself, for no human reader had the ingenuity to find more than God had put there.

The twelfth century attempt to take the literal sense as the foundation saw it not in terms of the old architectural metaphor which made it merely the crude base of rough-cut stones on which the beautiful superstructure of the spiritual senses was erected, but as the most important of the senses, yielding far more to analysis than had hitherto been dreamed of.[2]

It had long seemed that certain passages of the Old Testament demanded allegorical interpretation because their literal sense was unacceptable. There was an attempt in the late twelfth and early thirteenth century to reassess the ceremonial precepts of the Mosaic Law, and to determine whether they were merely 'foreshadowings' of the laws by which the righteous must now live, or intended to be fulfilled literally.[3] It may be that the rejection of the Old Testament by Cathar heretics in the south of France and northern Italy prompted efforts to retrieve the literal sense. William of Auvergne (who taught theology at Paris during the 1220s, and who wanted to see reform of corruption in the Church and a tightening up of standards), took a fresh look at the matter in the light of the teaching of

Aristotle, which was newly available. He argued that the law set out in the Old Testament must reflect the law of nature. Moreover, God as divine Lawgiver could have given no unworthy precepts. He concludes that the law of the Old Testament is a part of the perfect and eternal law of the Gospel, and that it takes the form it does because it is designed to teach an uneducated people and prepare them to receive the Gospel. The Old Law is suited to its time and place, and within that context necessary and useful. It contains so many detailed rules because, just as children cannot understand large general ideas, so the people of the Old Testament needed simple, precise instructions.[4] Something of the same notion persists in Tyndale's account. He says that 'the ceremonies . . . were chiefly ordained of God . . . to occupy the minds of that people the Israelites . . . that their consciences might be stablished, and they were sure that they pleased God therein; which were impossible, if a man did of his own head that which was not commanded of God . . . Such ceremonies were unto them as an ABC, to learn to spell and read; and as a nurse to feed them with milk and pap, and to speak to them after their own capacity . . . And as the shadow vanisheth away at the coming of the light, even so do the ceremonies and sacrifices at the coming of Christ'.[5] The precepts of the Old Testament could, then, be taken literally, but as applying literally in their time and place; as not unworthy but, on the contrary, a merciful dispensation of the divine lawgiver.

In order to rescue the Old Law in its literal sense, scholars had to make a concession to the idea that historical circumstances may affect interpretation. The resort to the spiritual sense had given an eternal validity to these particularities and lifted them out of their local context of time and place.

A further concession was to look upon the literal sense as that consciously intended by the human author of the text, and therefore to draw attention to the human element in the Bible's authorship. That made it possible to include in the literal sense a number of metaphors which could confidently be shown to have been in the human author's thoughts when he used them. The point of separation between the literal and spiritual senses now lay between meanings consciously put there by human authors, and meanings unknown to the human authors and of eternal validity, put there by God, who had guided their conscious and unconscious work.

William of Nottingham in the fourteenth century provides a clear account of this inclusion of the figurative within the literal sense. He explains that the literal sense is what the author first intended (*qui primo intenditur ab auctore*) and that it is a *duplex sensus*. There is one 'proper' sense, where the text simply means what it says ('In the beginning God created heaven and earth'). There is also a *sensus litteralis figurativus* which comes from the secondary or metaphorical signification of the term, again as the author clearly intended it (*ex secunda vocis significatione ab auctore intenta vel ab auctoris intentione elicita*). There is, it should be noted, provision for the interpreter to 'draw out' this metaphorical meaning. An example is Genesis 49.27, where Benjamin is called a ravening wolf. It is obvious that the primary signification of the words here will not do. Benjamin was Joseph's brother, not a wolf. So the word 'wolf' must be used metaphorically.[6] By the time of Nicholas of Lyre it was common doctrine that the author's clear intention is the defining characteristic of the literal sense.[7]

William of Auvergne attacked the traditional doctrine of the three spiritual senses in his *De Legibus*, speaking, it is clear, for others who were of the same opinion. He argues that prophetic signs, expressed by means of deeds or speech, were intended by the prophets themselves to be understood figuratively; they are the human authors' metaphors. It is legitimate within the literal interpretation (*secundum litteram*) to draw out the consequences or implications of the literal sense for behaviour in the Christian life. Comparisons would also be legitimate if interpreters would acknowledge that they were no more than comparisons and would refrain from regarding them as significations.[8] He will have nothing to do with 'spiritual' interpretations of the conventional sort.

As an illustration of the difficulties in which interpreters were now finding themselves, we might look at the last of these points. Writing in the aftermath of William of Auvergne's challenge, Aquinas notes that things are signified by words both properly and figuratively,[9] and that it is the business of the literal sense to deal with the way in which words signify things. Aquinas seems a little uncertain in his placing of *similitudo* under the literal as distinct from the spiritual sense. He explains in the tradition of Augustine and Hugh of St Victor that the Bible is unique in that not only the words in it but also the things signified by the words have meanings. The meaning whereby words signify things belongs to the first sense, the historical or literal. The meaning whereby the things signified by the words have themselves also a meaning, is called the spiritual sense.[10] But here Aquinas is doing what William of Auvergne says should not be done: he is reading a comparison as a signification. Things, says Aquinas, can 'signify' only by likeness.[11]

Behind these discussions lie two reservations which were clearly being voiced in the thirteenth century and which Aquinas attempts to deal with in his defence of the use of the spiritual senses. Viewed as falling under the 'spiritual' senses, the use of *similitudines rerum*, comparisons with things, seemed to some of those for whom William of Auvergne was speaking to be corrupt (*abusivum eis videtur res ad* [*in*]*signa trahere*), because they were not created in order to signify in that way (*quae non ad haec facta sunt ut significent*). Those who thus objected found the teaching that things signify by *similitudo* a stumbling-block (*et haec est quae multos offendit*).[12] Bonaventure makes an attempt to distinguish between *similitudines* which compare created things with one another and those which involve a comparison between God and a creature: a type of analogy which seemed to many to be simply impossible.[13] Aquinas asks whether any creature can be like God, again distinguishing between mutual likeness and identity (which can exist between things of the same order), and the 'image and likeness' to God in which man is made (Genesis 1.26), and with which we are concerned in postulating the existence of *similitudines* between created things and God in the Bible's use of things to signify.[14] These debates struck at the first principle of the Bible's authority outlined by Alexander of Hales when he described how God testifies to his own words through signs and events in the created world.[15] Aquinas and the other conservatives who defended the use of the spiritual senses saw much at stake.

A second reservation lay in the belief that the use of metaphors and other figures of likeness or comparison in which the thing signified by the word in the first instance is actually being used (by a transference of signification) to signify something else, is a poetic device. Yet poetry is the lowliest of the sciences. It would therefore seem that it is inappropriate for the highest of the sciences, theology, to use its props. That link between poetry and the use of figures in the three types of spiritual interpretation still came naturally to mind when Sir John Harington composed a preface to his translation of *Orlando Furioso* in 1591:

> The ancient poets have indeed wrapped as it were in their writings divers and sundry meanings, which they call the senses or mysteries therefor. In the literal sense we find in manner of an historie the acts and notable exploits of some persons worthy of memorie: then in the same fiction . . . as it were nearer to the pith and marrow, they place the Morall sense profitable for the active life of man . . .

Manie times also under the selfsame words they comprehend some true understanding of natural Philosophie, or sometimes of politike governement, and now
and then of divinitie. (All these are forms of allegory.)[16]

Both these objections – that comparison with created things is an
inappropriate, or indeed ineffectual, way of speaking of God and
that the use of figures properly belongs to poetry – had been raised
in early Christian exegesis and they continued to be made. Meister
Eckhardt raised both points in defence of figurative interpretations
in his *Liber Parabolarum Genesis*; Wyclif touches on the first.[17] But
the thirteenth century debate had its own consequences.

This, then, is the cauldron of debate from which William of
Auvergne lifts the lid for us in his remarks on the use of *similitudines*.
Aquinas responded by putting forward a largely conservative
defence of the spiritual senses in the *Quaestiones Disputatae* he gave
during his first regency in Paris (1256–9), and which may have been
among the subjects debated at his inception as a teaching Master.[18]
Much the same points were represented rather more briefly in the
Summa Theologiae (I^aQ.1.a.8–10), and it is clear that he took up a
position from which he did not later depart.

Some of the new technicians were arguing that a single word or
statement must be made with a single meaning, or it is in fact not one
but several *locutiones*. 'Therefore several senses cannot be hidden in
the same *locutio* of Holy Scripture', they argued (obj. 1). Some said
that a multiplicity of meanings confused the understanding. Holy
Scripture was intended to be understood (*ordinata ad intellectum*).
Therefore it ought not to contain many senses (obj. 2). Some said that
errors will arise if there are several senses, because the possible
interpretations will be too numerous; the interpreter will be free to
make what he likes of a passage (obj. 3). Since the literal sense alone
has authority in argument and can be used as proof, what is to be
gained by positing the existence of spiritual senses (obj. 4)? If a sense
not intended by the author is read into a passage, it is not a proper
sense. Many senses cannot all be 'proper' in this way.[19] Aquinas
takes a moderate but conservative position. The literal sense is that
which expresses the author's intention. The spiritual sense is indicated by things, persons, events which are described in order to signify other things, persons and events. The literal sense is the only
sense which is valid for theological argumentation. (This point
became a commonplace – it had Augustinian authority – and greatly
strengthened the importance of the literal sense in scholastic

circles.)[20] The spiritual sense is not a personal or private interpretation which the reader is free to make for himself; it is a sense
intended by the Holy Spirit: as when we see Christ as the new Adam
or as the brazen serpent which Moses raised aloft in the desert, or as
the paschal Lamb. There are three sorts of spiritual sense: the allegorical, the anagogical and the tropological.[21]

Aquinas's defence and the sheer weight of long tradition kept the
spiritual senses in use. Aquinas himself found multiple meanings,
literal or figurative, an indispensable help in interpretation. In
Luther's early sermons we find exclamations: 'Wonderful is the
emphasis in those words and the propriety, as is the way of the Holy
Spirit . . . That is well demonstrated in the figure, that he appeared in
tongues of fire: propriety is in the tongue and energy in the fire.'[22]
Nevertheless, the accommodation of the figurative within the literal
and a new willingness to look to the particular circumstances in
which a word was used were of great long-term importance in the
development of exegetical methods, for Counter-Reformation as for
Reformation scholars. The literal sense, says Bellarmine, is that to
which the words immediately refer, the spiritual senses something
beyond their immediate reference. There are three sorts of spiritual
sense: the allegorical, the tropological and the anagogical. The literal
sense is *duplex*: there is a simple literal sense, which consists in the
proper signification of the words (*in proprietate verborum*), and a
literal sense which is *figuratus*, which involves figures, in which
words are transferred from their natural signification to another, and
there are as many variations of this as there are figures.[23]

The revolt against the spiritual senses did not, then, blot them out
in the later Middle Ages. Jacobus Faber Stapulensis (c. 1455–1536)
sustained spiritual exegesis enthusiastically.[24] Its use was kept up in
devotional and spiritual writings. It was defended from the text of
the Bible itself. Johann Eck argues from the opening of John's
Gospel: *In principio erat Verbum* rather than: *In principio erat Filius*
that the (figurative) use of 'Word' is designed to remind us that the
Son was not begotten *per modum nature* in the way human sons are
begotten, but *per modum intelligentie*.[25] The notion that Old Testament characters and events prefigure those of the New as 'types' continued in use well beyond the Middle Ages. What would it benefit the
whole church to know that there was a man in the land of Hus who
suffered many calamities patiently, and whose story is related in a
canonical book inspired by the Holy Spirit and forty-two chapters
long, if it had no meaning beyond what is related? Job is a *typus*, a

type; the purpose of the book of Job, the *principalis intentio libri*, is
to show that human affairs are governed by divine providence.[26] A
clear parallel can be drawn between the four animals of Ezekiel's
vision and the four evangelists, between the vision of Ezekiel and the
vision of John on Patmos.[27]

Faced with their continued use, the reformers are sometimes vocal
on the dangers of the spiritual interpretations. Calvin contests a traditional understanding of II Corinthians 3.6–10, where Paul says
that the letter kills and the spirit gives life. He cites Origen as the
source of the idea that the 'letter' is the 'grammatical' meaning of
Scripture and the 'spirit' the allegorical sense. 'Thus, through the centuries, it has been commonly accepted and passed round that here
Paul has provided us with a key for the allegorical interpretation of
Scripture.' Nothing, says Calvin, was further from his mind. By
'letter' he meant preaching which does not touch the heart and by
'spirit' he meant live, powerful preaching, which works upon men's
hearts by grace. Origen and others have given rise to a pernicious
error, and led many to believe that unless Scripture is interpreted
allegorically it is useless.[28]

The unreformed interpreters to whom he addresses his reproaches
'divide the Scripture into four senses', says William Tyndale. These
are the four which had become traditional in the Western Church
under the influence of Augustine and Gregory, 'the literal, tropological, allegorical and anagogical'. As a result, Tyndale says, 'the literal
sense has become nothing at all: for the pope hath taken it clean
away, and hath made it his possession. He hath partly locked it up
with the false and counterfeited keys of his traditions, ceremonies
and feigned lies; and partly driveth men from it with violence of sort.'
In this polemic of the late 1520s, Tyndale saw the fourfold exegesis
of Scripture as the enemy of that correct reading by which the
Christian learns from the Bible what God wants to teach him. He
holds up the literal sense as the only sense, and like Calvin he thinks
'the greatest cause of' the 'captivity' and 'the decay of faith, and this
blindness wherein we now are, sprang first of allegories'.[29]

Luther, too, saw spiritual interpretation as something he had
deliberately put behind him:

> When I was young I was learned, especially before I came to the study of
> theology. At that time I dealt with allegories, tropologies, and analogies and did
> nothing but clever tricks with them. If somebody had them today they'd be
> looked upon as rare relics. I know they're nothing but rubbish. Now I've let them
> go, and this is my last and best art, to translate the Scriptures in their plain sense.

The literal sense does it – in it there's life, comfort, power, instruction and skill. The other is tomfoolery, however brilliant the impression it makes.[30]

When I was a monk I was a master in the use of allegories . . . Afterward through the epistle to the Romans I came to some knowledge of Christ. I recognised then that allegories are nothing, that it is not what Christ signifies but what Christ is that counts . . . I reflected on the histories and thought how difficult it must have been for Gideon to fight with his enemies in the manner reported . . . It was not allegory but it was the Spirit and faith that inflicted such havoc on the enemy with only three hundred men. Jerome and Origen contributed to the practice of searching only for allegories. God forgive them.[31]

The late mediaeval revision of the definition of the literal sense made this rejection easier because it made it possible to retain a large number of figurative usages within the conspectus of the literal sense. Tyndale himself exemplifies very well the way in which the device of thirteenth century scholars which brought some figurative usages within the conspectus of the literal sense continued in use and made available an additional dimension of interpretation to the reformers who wanted to employ it. Tyndale explains that the Bible contains figurative language which is quite clearly deliberately used, and where there is no question of our reading into it an interpretation of a fancifully 'spiritual' sort.

That literal sense is the root and ground of all, and the anchor that never faileth, whereunto if thou cleave, thou canst never err or go out of the way. And if thou leave the literal sense thou canst not *but* go out of the way. Nevertheless, the Scripture useth proverbs, similitudes, riddles, or allegories, as all other speeches do; but that which the proverb, similitude, riddle, or allegory signifieth, is ever the literal sense, which thou must seek out diligently: as in the English we borrow words and sentences of one thing, and apply them to another, and give them new significations . . . 'Look ere thou leap': whose literal sense is, 'Do nothing suddenly, or without advisement'. So in like manner the scripture borroweth words and sentences of all manner things, and maketh proverbs and similitudes, or allegories. As Christ saith, Luke IV, 'Physician, heal thyself': whose interpretation is, 'Do that at home, which thou doest in strange places'; and that is the literal sense. So when I say, 'Christ is a lamb'; I mean not a lamb that beareth wool, but a meek and patient lamb, which is beaten for other men's faults . . . The similitudes of the gospel are allegories, borrowed of wordly matters, to express spiritual things.[32]

This sort of 'similitude' is different from the use of comparisons invented by the interpreter. Such figurative interpretation is legitimate, within certain bounds. Tyndale would rate the use of a method which Scripture itself employs beyond the point to which Scripture itself uses it (that is, a mere 'borrowing' of similitudes and allegories from Scripture) as 'no sense of the Scripture, but free things besides

the Scripture'. Their use must be confined within 'the compass of the
faith'. There must be no 'wild adventures'. Thus, 'of Peter and his
sword make I the law, and of Christ the Gospel'. This allegory proves
nothing, nor can do. 'For it is not the Scripture, but an ensample
borrowed of the Scripture to declare a text of a conclusion of the
Scripture more expressly, and to root it and grave it in the heart.'[33]
This is the essential principle: literal interpretation, including
interpretation of figures put there deliberately by the human author
of the text, is one thing. The human authors of Scripture sometimes
borrow a similitude or figure from the Old Testament. Here 'doth the
literal sense prove the allegory, and bear it, as the foundation beareth
the house'.[34] Free figurative interpretation as the reader chooses is
another. It can prove nothing. Its value is that 'a similitude, or an
ensample, doth print a thing much deeper in the wits of a man than
doth plain speaking'.

This separation of the literal sense with its own proper figures
from the spiritual senses which involve the making of artificial comparisons is put into practice throughout Tyndale's Prologues to the
books of the Bible. 'There is no story nor gest, seem it never so simple
or so vile unto the world, but that thou shalt find therein spirit and
life and edifying in the literal sense',[35] he insists. Allegories made by
man 'worldly similitudes', 'prove nothing'; their function is only to
'express more plainly that which is contained in the scripture'.[36]
'Cleave unto the text and plain story, and endeavour thyself to search
out the meaning of all that is described therein, and the true sense of
all manner of speakings of the scripture; of proverbs, similitudes, and
borrowed speech, . . . and beware of subtle allegories.'[37]

In this way Tyndale is able to retain what seems to him the best of
the old system – the reference to Augustine's *modus loquendi* comes
naturally – and to retain something of the advantages of the figurative interpretations, while elevating the literal sense to the status of the
only sense which is acceptable:

The scripture hath a body without, and within a soul, spirit and life. It hath without a bark, a shell and as it were a hard bone, for the fleshly-minded to gnaw
upon: and within it hath pith, kernel, marrow, and all sweetness for God's elect.[38]

The old image of chewing and sucking Scripture and coming to the
heart of its flavour, which in the earlier Middle Ages had made the
spiritual senses the kernel, is now adapted for the literal sense alone.

8

VIS VOCIS

1 The Bible's language

Wyclif speaks of the *vis vocis*, the intention of the words of Scripture. This, he holds, makes it possible for the literal sense to carry a force of proof which the spiritual cannot.[1] To abandon the use of 'spiritual' interpretations in argument and proving is to lose a number of the ways devised by patristic and earlier mediaeval scholars of getting round difficulties in the text – especially the method of resolving apparent contradictions by regarding one or both passages as 'spiritual' in meaning. Some of these solutions could be retained by including metaphors and some figures within the literal sense, but not all. The new work on the theory of language which had prompted the strong interest in the literal sense of twelfth and thirteenth century scholars provided some solutions in its own terms of deeper investigation into the nature and working of language.

As a rule, the endeavour was still to find a way to interpret the text as it stood. The possibility that some of the difficulties might arise from corruptions in the text was considered, and some scholars, as we shall see, tried to arrive at a correct text. But this second, and in the long term immensely important development, belongs in its full implications to the period of the humanists and reformers. For the most part, mediaeval grammar and logic pursued the hard road of trying to make sense of the text available, and we must begin with that.

William of Auvergne pointed to a distinction between making comparisons between things and events in the natural world and the divine, and regarding things and events as actually signifying the divine. The latter he thinks a dangerous practice. He gives as an example the adultery of David with Bathsheba. If this is taken (as had become usual) to signify Christ's union with the Church, it seems to many to be offensive in its implications, because the unedifying

aspects of the tale are included by implication with the points of simi-
larity. If it is merely used as a basis for comparison, the relevant
details can be separated from the irrelevant and the analogy limited,
as it must be, since there can be no equivalence in reality between
creature and Creator.[2]

The discussion of signification in all its ramifications was the first
task of the late mediaeval study of the Bible's language, as it had been
in the West since Augustine pointed to its importance in the *De
Doctrina Christiana*, but with a new technical refinement made
possible by the work of the twelfth century. By the beginning of the
thirteenth century, the study of grammar and logic was highly
sophisticated, providing, its practitioners were confident, a means of
access to the solution of deep problems about the nature of language
and its function of enabling us to speak of things created or divine.
Technical terms were used freely in commentary and discussion, on
the assumption that all students were familiar with them by the time
they came to the study of the Sacred Page. Early in the century
Alexander of Hales, for example, addresses himself to a passage in
Peter Lombard's *Sentences* (Dist. II.7), like this: 'Father and Son and
Holy Spirit are (*sunt*) of one substance.' He notes that Augustine was
uncertain whether the verb ought to be in the singular or the plural.[3]
Should we say Father, Son and Holy Spirit 'are' of one substance or
'is' of one substance, since the subject of the verb is one God not
three? Alexander considers, without feeling it necessary to explain
his choice of terms, the way in which the word *Deus* is made to refer
to the thing it signifies (*impositum*), its signification (*significatio*) or
any additional signification (*consignificatio*) and the way of speaking involved (*tropus*); he takes it that the student will appreciate the
bearing of a parallel example in Psalm 81.6;[4] and he makes a resolution of the problem which depends on certain assumptions about
the way words signify things.

Another thirteenth century commentator, Albertus Magnus,
writing on Isaiah, illustrates the role grammatical considerations
might play. Discussing *trans Iordanem Galilaeae gentium* (Isaiah
9.1), he examines *trans* in its context and explains that it is behaving
here not as a preposition, which would signify being opposite to the
speaker (*'trans' praepositio non notatur ibi sicut oppositum
loquenti*), but as part of a *circumlocutio*, *trans-Iordanem*, which signifies a piece of land which is across-the-Jordan (*sed situm . . . 'trans
Iordanem'*).[5]

The 'speculative' grammar which looked at language in ways close to the concerns of the logicians began in the twelfth century, had a relatively brief flowering during the thirteenth century and was already fading in the first decades of the fourteenth century, as it became absorbed into the 'modern' logic of the day. Textbooks of speculative grammar had always travelled with treatises on *sophismata* and *quaestiones*, in scholarly notebooks and relatively independently of the ordinary grammars based on Donatus and Priscian,[6] although some of the technical terminology (perhaps inevitably) crept into the latter. But in the period of its influence it entered deeply into the preoccupations of the logicians and made them think about the mechanical operations of language in ways which are partly grammatical in inspiration. This duality of grammar and logic in mediaeval thinking was never fully fused into one in the Middle Ages. The 'modists' among the grammarians, with their emphasis upon the range of 'ways' in which a word might signify, tried to establish a theory of 'double imposition'. A sound first acquires a meaning by being attached to a *ratio significandi*, that is, some link with a property of the thing or things it is to signify, which makes it a *dictio* or word. Secondly, it is further and more closely associated with the thing signified. At that stage it becomes a part of speech which can be susceptible of grammatical accidents, declined or conjugated.[7]

Despite attempts to define their relationship, grammar and logic persisted in their duality until the influence of humanist ideas began to encourage a different emphasis: on the literary and philological aspects of grammar, on correctness and elegance.[8] Something of both philosophical and practical value was thus lost to students of the Bible's language. It ceased to be a matter of course to distinguish between the lexical meaning or signification of a word and its function in the sentence. *Dictio*, word, and *pars orationis*, part of speech, became synonymous. Interest passed from language as a system of signs[9] for things, and for concepts of things, whose relationship was the nub of the epistemological debates of the Middle Ages.

2 Ways of signifying and the properties of terms

Wyclif provides an excellent vantage-point from which to look at mature mediaeval criticism, in which logic had taken grammar as far as possible to itself and developed a large apparatus for use in all scriptural contingencies. His early *Logica* was, he says, written to help students of the Bible who confuse technical terms of logic in their reading and fail to come to any valid conclusion. The *Logica* is not an important logical work in its own right; its value for our purposes is precisely that it sums up the assumptions in which Wyclif was trained and which underlie much of the exegetical work of the later Middle Ages. Everywhere in his discussions Wyclif shows himself concerned with the use of terms and the analysis of terms which the special difficulties of the Bible's language necessitate. He claims that all the range (*variatio*) in the proofs which may be drawn from propositions is derived from terms (*habeat ortum ex terminis*). As he divides and classifies terms he emphasises the way they work as building-blocks for propositions.[10] We must look at this logicians' doctrine in some detail if late mediaeval thinking on the Bible's language is to be intelligible.

Augustine's relatively loose talk of Scripture's usages (*usus loquendi*) and modes of speaking (*modi locutionum*) had been designed to make it possible to get over difficulties of interpretation by distinguishing between the special constructions necessary in the Bible if it is to speak of the divine, and those of ordinary speech. In the hands of mediaeval logicians from the time of Anselm[11] this device became more technical and progressed towards a developed doctrine of the properties of terms, in which the emphasis is upon their behaviour in different parts of a proposition.

The *modistae*, who flourished for a period up to the middle decades of the fourteenth century, had much to offer the readers of the Bible. As Wyclif comments, from the standpoint of a scholar who was able to make use of a number of their ideas, Christ 'like a *celestis et realis philosophus* loaded his words with a multiple and subtle meaning (*multiplici et subtili sentencia*)'.[12] He looks at some of these *modi loquendi* in detail,[13] with the aid of the logic and metaphysics which he believes to be necessary helps in finding solutions to puzzling passages.[14] The same consciousness of *modi loquendi* is apparent in Bellarmine. 'If we consider the *modis dicendi*,' he says, 'we shall find innumerable points of difficulty, things which seem contradictory, ambiguous words and sayings, incomplete statements, preposterous statements, phrases peculiar to Hebrew, many figurative expressions'. The 'thing' and the *modus dicendi* are for Melanchthon as for Bellarmine the two elements which must always be considered in reading the Bible, and the function of the *modus dicendi* is to throw light on the *res*.[15]

It was common doctrine, but by no means a straightforward rule, that a word becomes attached to the thing it signifies by a process of 'imposition', that is, by being applied to it or made to refer to it. Bonaventure provides an example of the use of the notion in the study of the Bible, in a particular case (of giving names to individuals) which throws the principle into relief. Did Jesus 'impose' the name 'Peter' on the apostle Simon at the moment when he said, 'You will be called Peter'? It seems not. The interlinear gloss says that Jesus did not name him then, but he indicated what he would be called (*nondum imponit ei nomen, sed praesignat*). Mark says in his Gospel that the Lord called the twelve and then gave Simon the name of Peter (*et tunc imposuit Simoni nomen Petrus*) (Mark 3.17). Matthew says that he gave it him when he confessed him Son of God (Matthew 16.16ff). Bonaventure marshals Augustine's view and Bede's, in an effort to establish the precise point at which Peter was given his name and proposes a solution which involves distinguishing between the 'giving' of the name and its 'general use' (*vulgatum*).

Involving deeper difficulties still is the problem of the naming of Jesus. Was the name 'Jesus' a proper name given to Christ as a man? In Luke 2.21 we read: 'His name was called "Jesus" ' in a context where it seems a proper name (*nomen proprium*) which belongs to his humanity (*convenit humanitati sue*). But in Ecclesiasticus 46 and 50, Haggai 2, Zechariah 3, Habbakuk 3, the 'prophetic' reference in such passages as *exultabo in Deo Iesu meo* would suggest that it is a *nomen appellativum* signifying the divine nature and the human nature in hypostatic union (*naturam divinam et naturam humanam ypostatice copulatae*).[16] Underlying all these discussions is the assumption that the student will understand something of the technicalities of the act of 'imposition' by which words are made to refer to things, and of the complexity of this process of 'naming'.

There is a preoccupation in both these examples with the difference between naming in particular and naming something general or common: in the first case with the imposition of 'Peter' at a particular time and place as the name of one individual and its common use as his name at a later date, and in the other with the imposition of 'Jesus' as the name of a particular new-born human child and its use timelessly to refer to the Incarnate Word. These are special cases arising in Scripture of the central problem of separating the imposition of words as names (for particular things), from naming the general or abstract idea or concept (those notions which are common to all rational minds and which make it possible to do more with language than simply point to particular things).

This way of thinking required an approach which rested on the assumption that the ways in which a word signifies form a connected system with the ways or modes of being of the things signified, and of rational understanding, human or divine. Already in the twelfth century there had been discussion of the notion that at a deep level grammar is universal. Boethius of Dacia was able to assert in his *Modi Significandi* of the last quarter of the thirteenth century (a set of Questions on Priscian linking grammar with logic) that there is only one grammar underlying all languages. Anything which can be conceived by the mind can be signified by a word which can be identified as some part of speech. All meaning and reference is interlinked in a vast and complex system of signs and significations, and rules of procedure for setting them out.[17]

Wyclif recognised clearly that the imposition of words is a technically complex process, involving all these considerations. He defines a 'term'[18] as what the grammarians would call a *dictio*, something *artificialiter inventa*, designed by man to make propositions from (*propter composicionem proposicionis*).[19] But though the name of the thing may be artificially chosen, the thing it names is inseparably linked with a concept, and that means that the operations of language are firmly fixed in reality. Wyclif divides terms into the simple (*simplex*) which corresponds to a single conception in the mind (*conceptus in anima*) and the composite, such as 'holy man' (*homo sanctus*), where two or more different concepts are brought together,[20] and he discusses some of the difficulties into which the logicians had got themselves in trying to work out the relation of word to concept and thing.

For those who held a Realist view of the nature of language, the primary signification of a term (*quod primo et principaliter apprehenditur toto signo*)[21] was the universal or concept to which it referred, and its secondary signification the particular thing to which it referred.[22] The term 'man', for example, is used primarily to denote each and every man in his humanity, and only secondarily to refer to a particular man.[23] This secondary signification may point to the particular in various ways: by an association of ideas, or by extending the general meaning of a part in relation to a whole, for instance,[24] and in this and other complexities of the mode of signification there was ample scope for the exegete to find ways of penetrating to an understanding of the signification of what was otherwise hard to understand in the text of the Bible.

In one widely-used account *significatio* has three 'functions' in the context of a statement or proposition: *suppositio*, *appellatio* and *copulatio*. William of Sherwood set out the four general headings (*significatio, suppositio, copulatio, appellatio*) in his *introduction to Logic* before the end of the thirteenth century.[25] The last three involve the reference in particular contexts of words which may be capable of various *significationes*. The *copulatio* was sometimes regarded as, in a sense, the least 'significant'. Paul of Venice in his *Logica Magna* of the turn of the fourteenth century (d. 1429) maintains what is inevitably one view of many in a controversial milieu where every point has to be argued against alternative opinions even in what promised to become a standard textbook.[26] He suggests that a *copula* in a proposition has in fact no reference of its own. Its task is solely to express the relationship between what the predicate signifies and what the subject signifies.[27] Walter Burleigh was already taking the same view a century earlier. He explains that *est* may be itself a predicate, as in *homo est*, and then it is a term with reference in its own right in the context. If it acts as a copula between subject and predicate it becomes a sort of 'third party' (*tertium adjacens*), and then it does not signify in context in its own right.[28] Its power of signification is frozen by its use in such a context.

Appellation and supposition, on the other hand, have to do with the reference a term may have when its signification is modified by being put into a subject or predicate. The term *appellatio* may have been derived from Priscian's term *nomen appellativum*,[29] but whatever its grammatical origin, it was held by logicians to apply to the use of a term in a proposition, normally in the predicate. When a term was used in a predicate its signification would be limited to a particular reference, and then that signification would be called *appellatio*. A number of logicians also maintained that a term could have *appellatio* only if it applied to something which existed at the time of speaking, that is, if it has a *presens convenientia*.[30] *Appellatio*, says William of Sherwood, is 'in a term insofar as it is capable of being predicated of the things which are subordinate to it through the use of the verb "is" ' (*appellatio . . . inest termino secundum quod est predicabilis de suis rebus mediante hoc verbo*).[31] Walter Burleigh defines *appellatio* as a property of a common term (*terminus communis*) which is predicable of things inferior to it (*suis inferioribus*). It is strictly a property of the predicate. It can be said to 'name' (*appellare*) things subordinate to it but not to 'signify' them.[32]

In supposition, too, there must be a context which limits the signification. Originally that context was conceived of grammatically. Just as the term *appellatio* is seen to derive from a technical term of

grammar, so the term *suppositio* first refers to the grammatical subject of a verb in a proposition, and was extended to refer to the substance of the individual thing it signifies, together with its 'quality' or
universal nature.[33] Walter Burleigh gives a general definition of
supposition[34] as 'taking' a term to stand for something (*acceptio
termini pro aliquo*), whether the 'something' is a thing or a word or
a concept.[35] *Acceptio* is used in rather this way by Bonaventure for
such 'taking'. He says that *principium* is sometimes taken (*accipitur*)
essentialiter, as when it is said with respect to creatures and refers to
their really having a beginning of their beings; and sometimes
notionaliter, as when it is said that Father and Son are the *principium*
of the Holy Spirit, whose being has no beginning.[36] The signification
of the word *principium* may be either of these. Its supposition will be
determined by the context in which it is used.

Strictly, *suppositio*, like *appellatio*, is confined to propositions.[37]
Wyclif, like Bacon, Burleigh, Ockham, takes that as a first principle.
'No term supposits (*supponit*) outside an *oratio*.' It is a 'function' of
signification in a context. More strictly, in many authors it came to
be restricted to a subject-term. When a common noun or similar sub-
stantive occurs as a subject in a proposition its meaning is subordinated to that of the predicate. This we speak of as *sub-positio*. The
presence of the predicate limits the signification of the subject-term,
just as the presence of the subject limits that of the terms in the
predicate.

In line with developments in signification theory at large,
supposition came to be divided into two types: material and formal.
In material supposition the term supposits for itself, as in: ' "I" is a
pronoun'; ' "lord" is a noun', that is, for a grammatical category.
The word itself is a grammatical object. Formal supposition is either
simple or personal. When it is simple, it supposits for a universal or
general notion, such as occurs in 'Man is predicated of every man',
where 'man' stands for humanity as a whole. In 'personal' supposition, the reference may be single ('Peter is a man') or common, as
when the term supposits *confusa pro multis*, for many individuals
indiscriminately. This is the distinction which lies behind one of the
points debated in Ockham's *Quodlibets*: whether *homo* or
humanitas are synonymous (*nomina synonyma*) according to
Aristotle's intention (*secundum intentionem philosophi*).[38]

Paul of Venice sets out one accepted late mediaeval version in his
Logica Magna. There are three types of reference by which words
signify things: in the first, material reference, the term refers to itself

as in a grammatical category ('man' is a noun): (Paul of Venice recommends the use of quotation marks for greater clarity). In the second simple reference, the term refers to a concept (humanity is a species). In personal reference the term refers outside language and outside thought to a particular individual or individuals, and at the same stage additional complications arise in the form of words such as 'all', 'every', 'some', which affect the reference.[39] We shall come to these *syncategoremata* shortly.

First, a word about 'improper' supposition. This, as Wyclif describes it, takes a signification other than would be common usage (*usus loquendi*). If we say 'England fights' (*Anglia pugnat*) the word 'England' supposits for (*supponit pro*) 'Englishmen'.[40] This is Walter Burleigh's definition, too: 'Improper supposition is when a term supposits for another by transference (*ex transumptione*) or *ex usu loquendi*.[41] Some scholars ruled improper supposition out of the logician's province. Paul of Venice does so. But he concedes that figurative statements such as 'I drink a cup' (*bibo cifum*) and 'England fights' (*Anglia pugnat*) have reference. It cannot be classified into material, simple or personal.[42] Yet it is supposition, and its functioning was, in practice, of the first importance in the study of the Bible, especially when the literal sense was extended to include just such metaphors. The stock examples of the logicians show an admixture of Biblical examples: *pratum ridet* is given as an example of a metaphor; as an example of taking the container for the contents or the reverse, *audiat terra verba oris mei*, where the 'earth' is said to hear rather than the people in it; as an example of taking the common term to stand for the individual, *apostolus praedicat*, where Paul is meant, as an individual, but the common term 'apostle' is used.[43] Similar instances are found in more than one author.[44]

Wyclif has a good deal to say about the Bible's use of figurative language in his discussion of Hebrews 1.1–2 (*multiphariam multisque modis olim Deus loquens patribus in prophetis*). God spoke in many ways, in figures and mysteries in the youth of the Church; in more recent times he spoke through his incarnate Son, in plain language (*plane sermone*) and literally.[45] Similarly, in his own day, Wyclif finds images helpful to simple men; images are the 'books' of laymen. They are *signa sensibilia*, signs which can be perceived by the senses.[46] Even Jesus spoke sometimes in parables, so that the hidden and saving meaning (*sentencia latens et salubris*) might be more firmly imprinted on the memory.[47] When Christ mounted an ass (Matthew 21.2) he signified *ad sensum allegoricum* that he had assumed human nature; and the tropological sense of the colt is that the gentiles were brought into the Church by his coming.[48] The fact that the apostles returned safely from their errand to the *castellum* (which Wyclif understands to have been fortified against them) shows in the anagogical sense how the blessed are safe from their enemies.[49] In these and similar ways Wyclif incorporates the traditional modes of analysis by the spiritual or figurative senses of Scripture into the talk of improper signification and supposition with which contemporary logic expressed them.

A free adaptation of the doctrine of signification is to be found in John Hus's commentary on the *Sentences*. This scholarly jest, for all its technical informality, underlines admirably the extent to which the doctrine of signification was common doctrine for late mediaeval exegetes. 'Scripture is said to be holy *primo significative* and *secundo effective*', he said at his inception as a Master. The pun on the theory of signification is developed. Scripture 'signifies holy things'; and it has a causative effect in bringing about holiness in men.[50]

3 Syncategoremata

Terms are commonly divided by mediaeval logicians into those which can signify by themselves (*termini significativi* or *categorematici*), such as nouns and verbs, and those which can signify only in conjunction with *termini significativi*. These last are known as *termini consignificativi* or *syncategorematici*. The principal terms are called 'categorematic' because they can form logical predicates: that is, they can be affirmed or denied of the subject of the proposition in ways which correspond to the 'categories' or *praedicamenta* of Aristotle's *Categories*, explaining what it is or what it is like, or what it does, and so on. The second are called *syncategoremata* because they must be joined with (*syn-*)*categoremata* before they can do any work in the proposition. They include such parts of speech as prepositions and conjunctions. For example, like other *syncategoremata*, prepositions modify the principal terms in some way, but have, for practical purposes, no independent signification; their signification becomes fused with that of the categorematic terms they influence or with the whole predicate, making it, for the purposes of the proposition, into something different. William of Sherwood explains this change in his definition of the way a preposition is used. A preposition is, he says, used to indicate definitely (*definite*) a state of things (*habitudinem*) which signifies indefinitely (*indefinite*: that is, for the duration of the proposition) something fortuitous (*casuale*: that is, which depends on the chance juxta-position of preposition and categorematic word).[51]

The terminology which labels these *consignificativi* is ambiguous. The term *consignificatio* has a prior sense in the textbooks of the old logic. A verb is said to con-signify the time at which the action of the verb is done, along with the action of the verb itself. This property of verbs had a special application in the study of the Bible's language. In the Bible the use of tenses has a unique characteristic of being in a sense independent of time. God is eternal and no act of God can be said to be in the past, present or future even if it takes place within the created world where such categories operate. Bonaventure raises a number of questions about tenses in his commentary on Ecclesiastes. 'Eternal', he said, may have various meanings: it may indicate that no end is fixed, as in the promise that the children of Israel will have the promised land *in possessionem aeternam*. It may mean that there will be no end in time: thus time itself is eternal for it cannot end in time. It may mean that the substance referred to will have no end, or that it has neither end nor beginning. This last is the eternity of God him-self.[52] Or we may look at time itself and ask what it is 'to do the action of a verb' *cum tempore*; *in tempore*; *sub tempore*; *pro tempore*.[53] If we apply considerations of this sort to the actual use of verbs in the text we might ask of the word *erat* whether, if it is in the past imperfect, it is incompatible with eternity (*omnino repugnat aeternitati*). Commenting on John, Bonaventure is able to give a number of instances in Scripture of tenses which do not behave as tenses normally do, and to break down the ways in which, as they sig-nify divine actions, they may behave differently.[54] We shall come to some of the further ramifications of all this when we look at the Bible's future tenses.

To return to *consignificativi* in the later technical sense of *syn-categoremata*.

Peter of Spain sets out one of the implications in his *Tractatus Syn-categorematum*. The syncategorematic words, he says, 'cause' truth or falsity in a proposition.[55] But, as William of Sherwood points out, that means that they cause difficulty,[56] not least because they pertain in some way both to the subject and to the predicate.[57]

Among such terms, as listed by William, are 'every' or 'all' (*omnis*), 'whole' (*totum*), number words, 'no' (*nullus*), 'nothing' (*nihil*), 'neither' (*neutrum*), 'but' (*praeter*), 'alone' (*solus*), 'only' (*tantum*), 'is' (*est*), 'not' (*non*), 'necessarily' (*necessario*) and 'contingently' (*contingenter*), 'begins' (*incipit*), 'ends' (*desinit*), 'if' (*si*), 'unless' (*nisi*), 'but that' (*quin*), 'and' (*et*), 'or' (*vel*), 'whether' (*utrum*), 'or' (*an*), the particle *ne*, 'whether . . . or' (*sive . . . sive*).

Peter of Ailly, a century after William of Sherwood and Peter of Spain, was able to classify categorematic and syncategorematic terms with a comparative tidiness made possible by a good deal of scholarly labour done in the meantime by others. His analysis was used by most of the later authors at Paris. Peter of Ailly's (1350–1420/1) distinction is between the use to which a term is put in a particular proposition (its function) and its signification. A word may be categorematic both in its signification, that is, in being able to signify on its own, and in its function in the sentence as subject or predicate ('horse', 'John'). Or it may be categorematic only by virtue of its function: *est* needs to be joined to a categorematic term in order to signify, but if it serves as a predicate (*equus est*) it becomes categorematic by its function. '[There] is a horse' is a satisfactory statement. Some words are categorematic by signification alone. An adjective which is qualifying a noun does not stand alone in the statement and is not categorematic by function. Nevertheless, it is capable of signifying independently (*grammaticus* may mean 'a grammarian'). Similarly, terms may be syncategorematic by both function and signification, as are many of the terms William of Sherwood lists, all logical connectives, and quantifiers, and negation. Syncategorematic by function alone are those terms which are categorematic by signification alone, and syncategorematic by signification alone are those terms which are categorematic by function alone.[58]

Peter of Ailly's classification by function and signification helps to clarify areas of difficulty in identifying syncategorematic terms, but there remains the difficulty of putting *syncategoremata* themselves into order. Walter Burleigh attempts a classification into hypotheticals which are explicit (copulatives, disjunctives, *an*), or implicit (four types: exclusives, such as *nihil*, *tantam*, *solus*; exceptives, such as *praeter*, *nisi*; reduplicatives, such as *inquantum*, *secundum quod*; and *incipit*, *desinit*, which form a class by themselves).[59] William of Sherwood tries out a division of syncategorematic words[60] pertaining to the subject from those pertaining to the composition of a predicate and a subject. There are, he finds, signs distributive of *supposita*, such as 'every', 'all', 'whole', number words, 'infinitely many', 'both'; signs distributive of *copulata*, such as *qualelibet*; negative signs, such as *nullus*, *nihil*, *neutrum*. There are exceptive words, like 'but', and exclusives ('alone', 'only'). Among words which connect predicate and subject, 'is' and 'not' are of primary importance, but William of Sherwood includes 'necessarily', 'contingently', 'begins' and 'ceases', 'if', 'unless', 'but that', 'and', 'or', 'whether . . . or', *ne*.

These classifications are not fully satisfactory, and they differ from author to author. Each scholar is to some extent feeling his way. William of Sherwood relies a good deal upon Priscian, whom he cites frequently as he puzzles out instances where a term is syncategorematic in logic but not in grammar (*omnis*, for example). But certain common patterns emerge. Standard elements in the treatment of *syncategoremata* are definitions and analyses designed to identify syncategorematic terms, classifications like William of Sherwood's, discussions of the grammatical, semantic and logical rules which operate in propositions containing syncategoremata, examples, sophismata resolved so as to show up misunderstandings in analysis, and questions arising from these explanations.[61] The root of the difficulty is that *syncategoremata* are a vast and far from homogeneous group of terms which have in common only their failure to signify independently in propositions; they include and involve a wide range of highly problematic areas.

Our scholars recognise that much may be 'implicit in Scripture'. One of the difficulties facing the logician is the presence, in both deliberately sophistical and quite innocent arguments, of embedded or implicit[62] features of what is being said which, once they are brought out, prove to alter the propositions which contain them. It is again largely a matter of the logic of terms. Wyclif includes among these terms a number of the standard *syncategoremata*.[63] 'Scripture is not to be despised for its simple or childlike language' (*pueriles significationes*), Wyclif insists. Such passages signify 'primarily' a truth which reflects their divine Author's truth. So it is as 'foolish' to ask what 'and' and 'not' and 'therefore' 'or any other syncategorematic term signifies completely as it is to ask what is signified by "God is not" '.

Wyclif draws a parallel between the well-known phenomenon of incomplete signification in syncategorematic terms of this sort, and the behaviour of certain passages in the Bible. Syncategorematic terms seem far from *inadequate* when their function in a proposition is understood; properly linked with categorematic terms they signify completely. So it is with certain texts of Scripture. Once the behaviour of the terms they contain is understood, their full signifi-

cance and truth is apparent.[64] 'Something is true when its sense
(*sensus*) is true and false when its sense is false. I call a sense true by
which someone . . . conceives the truth.' Thus if good men hear the
statement 'a man is an ass', it does not signify to them that a man is
an ass, but on the contrary, in the light of the true sense they perceive
as good men, it signifies that nothing of the sort can be proved; and
similarly with incomplete significations: they make the sense they
should in good men's minds.[65]

Like Wyclif, Martin of Alnwick distinguishes those terms which
are 'discrete' from 'common' terms. Discrete terms are those which
do not have any others *inferiores se secundum predicationem*, subordinate to them in predication, into which they can be resolved.
Common terms are more complex. They have hidden contents,
which may be of various sorts: *resolubiles, exponibiles, modales*.[66]
Resoluble propositions contain a common noun which can be
resolved from a general into a discrete application.Modal propositions contain terms such as 'necessary' and 'possible', which affect
the signification of the other terms in ways which must be clarified if
they are to be understood correctly. Exponible propositions consist
of several propositions taken in conjunction in such a way that they
look superficially like a single proposition. They contain a *dictio
exclusiva* or *exceptiva*, such as 'differs', 'begins', 'ends'.[67] To be
understood, all these require 'unpacking'. Many of these compressed
propositions with hidden elements contain syncategorematic terms
which are affecting the signification of the terms they contain.

Bonaventure comments more than once on the difference a preposition can make to the interpretation of a passage of Scripture. It is
different to say 'glorified in', 'glorified through' (*per*), 'glorified by'
(*ab*), he says in his remarks on John 6.19, 'signifying by what death
he was to glorify God'.[68] Again, the Manichees argue from *Vos ex
patre Diabolo estis* that wicked men have the Devil for their father,
and so God is not the creator of wicked men, and again the argument
turns on the use of the preposition *ex*.[69]

A typical – and indeed very common – problem involving *syncategoremata* in Scripture concerns wholes and parts. Bonaventure
answers a question which has been raised concerning John's Gospel:
Omnia trahet ad se. This is clearly not the case. Not everyone
(*omnes*), nor even most people (*nec maior pars*) are converted to the
faith. There are more wicked men than good men. Bonaventure
replies that Augustine says that those who are moving towards non-
existence (*non-esse*) ought not to be counted; evil is nothing, and the

wicked are moving towards being nothing. The *omnia* of the text therefore applies only to the elect (*non fit distributio nisi pro electis*). The whole has been shown to be a part and the difficulty vanishes. Another difficulty arises elsewhere. The text says (John 1.14): *Quod factum est in ipso vita erat*. The following argument is proposed:

> What was made in him was life.
> All things were made in him.
> Therefore all things are alive.
> Therefore a stone is alive.

Bonaventure meets this argument in several ways, technically identified in contemporary terminology, but attributed to the Fathers in each case. Chrysostom says that the *quod* belongs to the previous *clausula* and is to be taken *implicative*. Hilary punctuates differently and sees the *quod causaliter* as 'causing' our life and salvation. Ambrose sees the construction as *appositiva*, Augustine as equivocal, and so on.[70]

PART III

PRACTICAL INTERPRETATION

9

THE TEXT

1 What is the Bible?

The apocrypha might be regarded as of secondary authority (*secundae auctoritatis*),[1] but they had an attraction for preachers because of the stories they contained which could be used as *exempla*. They were in an important sense part of a secure and fixed whole, although the debate about canonicity went on into the Reformation period.[2] The question of what was or was not part of the Bible and what kind of a whole it constituted is not our immediate concern here. But the debate points to the development of ideas about the identity of the Bible. Robert Bellarmine divides the *libri sancti* into three 'orders'. The first includes those books over whose canonicity there is no doubt. In the second order he places Hebrews, the Epistle of James, the second Epistle of Peter, parts of Luke, Mark, John, Tobias, Judith, Ecclesiasticus and other books whose authorship or canonicity has been brought into question. The books of the first order have the testimony of the Church in every age to support their divine *auctoritas*. In the case of books and parts of books of the second order there are sometimes major difficulties to be got out of the way. Books of the third order, 'even though some of them seem canonical' are called 'apocrypha' because their status is not clear. But they contain nothing misleading or erroneous.[3] He wanted to bring the Scriptures together as a whole for its readers, despite the complex nature of the claims to authenticity of its parts.

The liturgical use of the Bible presented it in fragments as it was read at services. Several mediaeval authors made an attempt to see it as a whole, or to see its parts in relationship to one another – not a minor matter when its books were so often bound separately and must have appeared physically as a collection of separate entities – and to identify the different functions and purposes of its parts. Jean of la Rochelle, for instance, took the motif of the Law, Psalms and Prophets and worked out an arrangement of the books of the Bible

under those heads.[4] A more common arrangement – found in
Aquinas and Nicholas of Lyre, for example – is built on Origen's
threefold division which makes Proverbs a book of moral science,
Ecclesiastes a book of natural science, the Song of Songs a book of
contemplation.[5] Peter Lombard took as the *principia rerum* questions concerning the place of the Pauline Epistles in the whole corpus
of Scripture;[6] again, he was making an attempt to see the Bible as a
whole.

This pattern-making is, however, a rather different thing from the
robust familiarity to which Luther came after he had had a whole
Bible to read for a time. He could compare one book with another:
'In Proverbs the eighth chapter is the best. Similar to this is the first
chapter of Ecclesiasticus . . . The Psalter, Isaiah, Jeremiah and even
Daniel are far superior to the books of Solomon as far as prophecies
are concerned.'[7] 'A doctor of the Scriptures,' he says, 'ought to have
a good knowledge of the Scriptures and ought to have grasped how
the prophets run into one another. It isn't enough to know only one
part – as a man might know Isaiah, for example – or to know only
one topic of the Law or Gospel.'[8]

Calvin puts his finger on the nub of the matter. 'All these witnesses'
(that is, the prophets and the apostles) 'come together into a unity so
well, and they are of one accord among themselves so fully, that it is
easy to recognise in such agreement most certain truth.'[9]

George Bull states the principle squarely in the seventeenth century: 'It is not to be supposed, that St. James hath advanced any
paradox or dogma peculiar to himself. No. What he says is the voice
of the Holy Spirit, which every where utters the same sound. The
Prophets, the Apostles, Christ himself, all give the same evidence.'[10]
All these ideas are important if the Bible is to be seen as something to
which it is possible to point and say that this, and not that, is the
Bible. This problem of the identity and integrity of the sacred text
underlies much of the debate we are to look at next.

2 Textual criticism: the Vulgate

Attempts were made as early as Carolingian times to remove corruptions in the text of the Bible. Lanfranc of Bec was an insistent correc-
tor, and the early Cistercians tried to purge their Bibles of accretions
and errors.[11] What was at issue here was the arrival of late corruptions in what was believed to have been a previously sound text. The

human authors of Scripture were not to blame: merely copyists of recent generations.

There was good reason to blame careless copying, particularly in the universities, where the demand for copies seems to have tempted the stationers to have more of an eye for profit than for accuracy. The Friar Thomas Waleys comments that good copying ought to be accurate copying. An exemplar is given to a copyist so that he may transfer what it contains to another sheet or volume, adding nothing and leaving nothing out, because as a rule copyists are not so knowledgeable that they can make such alterations without error. Notwithstanding, a false copyist will often leave something out which is in the exemplar because he is in a hurry and will not stop to make sure that the lines and punctuation match. He hopes his error (*falsitas*) will not be discovered until after he has been paid. Such a man deserves not payment but punishment. Thomas Waleys advises the buyer to examine the work carefully before paying the scribe, in case he has cheated.[12]

Not all changes were the result of carelessness. There is some evidence that the need to make the text make better sense, or to accord with the form or direction of some comment in the Fathers, encouraged some alterations. Aquinas provides an example: ' "Of them who seemed to be something" (Galatians 2.6). The text is deficient and should be amended to read, "Of them, namely Peter and John". So that it is as if Paul said, "Although I would have yielded to them at the time, yet I received from them no new power or teaching".'[13]

Roger Bacon wrote angrily in the mid-thirteenth century that there is greater and more dangerous error *in textu Dei*, in the Bible itself, than in philosophy books. 'The letter is false everywhere in the Vulgate,' he complains, 'and if the letter is false or doubtful, then the literal and spiritual sense will contain unspeakable error. He suggests the adoption of Augustine's principles, that an older manuscript should be preferred to a more recent and the majority reading to that of a minority of manuscripts; Augustine also suggests that when any doubt remains, the reader should go back to the original languages. In Bacon's experience, the Greek and Hebrew agree with the older manuscripts against the Paris text. He gives examples of additions, subtractions, false juxtapositions and errors of all sorts.[14]

In the second quarter of the thirteenth century the Dominican Chapter General – probably moved by Hugh of St Cher – ordered the Bibles of the Order to be standardised according to a list of corrections prepared by studying readings in the Fathers and in Greek and

Hebrew copies, and in the oldest manuscripts of the Latin text that could be found. There is some discussion in the prologues to these improved versions, of the merits of modern Hebrew manuscripts or of Greek and Hebrew against Latin, or of the value of alternative readings in the Fathers. There was an attempt to provide a critical apparatus of sorts.[15] These efforts were exploratory and they did not lead on uninterruptedly to the emergence of a mature system of textual criticism, or to the establishment of firm editorial principles. Their purpose was to put right mistakes of, it was believed, comparatively recent origin and not to take a critical look at the Vulgate text to see how satisfactory it was. A definitive text was thought to exist already, under the slips and miscopyings.

Something of the rather modest scale of the enterprise is clear from such works as Thomas Docking's collection of corrections in which the accurate spelling and declension of words in the text are the principal consideration.[16] There is sometimes no more than a mention of the existence of textual variants, a note perhaps that the Greek reads differently, often only a comparison of the different Latin versions, and the principle on which the correct one is identified may be no more than its conformity with the rules of syntax. The dominant discipline is grammar. An emendation is primarily designed to make good Latin.[17]

A brake was put on attempts to improve the available Latin translation wholesale by the profound respect in which Jerome continued to be held as a translator. Jacobus Faber Stapulensis (1455–1536) begins his commentary on the Pauline Epistles by discussing the problem of the many unsatisfactory passages in the text in common use in the Church. He would not feel it proper to alter Jerome (*neque enim id praesumpsissemus*); but he canvasses the view that the corrupt parts are not Jerome's at all, but survivals from an earlier rendering; he is able to point to 'many of the oldest manuscripts'. He has done what he can by putting a fresh translation (*intelligentia ex Graeco*) beside that of the Vulgate in his book.[18]

Robert Bellarmine discussed the question thoroughly as it looked to a scholar of the later sixteenth century who had not adopted the methods of the new criticism. Has the text of Scripture come down to us safely in the Vulgate? He looks at the *variae editiones* of Scripture: Hebrew, Chaldean, Greek, Latin, German, and so on. Can we take it, he asks, that the Hebrew text has come down to us as it was written by Moses and the prophets? Or is it so corrupted by the *perversum studium* of the Jews that it deserves to carry no authority in the Church? He examines various points in detail. The collation of manuscripts demonstrates that there are many places where the Hebrew text does not coincide with the Vulgate. Bellarmine believes that it is best to trust the Vulgate even where it is clear that something went wrong at an early date, for these variants are themselves in a sense parts (*partes quaedam*) of Holy Scripture and they have been there so long that they cannot be taken out now without causing distress to the people of God.[19] He looks at the Greek text. Who wrote it? The apostles and evangelists whose names appear in the titles of the books of the New Testament. What is the authority? There can be no doubt that the *editio apostolica* is of supreme authority. But there are corruptions, as in the Hebrew version. Some parts are missing in various Greek manuscripts, as the adulterous woman in John 8 and the last chapter of Mark.[20] What, then, of the Vulgate? The heretics, who disagree with one another wonderfully on all sorts of matters, agree in condemning it as an unreliable text. Bellarmine replies that if it were a recent version it might indeed be suspect. But it is a thousand years old. All the things the reformers criticise in the Vulgate were cited in that form by the Fathers and have clearly always been there. Certainly the 'spring' of the original languages ought to be preferred to the 'stream' which flows from them in the Vulgate, if the springs were unpolluted. But they have been shown to be muddy. The Hebrew and Greek are both corrupt. So the Vulgate remains, on balance, the safest text to use, with some recourse to texts in the original language in certain precisely defined circumstances: notably, when the Latin manuscripts disagree so that it cannot be determined from them what is the true Vulgate reading; when the word or *sententia* in the Latin is ambiguous, we may turn to the Greek or Hebrew, in case they are not ambiguous; it is permissible to look to the Greek or Hebrew to get the force of a word or its exact meaning (*ad energiam et proprietatem vocabulorum intelligendam*).[21] By and large these are the purposes for which mediaeval scholars had had recourse to the Greek or Hebrew where they had been able to do so. These procedures represent a nascent textual criticism, but one inexorably focussed on getting the Vulgate text right, as the only text proper for Bible study.

3 The original language

Some of the friars of the early fourteenth century in England showed a bent for the classics. Between about 1320 and 1350 they introduced a noticeable proportion of classical references into their lectures on the Bible, drawing parallels with Virgil or Livy or Seneca.[22] They were not uncritical of these sources. Virgil's account of the founding of Rome is recognised as a *fictio poete*, for it cannot correspond to the *veritas historie*. (Aeneas never saw Dido, who founded Carthage and was queen of that city, for Aeneas had been dead before Carthage was founded 'for thirty years and more'.)[23] Matters of historical interest are drawn out of the ancient sources repeatedly – there are many references to Livy and Seneca. ('Livy says that it was the custom among the Romans that when an Emperor wanted to make a law, and he intended it to be followed in one particular place, he caused it to be announced by messenger.'[24] 'We have an example in Seneca. He tells us that it was the ancient law among certain peoples that the elder brother divided the inheritance and the younger chose [between the parts] because it requires a more mature judgement to divide than to choose'.)[25]

They used such material not without an awareness that they were doing something contentious. John Lathbury, an Oxford Franciscan, addresses himself directly to the question: 'Surely the sayings of heathen poets and philosophers ought not to be applied to the holy purpose of the theologians?' He gives four familiar reasons why they should. Poetry and philosophy help and adorn the study of Holy Scripture. The sayings of poets and philosophers are humble *instrumenta* of divine wisdom and holy eloquence. They constitute a *media subtilia* for teaching and learning. When the sayings of poets are *nobilia*, they ought to be taken from the pagans as spoils and distributed to Christians.[26] A Carmelite of the early fourteenth century, John Baconthorpe, remarks on the same question that he himself has no objection to 'spoiling the Egyptians' in this way as an aid to preaching the Gospel (although he does not like to see fables and tales used as moral *exempla* as was increasingly common practice among the friars in their work among the laity).[27]

Pleading the same cause in the circumstances of the sixteenth century, Melanchthon says that it is fitting (*decet*) for Christians to 'cultivate this civil society' (*hanc civilem societatem colere*),[28] as long as it is clear that 'the fragrance of the unguents of the Lord is sweeter than the scent of human disciplines'.[29] By imitating classical models, Christians can learn to write well and that will enable them to argue better in the great cause of the faith.[30] A knowledge of the Aristotelian sciences is valuable, too, and for the same reason. 'The theologian is without a great instrument if he does not know those most learned discussions on the soul, the senses, the causes of appetite and desires', and so on.[31]

Melanchthon is saying that both the content and the form of the works of classical authors stand the Christian in good stead. He adds in this way to the borrowing of these English friars an additional dimension which their limited Latinity could not allow them to envisage. That is something rather different in its emphasis from the long-standing debate about the use of the liberal arts and the sciences in Christian learning, although it takes in the old debate. Melanchthon speaks of the borrowing of outstandingly beautiful figures (*insignes figurae*) and of pleasing stories (*iucundae narrationes*) and memorable sayings (*sententiae maximae memorabiles*) to make the Christian author's compositions *locupletior*, running together elegancies and scraps of material, form and content, as though they were of a piece.[32]

The new emphasis upon elegance and clarity was envisaged as a deliberate movement away from the bad habits of the scholastics of an earlier generation. 'In the last century,' says Melanchthon, Latin was scarcely comprehensible. 'Who can understand Scotus or any writer of that time?'[33] The aim of the new reading of the classical authors is to learn not only from what they have to say, but from the way they say it, so that what is said is clear (*dilucide ac perspicue de re quapiam dicere*).[34] It is most difficult to place words in their proper position, to move and take away and abbreviate, to expand, cover over or uncover, so that it is as though lights shone out brightly in the darkness and there is no *tumultuaria verborum congeries*, no jumble of words.[35] It is best done by joining Latin studies to Greek and reading as wide a range of works as possible,[36] with an eye always to that elegance which is also eloquence,[37] controlled and brilliant and clear.

Two factors above all made a difference in what Melanchthon is saying here: the cultivation of a Latin style in imitation not of the best Christian models (Augustine's *eloquentia*)[38] but of the best classical models; and the study of Greek. Both these developments were being made in the century after the classicising English friars – not as a direct result of their work (when humanism came to England it came afresh from the continent) – but under the influence of longer-term historical and cultural events.

The depredations of the barbarian invaders in the last years of the Roman Empire were so great in Italy that even major libraries were left without key texts; northern scholars since the days of Benedict

Biscop had searched for texts and collected them. The Italian humanist scholars of the fourteenth and fifteenth centuries were therefore in some measure rediscovering classical works which had been familiar friends in the north for centuries.[39] This is remarked on by Melanchthon himself: *interim frigebat Italia, frigebat Gallia*, while Bede and others in the north were, he considers, respectably proficient in Greek and Latin. When Charlemagne wanted to learn letters, he took Alcuin from England and brought him to his court.[40] Certainly it was from northern Europe and especially from Germany that the formidable combination of humanists and reformers came (although they were not always at one).

A number of German towns became centres of humanist studies. To take Strasbourg as an example: it had not been a centre of learning during the Middle Ages, but for a period between 1480 and 1520 it became an important focus of humanism. Martin Bucer was the most notable of seventeen or so scholars who came to the city to take up positions in the civil service and in the Church, with an education in the German universities behind them: five from Freiburg, five from Heidelberg, five from Basle (where classical studies already formed a staple part of the curriculum). Those from Freiburg and Heidelberg, where the old syllabus still ran, had still had an opportunity to take advantage of the 'humanist' courses operating on the fringes of the university. These young men were unusual in various ways, not least in their willingness to take on the work of parish priests, which had long been despised. They helped to popularise the new ideas.[41] It is possible to list a number of German humanists of this period who were turning from the late mediaeval scholastic tradition, as the reformers were.[42]

Melanchthon draws a parallel with Florence, which attracted Greek scholars in exile from their native land after the fall of Constantinople by offering them large salaries to come and teach there. If the city had not done so 'we should have lost the Greek language and Greek literature with Greece herself', and the Latin language, which was decaying into barbarism, would not have been rescued by the effects of the new study of Greek upon the literary sensibilities of learned men, not to mention the loss of a key to the Bible in the original language.[43] His immediate purpose was to congratulate the founders of a new German school and to suggest to them that their action might prove as important as that of Florence. But his remarks underline the association not only between the Italian movement and the humanism of northern Europe, but between the new classicism and the study of the Bible in the original language, which was a more marked feature of northern than of Italian humanism. A new appreciation of the Latin classics was, by the early sixteenth century, largely inseparable from an interest in Greek. In Germany, the Netherlands (Erasmus), and England (Colet, Thomas More), it was also inseparable from questions of its proper application in Christian scholarship.

A similar pattern of continuity and discontinuity marks the progress of Hebrew studies. Jerome had of course pointed the way. In the twelfth century Andrew of St Victor and others[44] had talked to Hebrew scholars among the Jews and asked their help in explaining puzzling words and phrases. Some elements of Hebrew had persisted in Biblical interpretation and Nicholas of Lyre (c. 1270–1340) produced a standard commentary which was printed with many of the early printed Bibles and which made literal sense of the Old Testament with the aid of a knowledge of Hebrew. But the study of Hebrew did not become usual as a direct result of these pioneering endeavours, any more than the few Greek speakers of the West in the earlier Middle Ages had succeeded in encouraging others to follow their example in any numbers. In short, there were precedents for the new work, but no steady line of development. The new departure was made by Johannes Reuchlin, stimulated by the work of Pico della Mirandola (1463–94), who had been comparing the Vulgate with the original Hebrew text of the Old Testament. Pico found six hundred mistakes in a version of the Psalms. Reuchlin was a German humanist who had already mastered Greek and who took advantage of a journey to Italy as a civil servant and diplomat to study Hebrew. He associated himself with Jerome and Nicholas of Lyre only to stand away from them. 'Although I venerate St Jerome as an angel and respect Lyre as a master, I adore the truth as God.'[45] He also had a sense of having departed from the *eloquentiae studium* of the day which had called him as it called to others, like the siren's call to Ulysses.

He thought it important that the Bible's readers should be brought to see it with new eyes. They are bored with the familiar words. If they can be presented with it in its original language (*nativum dicendi genus*), the very words in which God delivered it (*quale os dei locutum est*), it will burst upon them afresh (*Lexicon Hebraicum*, Prefatory Letter). He began accordingly from first principles and set out to be thorough, not to nibble at individual textual problems as his predecessors had done. The first need was for a Hebrew grammar

and a word-list. His *De Rudimentis Hebraicis* (1506) appeared in
three volumes. The first two contain a Hebrew dictionary with Latin
definitions and an elementary grammar, the third a fuller grammar.
It sold well. He relied on mediaeval Jewish grammarians for his
information, but he arranged the material in a way which would give
it the freshness of appeal he thought important. After an outline of
the alphabet and a discussion of syllables in his Hebrew dictionary
there is a little exercise designed to give the student a sense that he is
beginning to master the language. The names in the genealogy of
Christ (Luke 3.23–38) are given in order from Adam, the Hebrew
first and then the Latin name.[46] The grammar itself follows the tradition of Latin grammar, describing the parts of speech beginning
with the noun, its declension, number, gender and so on, and placing
consignificativa under a heading in the mediaeval way, with an explanation that they are the indeclinable parts of speech which take
their meaning from their connection with a noun or a verb, adverbs,
prepositions, conjunctions.[47] The study of Hebrew is made to seem
manageable, even a familiar kind of task, and the Bible in the original
Hebrew correspondingly accessible.[48]

In May 1515 Erasmus wrote a letter to Martin Dorp in which he
tried to convince him that something more thoroughgoing than the
minor modifications which had been timidly made by earlier critics
was needed if a reliable text of the Bible was to be arrived at. 'You do
not want me to change anything except where there might be,
perhaps, a little clearer meaning in the Greek. You deny that there are
faults in the edition we commonly use, and you think we are forbidden to alter in any way something approved by the agreement of
so many ages and so many synods.' This pusillanimous approach
does not, Erasmus contends, allow for the correction needed in cases
where Jerome, Augustine or Ambrose have different readings from
the ones we have, or more significantly still, where not only Jerome
gives a different reading, but the Greek codices agree with him and
the most ancient Latin texts have the same reading, and that reading
fits better. 'Are you going to disregard all these facts', asks Erasmus,
'and still follow your own codex, which might have been corrupted
by a copyist?'

He tries to bring home to Dorp the distinction between saying that
there are 'mistakes' in the divine writings themselves and allowing
for the possibility that error has crept in later, that the Greek was
poorly translated because the translator was ignorant or lazy, that
copyists have introduced corruptions, and so on.

As to the argument that the Church's authority stamps the standard text, Erasmus says this: 'When you write that we should not put aside our present edition after it has been clearly approved by so many councils, you are acting like the commonplace theologians who are wont to attribute to ecclesiastical authority whatever in any way has crept into public usage.'[49]

Erasmus was thus taking up a position on important issues in the debates the reformers and their opponents were to continue. He did so because, given the alternatives of Dorp's position or his own, he found that as a scholar and a Christian, he had to sacrifice tradition for Scripture: that there was, in short, an opposition for him between the two.

In his *Annotationes in Novum Testamentum* he looked in detail at the implications of the new critical method he was proposing. He made extensive use of the Greek as a basis for his comments, corrected errors which had arisen in the received text, threw what light he could on unclear passages, clarified Greek idioms.[50] He shows a moderation of judgement, balancing a respect for the literal against an excessive liberalism. In 'This generation shall not pass away' the Greek will bear the rendering 'this age', and therefore we need not think that this was a prophecy unfulfilled. He believes that a translation should make good sense in itself. In John 11.28, Martha did not call Mary 'in silence' (*silentio* in the Vulgate); that would be impossible; rather, she called her 'secretly'.[51] If Scripture seems to contradict itself and we are driven to resort to the explanation that one or both passages must be taken as a figure of speech, let us at least keep such explanations simple.[52] Nevertheless, Erasmus did not have access to a sophisticated critical technique, to a good range of manuscripts or a method of evaluating those he had by their family affiliation; he did not know how to collate or compare manuscripts; he could not fall back on a body of contemporary scholarship; he had little knowledge of the historical background.[53] (An indication of the sometimes confused thinking of the day on the reliability of sources is to be found in William Whitaker rather later in the century: 'Jerome,' he says, 'relates that Porphyry the philosopher wrote a volume against the book of our prophet Daniel ... But we need not regard what the impious Porphyry may have written.'[54] Porphyry has no standing as a source for Whitaker because he was not a Christian.)

Erasmus's assumption of the priority of the Greek text over the Vulgate was shared by Melanchthon and by Faber Stapulensis,[55] who developed a passion for Greek learning on his travels in Italy. Although he wrote commentaries on the Latin text of the Pauline Epistles (1513) and the Gospels (1522) he added notes to clarify the meaning of the Greek. Melanchthon's *Oratio* of 1549 on the study of the Greek language sets out a comprehensive case for the precedence Greek ought to take over Latin on all fronts. He sees it as an urgent necessity in times when Satan threatens Church and schools alike with destruction.[56] Greek is the most elegant of the languages of mankind, beautiful and capable of expressing the highest truths.[57] God ensured that it was the language in which the New Testament was written.[58] We need to understand Greek in order to comprehend the New Testament rightly.[59] There are many words and figures and phrases and meanings which cannot be correctly interpreted in any other way.[60] Greek is also the medium through which we have learned the human *artes*.[61] The first patristic writers were Greek, and if we cannot read them we cannot return to the springs *(fontes)*.[62] If we are dependent on translations we risk misunderstanding because something is always lost or distorted in translation.[63] For all these reasons the study of Greek is a necessity, but above all because of the joy of 'speaking with the Son of God, with the evangelists and apostles themselves, with Paul, without an interpreter, and hearing their actual living voices'.[64]

To keep to Latin is to do without the history which continues where the Bible leaves off,[65] to limit oneself to a language which is dependent upon the Greek even for what elegance and power of expression it has,[66] to be unable to think clearly, for there is a connection between barbaric thinking and barbaric language.[67]

The connections between these studies of the text of Scripture in its original language and the work of the reformers are strong, but they are not straightforward. Calvin's commentaries owe a great deal to the work of Greek and Hebrew scholars, especially Erasmus. He read the portion of the text under consideration aloud in the original language in the classroom, and then made a translation into Latin on the spot.[68] Luther, too, acknowledges that 'one knife cuts better than another. So good tools – for example, languages and the arts – can contribute to clearer teaching.' But they do not always do so. 'Many, like Erasmus, are equipped with languages and the arts and nevertheless make damaging mistakes. The same thing happens with weapons, most of which are made for slaughter.' Luther's own emphasis is always upon the illumination of the Holy Spirit rather than upon Greek and Hebrew scholarship as the guarantee of sound interpretation.[69] He could not forget that Cicero was – if 'supreme in human wisdom' – nevertheless only a man. 'Human wisdom can't rise above its own level.' The new scholarship was human.[70]

4 The translation of the Bible into the vernacular

'We have translated . . . as faithfully as we were able according to the truth and the style of the Greek language, to enable all Christians, men and women, who know the French language, to understand and acknowledge the law they ought to obey and the faith they ought to follow' (Calvin).[71] Although the humanist scholars did not set out in the first place to provide a text on which translation could go forward, but simply to get the text right, the two processes, work on the original languages of the text and work on translations into the vernacular, became intertwined. Edward Stillingfleet (1635–99) was able to take a long historical view which placed the Latin text in context as the vernacular rendering of its time:

Wherever the Christian religion prevailed, the Scripture was translated into the Vulgar language for the Peoples benefit. Which I proved from the Ancient Italick Versions before St. Jerom's time, the Gothick, Persian, Armenian, Syriack, Coptick and Aethiopic Translations; without the least prohibition of the Common use of them. That where a Language grew into Disuse among the people there the Scripture was Translated into the Tongue which was better understood.

That continued even after primitive times. Gregory the Great was, he says, the first to forbid the use of Scripture and divine offices in the Vulgar Tongue.[72] It was possible to see the Vulgate and modern vernacular renderings as stages in a continuing endeavour.

The translation of the Bible into the vernacular was one of the matters on which the reformers and their opponents saw one another as conspiring against the truth most vigorously. 'There is,' says Bellarmine, 'a controversy between Catholics and heretics as to whether it is proper or indeed beneficial for there to be common use (*usus communis*) of the divine Scriptures in the vulgar tongue of every region.' The Catholic Church takes the view which underlies Stillingfleet's comment, that God himself arranged for the Vulgate translation to be made at that point in history when the Greek language ceased to be in common use in the West and Latin was a common language there, at least among the learned, throughout Italy, France, Spain, Africa and other regions. Today no language is common to the whole West except Latin, and for that reason it seems plain that that is the language in which the Bible must be read. If the

vernacular were to be adopted it would be necessary to alter the
translation in every age.[73] Speaking for the other side, Coverdale
put the reformers' case in language of the utmost hostility in his dedication of his own translation to Henry VIII of England in 1535. 'For-
somuch now as the Word of God is the only truth that driveth among
all lies, and discloseth all juggling and deceit, therefore is our Baalam
of Rome so loath that the scripture should be known in the mother-
tongue; – for he knoweth well enough, that if the clear sun of God's
word come once to the heat of the day, it shall drive away all the foul
mist of his devilish doctrines.'[74] Both sides were concerned for the
safety of the body of Christian revelation contained in Scripture; to
the Catholics it appeared that it could best be guarded by keeping it
protected from damage by the ignorant, and in the form in which it
had survived for a thousand years; to the reformers it seemed that
this was to risk it in the hands of wicked men who wanted to keep the
truth from the faithful and would deliberately misinterpret for them
what they were not allowed to read for themselves.

A nervous air of awareness that controversy was always in the
wind marks the translations themselves at times. Tyndale gives a list
of terms he has chosen in preference to other perhaps more obvious
renderings, in order to avoid using words which have associations of
which he wants to keep clear: 'congregation' is used instead of
'church'; 'elder' is used instead of 'priest'; 'love' for 'charity';
'favour' for 'grace'; 'knowledge' for 'confession'; 'repentence' for
'penance'.[75] Anything which might seem a technical term of theology
gives way to what may be hoped to be an uncontroversial substitute.

The oppositions of often bitterly disagreeing factions went back a
long way. The friar-preachers were the loudest opponents of the
translation of the Bible into languages which ordinary people could
understand. In the case of the Dominicans, whose Chapter General
of 1242 forbade the friars themselves to make translations to help
in their preaching, the reason may lie in the practices of the
Waldensians. The Waldensians seem to have been the earliest sect to
set out to master the Bible in their own language and the result of
their efforts was that many of them were able to match text for text
with those who sought to convert them. There was, then, a danger of
heresy in putting the Bible into the hands of laymen, which the
missionary preachers were the first to feel in its practical results.
They insisted that the 'naked text' at any rate could not be put into
their hands; they needed interpreters to guide them as to its meaning:

nudis terminis absque alterius interpretis vel expositoris admissione,
exponitur gravibus periculis et scandalis.[76]

The friars did, however, do a good deal to make portions of Scripture intelligible in their sermons[77] to lay people. Communities of
holy women were provided with Biblical material at one remove for
devotional use: texts such as the *Meditationes Vitae Christi* which
was written for a Poor Clare, it was believed by St Bonaventure, and
which was translated into a number of languages.[78] Women were
encouraged to lead lives of prayer and holiness based on devotional
reading, but they were not encouraged to read the Bible.[79] There are
instances of translations of the Sunday Gospels and homilies into
rhyme, sometimes in a rather free rendering, which the friar could
then read aloud to the congregation. An instance is Robert of
Greathem's translation of about 1300.[80]

Something more was at issue than the risk of putting Scripture into
the minds of ignorant men without interpreting it for them. Latin had
come to be regarded as one of the sacred languages, along with Greek
and Hebrew, as capable of expressing profound and holy things in a
way that the vernaculars were not. It is a commonplace of the Wycliffite tracts that 'witte stondis not in language but in groundynge of
treuthe, for tho some witte is in laten that is in Grew or Ebrew', with
the concomitant assertion that 'trouthe schuld be openly knowen to
alle maneres of folke', and the complaint that 'trowthe move mony
men to speke sentencis in yngelysche that thai have gedirid in latyne,
and here fore bene menc holden heretikis'.[81] It is not only possible for
the Bible to be translated; it is good that it should be available to all
Christians in their own language.[82] The Lollards gave Biblical support to their argument. Moses was told to read the law to the people
so that they should understand it. Peter said that the Christian should
be 'redi to fulfille to echeman that aske you in resoun, in feith and
hope'. Authorities from Bede to Nicholas of Lyre are cited ('I wole
rather fyve wordes be spoken to the understanding of men, than ten
thousand that the[i] understonden not').[83] A similar marshalling of
Scriptural and patristic authorities appears in the Prologue to the
Wycliffite Bible: 'Crist seith that the gospel shal be prechid in al the
world'; 'Ierom seith on that vers "Holi writ is the scripture of puplis
for it is maad that alle puplis shulden knowe it".'[84] It was claimed
that in England there was a long historical tradition behind the
rendering of the Bible into the vernacular, that Bede and King Alfred
had made translations, and that Alfred 'wolde more if he hadde lyved

lengere'. Translations in other vernaculars were pointed to: 'And also Frenshe men . . . and Britons han the Bible and othere bokis of devocioun and of exposicioun translatid in here modir langage.' And the idea that men are no longer holy enough to do such work is scotched.[85]

Even if the principle that translation into the vernacular is a good and desirable thing is conceded, the practical difficulties of making a complete rendering were immense. In Wyclif's case there was a large and well-educated group of enthusiasts who produced surprisingly quickly (between 1384 and 1396) a large collection of Biblical, patristic, canonistic and scholastic authorities in English known as the *Floretum*, and who put in hand the organisation of the translation.[86] Early English glosses on the Psalter constituted a translation of sorts, but since they rendered only individual words they could not be read in sequence as complete sentences.[87] The verse-translations of the Gospels which were available were not always exact.[88] There had been a tendency from about 1300 to read the stories of the saints on saints' days in place of the saints' day Gospels. There was much to be done to move from these incomplete and unsatisfactory substitutes to a full translation.[89]

The pressure was there, however, not only in England and not only in heretical groups such as the Lollards. Professional 'turners' were employed by royal patrons or by noblemen.[90] In Italy and Germany the Waldensians had been responsible for the first translations,[91] but the work had gone beyond their direct demand. The translations which were the result of heretical propaganda were mostly made in the mid-thirteenth century.[92] In regions where there was no notable threat of heresy, there was apparently little opposition to the making of translations.[93] The German mystics of the fourteenth century in particular were comparatively enthusiastic about the making of vernacular renderings of at least those parts of the Bible which were plainly intelligible, for the use of religious communities of women and for the lay people under religious direction who were known as the Friends of God. The matter became controversial; Charles IV prohibited the practice. But it began simply to meet a need.[94]

It had from the beginning been customary to translate the Fathers' comments as often as, or even instead of, the text of Scripture. A Wycliffite Gospel commentary on Luke 15.22–4 cites 'Crisostom', 'Teofile', 'Bede', 'Austyn' as the 'servantis' of the text and explains them as good angels or priests.[95] The use of spiritual interpretation is natural. 'A calf made fat' is explained as 'the Lord Iesu Crist', who is called a 'calf' because he sacrificed his body. 'He said him was made fatt, for he was so fatt and plenteouse that he suffice for the helpe of al the world.' Fine theological points are made: The Father did not offer the calf, but gave him to men 'to be offerid, for while the Fadir sufferide, the Sone consentyng was crucified of men'.[96] Within certain limitations of scale, the apparatus of academic Latin Bible study was taken over for use in vernacular Bible study.

Similarly, a scholarly perception of the problems of translation is apparent in the accounts the translators give of the way they went about their work. The Prologue to the Wycliffite Bible says disarmingly that 'a symple creature hath translatid the Bible out of Latyn into English'. This 'symple creature' has, with his helpers, gathered together 'manie elde biblis' and works of the Fathers and 'comune glosis', so as to establish as exactly as possible the text from which the translation is to be made. Then it has been looked at afresh ('to studie it of the newe'), in order to understand its meaning fully. Nicholas of Lyre has been especially helpful here on the Old Testament. All this preliminary work has been necessary because ('the beste translating is . . . to translate aftir the sentence and not onli aftir the wordis'; if that is done, without going far from the literal rendering ('and go not fer from the lettre'), then 'the sentence' will be 'as opin either openere in English as in Latin'. If it is impossible to render a passage closely without making nonsense of it, then literalness should be sacrificed to sense: 'Let the sentence evere be hool and open.' The Prologue shows considerable insight into grammatical differences between the structure of English and the structure of Latin which make this sometimes necessary. An ablative absolute may be 'resoluid into "the while", "for", "if", "as thus": "the maistir redinge, I stonde" mai be resoluid thus: "while the maistir redith, I stonde" ', and so on. In a spirit very different from that of Boethius or the rare Latin translators from the Greek of the earlier Middle Ages, the Wycliffite Bible moves away from a translation *de verbo ad verbum*; the compatibility of the two languages will not permit it, and, as the Prologue sums it up, there was an intention from the first 'to make the sentence as trewe and open in English as it is in Latyn, either more trewe and more open than it is in Latin'.[97] This awareness of the different characters of different languages is found in other reflections on the business of translating. If the *proprietates* of one language cannot be preserved even in a language governed by the same rules (*eisdem regulis regulata*), then *a fortiori* those *proprietates* cannot be preserved *in lingua barbarica*, in a language not governed by the same grammatical rules. And many Latin words do not have corresponding English words, and must be expressed in our language by paraphrases (*circumlocutiones*).[98]

Scholarship may, and must, lie behind the translating. But the Wycliffite Prologue speaks of the translator as a 'symple creature' and it remained a principle of Wycliffite teaching that the individual reader should check the translation for himself as he uses it, as well as he is able. He may make changes. Tyndale gives the same licence to translate it himself and put what he likes to 'any man' who finds faults in the translation. 'But loke that he examyne truli his Latyn bible, for no doubt he shal fynde ful manye biblis in Latyn ful false.' The individual has liberty, but only if he acts responsibly and ensures that his Latin text is reliable. Indeed, as the Prologue to the Wycliffite Bible points out, there is perhaps more likely to be corruption in a copy of the Vulgate than in the new English version over which such care has been taken.[99]

This problem was already driving the Wycliffite translators back to the Greek and Hebrew in places. The relationship between Greek and Hebrew scholarship and vernacular renderings manifests itself again in the sixteenth century from, as it were, the other end. Whereas the Wycliffite translators were bent on making an English rendering and set the Hebrew in the margin as a note where they felt it necessary, humanist scholars such as Erasmus began by studying the Bible in the original languages and from their work came translations into modern languages. The process of interaction between the two exercises, together with the rule that it was every man's duty to examine the text as fully as his learning allowed, led to new critical perceptions. The Wycliffite Prologue, for example, notes that it was in the Psalter that most discrepancies were found between Latin and Hebrew. The existence of more than one Latin translation was recognised.[100] It is not enough, says Tyndale, to have a translation in the vulgar tongue. We must also study to understand it. If parents bring a child into the world they also care for it and bring it up.[101] Rather than depart too far from the text in order to render in English a grammatical form which is natural to the Greek, it may be best to put 'a declaration in the margin' to explain the problem, he thinks; he expects the reader to familiarise himself with the behaviour of Greek and Hebrew at least sufficiently to understand that two tenses may look alike in Greek or that in Hebrew an interrogative may be used for a conditional.[102]

In one important respect the use of Greek and Hebrew was not indispensable to the translators into the vernacular among the reformers. They saw themselves both as seeking a rendering which would convey the teaching of the Holy Spirit and as scholars meticulously turning Greek or Hebrew into the vernacular. Luther said that he followed two rules in translating the Bible. 'First, if some passage is obscure I consider whether it treats of grace or of law, whether wrath or the forgiveness of sin [is contained in it], and with which of these it agrees better. By this procedure I have often understood the most obscure passages. Either the law or the gospel has made them meaningful, for God divides his teaching into law and gospel ... The second rule is that if the meaning is ambiguous I ask those who have a better knowledge of the language than I have whether the Hebrew words can bear this or that sense which seems to me to be especially fitting. And that is most fitting which is closest to the argument of the Book.'[103] The test is the fitness of the rendering as much as its excellence from the linguistic point of view. Elsewhere Luther gives three rules, also independent of the study of the original language: 'First, the Bible speaks and teaches about the works of God. About this there is no doubt. These works are divided into three hierarchies: the household, the government, the Church. If a verse does not fit the Church, we should let it stay with the government or the household, whichever it is best suited to. Second, whenever equivocal words or constructions occur, that one would have to be taken which (without however doing injustice to the grammar) agrees with the New Testament. Third, sometimes a sentence seems to be in conflict with the whole [message of the] Bible. So the rabbis have greatly corrupted all the Scriptures with their glosses and relate everything only to the coming of the Messiah, to his supplying us with food and drink, and to his dying afterwards. This is rubbish! Accordingly we simply throw it out.'[104]

Thus the hostility of some of the reformers to the classicists and Hebraists of their own day echoed the hostility of some of their precursors to the scholarship of the friars. If the Bible was to be everyman's, it could not remain the property of scholars any more than it could be kept in Latin and in the hands of the Roman Church. The driving force of the movement to make vernacular translations was from the first a little uncomfortable with the scholarly pursuit of the original text and, although it owed much in the end to that pursuit, it never perhaps fully felt its debt.

A knowledge of Hebrew seemed to Luther to be essential equipment for the reformer principally so that he could hold his own against scholarly opponents and hold his head up in scholarly company:

You, too, as future teachers of religion, should apply yourselves to the task of learning this language, unless you want to be taken for dumb cattle and uninstructed rabble who somehow teach the Sunday Gospels and the catechism with the help of books that have appeared in German. We need theological leaders, we must have fighters who stand on the battlefront against men of other nations and languages, men who are teachers, judges and masters in this language.[105]

10

LECTURING

1 Lecturers

In the twelfth century the decision to become a Benedictine or a Cistercian normally meant turning one's back on an academic life. Although that did not mean giving up scholarship, it largely determined the kind of work which would be appropriate; there was a concentration upon *lectio divina*, quiet, reflective reading of Scripture, rather than logical analysis of its contents. Some attempts were made to marry the two at the house of canons of St Victor at Paris, but the school's primary purpose was still to train the spiritual not the academic man. Early in the thirteenth century two new religious orders came into being, whose conception owed something to the canons' example of living under a rule but at the same time working in the world. Their members needed an education which would fit them to preach in the challenging circumstances of the day: against popular heretics and to articulate town-dwellers. They had to be trained thoroughly in academic theology so that there would be no danger of their leading the faithful astray through ignorance.

From the beginning the Franciscans and Dominicans involved themselves in the work of the new universities, matching the secular masters with such success that they were soon taking the foremost posts in academic life. The two orders were founded for distinct purposes, but by the end of the thirteenth century their scholars had been brought largely into line in their academic endeavours by rivalry. Some differences remained in their respective broad positions on, for example, the use to which the new Aristotelian learning should be put. The Franciscans tended to favour a conservative leaning upon Augustine and the Fathers. But even here it is impossible to make a clear separation: leading scholars from both orders proved to be able philosophers and logicians and no-one was untouched by the new learning.

The stated purpose of study for the mendicant orders was always the training of preachers. We shall come to the preaching itself later, but first something must be said here about the preliminary studies which grounded the preacher in the Bible and in various necessary secular subjects.

University students who were not friars began with the arts course and then (in relatively few cases) went on to one of the higher studies of law, medicine or theology. For the friars, the study of the Bible and whatever related to it was the principal and necessary subject-matter for their work as preachers. Some study of the *artes* could not be avoided; the friar had to be fluent in Latin and he had to be able to argue his case. But the mendicant orders did not regard a thorough-going course in the arts as a necessary preliminary to theological studies. Indeed, the Dominicans were inclined to the view that only someone already soundly grounded in theology should be allowed to take the modern arts course: in Oxford in 1253 the University statute requiring anyone who wished to graduate in theology to have a degree in arts first caused a violent dispute with the Dominicans, between whom and the secular masters relations had hitherto been largely very amicable.[1] The Dominicans' own arrangement was to take selected houses in each province and set up a *studium artium*, a *studium naturalium* or a *studium theologiae*[2] to which gifted students could be sent to learn, at a higher level than could be hoped for in the ordinary schools of the priories, whatever seemed to fit the needs of the Order and their own aptitude.

Those schools were often impressive in their organisation and in the level of learning to which they brought their students. It was the practice throughout the Order for Dominican houses to have a *lector*, normally a man who had had a full academic training and was competent to lecture at university level. He was indispensable; the divine office was kept short and to the point and manual labour set aside precisely so that the friars should have time for study; they were intended to be studying or reflecting in all their spare moments; those who were especially promising could be dispensed from certain observances to give them more time for uninterrupted study. Even if for some reason a *lector* was not available for a time, a replacement talked to the students about some edifying matter, such as the histories or the *Summa* of cases.[3]

In the *studia* of mendicant orders and in the schoolrooms of the secular Masters alike, the staple method of teaching was the lecture, in which the text was 'read' aloud to the students and explained bit by bit. Lecturing had been employed by the Masters in the schools of the eleventh and twelfth centuries. It was found to be as indispensable for teaching grammar or logic as for the study of the Bible.

The structure of the lecture proved to be capable of some variation and development as time went on. Even in the early twelfth century the questions the text raised were sometimes substantial and required lengthy answers. In due course they came to be held over for treatment on a separate occasion and the formal 'disputation' emerged during the course of the twelfth century as a second important method of teaching derived from the lecture although, as Simon of Hinton's commentary on the twelve prophets shows, *quaestiones* could still be treated within a lecture (Oxford, New College, MS.45).

The lecture itself became progressively more formal in its arrangement. During the thirteenth century lectures were divided into two types: the Bachelor lectured 'cursorily', merely reading the text, paraphrasing difficult passages and reading superficial glosses; the purpose was to make the student sufficiently familiar with the text to be able to make use of the Master's more advanced lectures – and to give the Bachelor himself a grounding on which he could go forward to mastery. When Aquinas lectured in the mid-thirteenth century, he read a portion of the text, then divided it into parts before giving a word-by-word commentary in which he made cross-references to other texts of Scripture and to the Fathers and other authorities and resolved any discrepancies by discussing the arguments on both sides and deciding for one or the other.

The separation of these two levels of lecturing came about gradually. The Bachelor's precise function was not fixed in the Paris regulations until 1231.

The apprentice lecturer normally began, then, with the cursory lectures, but in the case of the Dominicans the pattern was different, because each Dominican priory was obliged by regulation to have a lector of its own to lecture on the Bible, and his lectures were obligatory for everyone in the house. The Dominican student would therefore be able to pass directly to the next stage in his teaching career because he was already familiar with the text.

By the mid-thirteenth century the usual practice of the young lecturer was to go on from this point to give lectures on Peter Lombard's *Sentences* which had become, by the mid-thirteenth century if not before, a standard textbook. This topically arranged course of treatments of topics of speculative and systematic theology, with patristic authorities ready assembled, gave an excellent grounding for his later lectures and disputations as a Master. This stage was arrived at (according to the Paris statute) at the age of 29.

The Master who was eventually licensed after perhaps eight years' study of theology would then give his advanced lectures, usually on a book of the Old Testament and a book of the New simultaneously as parallel courses. He also held disputations at which questions arising were dealt with. We shall return to the *Sentences* and the Questions in due course.

From the fourteenth century the secular Masters began to assert themselves more effectively in competition with the friars, as did members of other orders, such as the Carmelite John Baconthorpe.[4] Wyclif is a notable case in point of a Master who rose to prominence outside the medicant orders, and we might look briefly at his career as an example of the training available in fourteenth century Oxford.

John Wyclif was at Oxford for most of his working life, as student and teacher; and for all the years when his habits of thought were being formed he was working within an academic tradition. He proved to be extraordinarily good at academic exercises, and he became prominent at Oxford. His academic ability launched him on a career in the royal service because it brought him to notice, and much followed from that, as he came into contact with the controversies of a wider world and involved himself in them with large consequences. But his later notability must not be allowed to blind us to the ordinariness of his beginnings as a scholar. Wyclif's mind had a long training in a discipline which required a particular rigour, and when he turned to politically contentious subject-matter and to views which brought him charges of heresy, he did not change his methods of analysis or his approach to problem-solving. The developed and novel views of his later years were arrived at by a process of steady unfolding of ideas he had long held but which were given a new direction and sharpness by his growing anger. The underlying conventionality of Wyclif's scholarship cannot be over-emphasised. The same is true of almost all the authors whose work formed part of the great mediaeval exegetical endeavour. A system of critical thought formed by a long training underlies all their work.

In Wyclif's case, his education at Oxford followed a pattern which had been evolving at Paris and Oxford and which was taken over with modifications by the late mediaeval university foundations in Germany and elsewhere. Four or five years as an undergraduate, studying the *artes*; then three or more years as *scholaris* and *sophista*;

followed by a year of performing the academic exercises of responding to questions, before his first 'determination' as a graduate. A further three years at least would have followed before his 'determination' and inception as a Master (*creatio Magistri*). The undergraduates of the day came to Oxford in pursuit of their careers without necessarily possessing the inclination or the aptitude for these studies, and only a comparatively small proportion achieved the Bachelor's degree and still fewer the Master's.

Wyclif was one of a still smaller number who went on to become theologians. We hear of him for the first time as a probationary Fellow at Merton. In 1360 there were six colleges with a total of less than seventy-five members. Most of these already had their Bachelor's degrees and were beginning to prove themselves. The colleges were designed to provide housing and support for poor but promising scholars,[5] while they worked towards a higher degree. With his doctorate (or mastership) in theology a man was almost bound to get preferment, and to become self-supporting. By 1360 Wyclif was a Magister and Master of Balliol. But these College affiliations were temporary, as they were designed to be. Before he continued his studies he retired for a time to a College living in Lincolnshire, and when he returned to Oxford in 1363 he took lodgings in Queen's College for a time. Queen's was at that period a poor college which let rooms rather as the halls did, to undergraduates in need of board, lodging and tuition. While he was living there, Wyclif began the course of hearing four years' lectures on the set books for theology. In 1365 he was offered the Wardenship of a foundation known as Canterbury College, one of a number of houses to which members of religious orders were sent so that they could study at Oxford. Wyclif's Wardenship was not a success and after five years he was ejected.[6] He continued to live at Queen's for the rest of his time at Oxford. There remained, after a fifth year of 'opposing' and a seventh year of 'responding', in which the art of formal disputation was mastered first by taking the part of the objector and then by taking the part of the Master who settled the matters, a period of 'reading the *Sentences*' in the form of lectures, and then a further two years before he became a *magister theologie*, during which the Bachelor of theology must preach and give lectures on a book of the Bible.[7] Wyclif seems to have reached this point about 1371. By 1372 he was beyond dispute the leading Master.[8]

The collegiate system was not common to the universities of Europe. Much of the syllabus was.

A striking feature of such a training is its length, the continuance year after year in the same exercises of hearing lectures put together in a similar way and engaging in formal disputations about questions arising. The system bred the habit of controversy, too. Senior Churchmen tried from time to time to check the speculative licence allowed in the schools, but with little success. The academics had considerable freedom of speech. When Wyclif applied his mind to abuses in the Church he won support from fellow academics who wanted to popularise his views. Academic controversy moved out into society at large. Until the early 1370s Wyclif wrote about matters of current debate in the schools. Then, soon after he entered the royal service, he began to produce new and contentious contributions to disputes which had a political colour.

Wyclif's training has been given space as an example; *mutatis mutandis*, it was undergone by most of the scholars with whom we are concerned, in a modified form by the earliest of them from the end of the twelfth century, and still in its essentials by the first of the reformers, who turned their backs on it as Luther describes himself as doing. That is to say, he tried. There is a perceptible difference between the tone and content of, for example, the early work of Luther on the *Sentences* and the Psalms and his later sermons and lectures, but old habits of thought die hard, and echoes remain. As late, for example, as Melanchthon's *Postills*, too, there are clear marks of scholastic method, quite unselfconsciously used because it is still the natural way.[9]

2 The commentaries

The commentary literature is both conventional and repetitious, but at the same time embedded in it are some of the most important new ideas of the age.[10] From post-patristic times, but especially after the end of the twelfth century, when the standard gloss, the *Glossa Ordinaria*, was extended to cover the whole Bible,[11] the fashioning of a commentary was principally a matter of borrowing and stitching together existing material. But matters of current interest or controversy were raised, other Masters' opinions considered, principles drawn from Aristotle or other works newly-available in the thirteenth and fourteenth centuries. Sometimes a Master stands away from what he is doing and takes stock of the whole enterprise of commentary and speaks about his approach and the methods he is choosing to use. But the essence of commentary is its workmanlike practicality as a means of instructing young men in the meaning of the text of Scripture.

The lecture-commentaries survive in two forms. A lecturer would arrange for a student or scribe to take down live what he said, and this *reportatio* or *lectura* in the form of lecture-notes sometimes survives unpolished, and in more than one version. Or he might make an *ordinatio*, a polished version or exposition, which he dictated directly to a secretary. Some surviving commentaries are a mixture of the two.

Most of the thirteenth century commentaries on the Bible which are still extant are the work of Masters of theology made during their teaching careers at Paris or Oxford or elsewhere among the universities of Europe. The same would be true for succeeding centuries. The lectures of the Bachelors were evidently thought to be less worth preserving. They had less meat in them, and anyway they were apprentice-pieces. The Biblical commentaries which were recorded and kept are primarily designed, then, for the instruction of students who are at a comparatively advanced stage of their studies and who, in many cases, want to equip themselves as preachers, and will need to have appropriate applications of the subject-matter drawn to their attention.

It is hard to put a value on these commentaries as more than the ephemera of a day in the lecture-room. Some (those of Peter Lombard, Hugh of St Cher, Nicholas of Lyre) became standard works. Luther, when someone referred to his lectures on Genesis and said that it would be useful to have them published, replied: 'The lectures are hastily thrown together and are imperfect. In them I offer others a stimulus to further reflection. Accordingly it wouldn't be prudent to make them public. They are too poor.' To make something of them worthy to stand would take time and concentrated work: 'A single work like this demands the whole of a man. I'm too busy for it. I can't do justice to such a thing while I'm busy with many tasks.' He saw a difference, as mediaeval scholars had done, between the lecture as delivered and the lecture as something polished for publication.

Commentaries on the Bible both rested and drew on a substantial tradition of commentaries on textbooks of every kind, which had been built up steadily in the schoolrooms of the twelfth century and after. If a topic needed explanatory notes they could be drawn from any source which was helpful. A case in point is the commentary on the Apocalypse of the Dominican Master Hugh of St Cher (Regent at

Paris 1230–35 and author of a commentary on the whole Bible).
Richard Fishacre, Master of Theology at Oxford from c. 1244 until
he died in 1248, compiled a commentary on Peter Lombard's
Sentences which, as we shall see, was the first of its kind at Oxford
and proved very popular. In it he explains how events will fall out in
the last days of the world, assembling a good deal of traditional
material. This account owes much to Hugh of St Cher's borrowing.[12]
Richard has gone, not to other Masters' remarks on the *Sentences*,
but to another source altogether.

Similarly, a certain interchangeability is apparent in the use of
texts to support one another, either *a* to support *b* or *b* to support *a*,
indiscriminately. Meister Eckhardt (c. 1260–1327) describes how he
has done this in his own commentaries: 'When expounding a [Scrip-
tural] text under discussion many other texts of Scripture are often
cited; and all these passages can be explained in their proper places
by means of this one, just as at present it is explained by means of
them.'[13]

The mixture of old and new in both questions and answers is
apparent everywhere in the commentaries of the later Middle Ages,
and it is still noticeable in the sixteenth century. There was no clean
break with the old ways, but rather a shift of emphasis to different
questions and different approaches to answering them.

When Peter Lombard wrote his commentaries on the Pauline
Epistles he did so at a time when the *Glossa Ordinaria* was more or
less complete and when new logical and scientific ideas were beginning to penetrate Scriptural commentary.[14] He helped to establish a
pattern from which later Masters were able to begin their own work.
It was a system heavily loaded with conventional material, for all the
glimpses of new thinking it occasionally affords. Peter Lombard was
a first-rate logician.

Yet settled criteria and points of reference, standard questions and
answers were persistent. When Peter Lombard looks at the authorship of the Pauline Epistles and the order in which they appear in the
canon he poses respectable questions of modern critical scholarship.
But he answers them in a traditional way. Some say that Hebrews
was not written by Paul but by Clement or Tertullian or Luke. They
are led to this view by the fact that the Epistle has no name in the title
and is in a finer style than the other Epistles. Peter answers that if the
absence of Paul's name is enough to make us question his authorship
it seems that the Epistle can have no author at all. The difference of
style is to be accounted for by the fact that the Epistle was written

first in Hebrew, Paul's native language, in which he was able to express himself fluently. As to the order of the letters: Romans comes first, although it was not written first, because it is Paul's most developed account of the faith and his most difficult letter, and because Rome then held a position of pre-eminence in the world which made it appropriate to put that letter first.[15]

Even in a writer as notable for his independence of thought and method as the Franciscan Master, and later Bishop of Lincoln, Robert Grosseteste (d. 1253), there is a solid base of common practice. Grosseteste taught himself Greek. He was able to bring to his commentary on the Hexameron an acquaintance with the commentary of Basil of Cappadocia. He was also a scientist and mathematician who is author of one of the earliest commentaries on the *Posterior Analytics* and who adopts its method (*inducens ad huius probacionem*)[16] here and there. But just as Peter Lombard uses the standard introduction or *accessus* to provide him with headings for his introduction (what is the reason for writing, the number and order of the works under consideration, the subject-matter and purpose and the method of treatment), so Grosseteste explains who Pythagoras was by the same standard method.[17] Grosseteste identifies a standard 'topic' of elementary logic in Jerome's *Prologue*: the argument that the statement that no art can be mastered without the aid of a teacher must be much more true for theology, which is the art of arts and deepest of all, is a *locus a maiori*.[18] He explains that a word can have many significations and he refers to *consignificatio*.[19] He marshals and compares authorities.[20] He knows that certain of the opening sentences of Genesis are used by the dualist Cathar heretics to support their case.[21] He is up to date in his emphasis on the literal sense.[22] He reflects on the art of exposition (*ars expositionis*). He demonstrates at every turn both how much common practice there was in the study of the Bible and how the commonplaces of contemporary scholarship found their way into each interpreter's remarks. It is this creeping invasion which gradually alters the emphasis of the investigation rather than any sudden break with the old methods of hermeneutics.[23]

The same scattering of devices of standard commentary method is to be found in Luther's early *scholia*: references to *res* and *verbum*, to the many modes of speaking in the Bible,[24] for example. Calvin retains certain assumptions: notably the fundamental patristic and mediaeval principle that, in the words of the Bible, God has 'lowered himself to the level of our ignorance', so that when we find God 'prattling to us in the Bible in an uncultivated and vulgar style' we must 'remember that he does it for our sake'.[25] He also continues to think – with modifications – of types.[26] Tyndale talks of glosses and of signs and similitudes.[27] The basis of monastic *lectio divina* had always been slow, reflective reading, exactly as Luther recommends reading and rereading an author 'until the author becomes part, as it were, of' the reader's 'flesh and blood'.[28] Tyndale places the same emphasis on careful, thoughtful reading with the promise that the reader will by that means come to the deep inner meaning; he uses a traditional image of the bark and the pith, when he speaks of those who are 'ever gnawing upon the bitter bark without, and never attaining unto the sweet pith within'.[29] Examples of the patristic and mediaeval legacy still in use in the commentaries of the reformers are both plentiful and varied. It is only to be expected. Well over a thousand years of endeavour underlay sixteenth century exegesis and although the methods used had not been wholly consistent they had been founded on a few settled ideas about the Bible; to leave them behind altogether would have been to abandon much that the reformers themselves held to be true about the Scriptures. We should not look for revolution in methods of exegesis all at once, but rather for evidence that the commentators are beginning to have their attention drawn to new aspects of the text.

That is not difficult to find. If we compare Melanchthon's notes on the Pauline Epistles with Peter Lombard's commentary we can see the interplay of convention and novelty.

Both begin by considering the *argumentum epistolae* (as was still standard practice in the sixteenth century), but whereas Peter Lombard says that the Corinthians had been corrupted by false apostles and the *verbosa eloquentia* of philosophers, so that the Apostle's task is to recall them to true faith and evangelical wisdom, for Melanchthon other points are significant. He contrasts the tone of the letter with that of Romans. He notes many topics (*varii loci*) which suggest that there were several occasions and reasons for writing.[30]

In treating the first chapter, Melanchthon passes over the first two verses of salutation and begins his analysis at: *gratia vobis et pax*. Peter Lombard stops to consider the opening. When he comes to *gratia*, etc., his treatment of *gratia vobis* is to see it as a salutation (*Ecce salutatio*). 'It is as though he said: "Paul and Sosthenes write you this letter and first of all they greet you, hoping that grace is with you, that it may remain with those in the faith and return to the lapsed".' 'Peace', he explains, is 'tranquillity of mind'. Peter's attention is not caught by the word 'grace' as Melanchthon's is. Grace, says Melanchthon, is the favour or mercy by which we are justified. He makes a comparison with Titus 3.7. He links grace with peace. When God shows mercy he pours out his spirit in our hearts and the faith thus created is quickly followed by peace (see Romans 5.1). Peace itself is a happy conscience concerning sins already committed and a sense of security against the threat of sin's further injuries. Again, several parallel messages are given to help the reader with the definition of peace. He also makes mention of Christ, Melanchthon explains, in adding 'From God our Father and the Lord Jesus Christ', not so much to signify that Christ is God as that all things are given through Christ. For he speaks of the human nature of Christ in order to establish and confirm faith because what we hear in Christ's name is held more surely.[31] Again, Melanchthon is reflecting a contemporary emphasis, while employing the same procedures as his predecessors, of taking a short piece of the text at a time, even a single word, and asking what it is intended to bring to mind, what it has to teach. He shows the same concern for definition, separating several meanings where he can.[32]

So we go on. *Gratias ago.* Here, says Peter Lombard, Paul thanks the Corinthians for the gifts of those among them who were good. There were good men in that congregation who deserved praise, and others worthy of blame. So after the salutation he first puts it to them that they should conform themselves to the good, etc. (PL 192.1535–6). Melanchthon sees an *ordo* in this. First he commends his duty and care and wins good will, by saying 'Thank you', and then he strengthens their faith when he speaks of the fullness of grace and awakens the memory of the inestimable goodness and mercy of god to help them live good lives.[33]

Here and there a difference in the text reminds us that Melanchthon is working from a revised translation. For *in omni verbo et in omni scientia* he prefers *in omni sermone et scientia.*[34] It is easy to see how such alterations can affect the interpretation. Peter Lombard keeps very close to the words of the text (*in omni verbo*); that is, in every mode of preaching (*in omni modo praedicandi*); that is, to the Christian of moderate stature, to the perfect and to those of less standing in the faith. *Et in omni scientia*, that is, in every understanding of Scripture (*scripturarum intellectu*) (PL 192.1536).

Melanchthon's picture of the text throws into relief the aspects which were of current interest: grace in particular. Peter Lombard's emphasis is different; but it also lacks that sense of new and direct insight which marks the later commentaries.

3 The wells of Abraham

Despite the persistence of old habits, then, something new was undoubtedly happening in the commentary of the reformers.[35] Luther thought it so important that commentary should be applicable to the needs of his own times that when he first read Erasmus's Prefaces to the New Testament he was filled with angry excitement because he thought they were not.[36] There was a sense of excitement abroad, as though the Bible were newly-discovered. Luther gave an account of his own first encounter with the Bible as a young man. He read 'by chance' the story about Samuel's mother in the book of Kings. He was much struck by it. Soon afterwards he bought a postill which also pleased him greatly because it had in it more Gospel texts than he could expect to hear sermons on in a whole year. When he became a monk he read the Bible so assiduously that he came to know what was on every page, and when a passage was mentioned he knew just where to look for it. 'If I had kept at it,' he said, 'I would have become exceedingly good at locating things in the Bible.'[37] Tyndale sees the 'discovery' as something far beyond the personal. What is happening, he says, is that Christ is beginning to restore the understanding of the Bible to the faithful, against the scribes and pharisees, who were hypocrites, false prophets and false preachers, and had corrupted the Scripture with the leaven of their glosses.[38] 'Wherein Christ, our spiritual Isaac, diggeth again the wells of Abraham: which wells the scribes and pharisees, those wicked and spiteful Philistines, had stopped and filled up with the earth of their false expositions . . . The wells of Abraham are the Scripture.'[39]

Tyndale explains what the 'scribes and pharisees' have been doing. They have given a false gloss, thus locking up the Bible's true meaning away from the understanding of the faithful. 'Then is the Scripture locked up, and henceforth extreme darkness and a maze, wherein if thou walk, thou wottest neither where thou art, nor canst find any way out. It is a confused chaos and a mingling of all things together without order, every thing contrary to another.'[40] He advocates a movement away from commentary to the reading of the text itself. In this way Christ's redigging of the wells is effective because the Christian can draw up the water of life from its source. In his *scholia* on the Psalms of 1513–15 Luther remarks that although perhaps no other book of the Bible has been commented upon more often than the Psalter, it is a text that still needs interpretation. He saw no end to the work of commentary.[41] But twenty years later we find him talking in a different vein. Certainly the Bible's possibilities can never be exhausted. 'I wonder whether Peter, Paul, Moses and all the saints fully and thoroughly understood a single word of God so that they had nothing more to learn from it?' he asks. 'Here one remains forever a learner . . . Who understands in all of its ramifications even the opening words, "Our Father who art in heaven"? . . . So this one word "your" or "ours" is the most difficult of all in the whole Scripture. It is like the word "your" in the first commandment, "I am the Lord your God" (Exodus 20.3) . . . '[42] It is, however, to the Bible itself that the Christian should turn, not to other men's explanations. 'The Scriptures are a vast forest, but there's no tree in it that I haven't shaken with my own hand,' he comments.[43] 'It is the greatest gift [of God] to have a text and to be able to say, "This is right. I know it." '[44]

It follows that if commentary still has a place, it is as a humble, brief, clear adjunct to the reading of the text itself, not a vast apparatus greatly exceeding the text in length. 'By God's grace,' says Luther at one point, 'the Psalter and the Prophets have now been completed in a good translation, so that we might get more from the bare text than from long commentaries . . . I used to be so fluent that I almost talked the whole world to death . . . There was a time when I could ramble on at greater length about a little flower than I can now about a large field. I don't like verbosity.'[45] 'I remember,' remarks Calvin in his Epistle to Simon Grynaeus on the Commentary in Romans, 'that three years ago we had a friendly talk about the best way of expounding Scripture. The method which you liked best, I myself approved most of all others. We both felt that the chief virtue of an interpreter consists in clarity combined with brevity. And indeed, since about the only business he has is to lay open the mind of the writer he has set out to explain, the more he heads the reader away from it, the more he deviates from his own purpose and is sure to wander out of the bounds.'[46]

4 The *Sentences*

Questions arose naturally in the course of commentary. Some attempts were made to order them and keep them within bounds as early as the twelfth century. Of these perhaps the most important single work both to prompt the enthusiasm for questions and to direct it in an orderly way was Peter Lombard's *Sentences* (*sententiae* – opinions). The Lombard was anxious that the limits set by the Fathers should not be exceeded in the interests of speculation. Therefore, he says, he has brought together in a short book the opinions of the Fathers on the topics of common discussion so that it will not be necessary to turn over the pages of many volumes in search of evidence (*Prologue*). Despite Peter Lombard's concern for security and orthodoxy, his work was regarded as controversial in some of its judgements at first. But it proved so useful as a collection of patristic materials and for reference that it became a standard textbook almost at once and it was used side by side with the Bible in the schools throughout the later Middle Ages, from the early thirteenth century. One commentator describes its use neatly: 'In the canon of Holy Scripture in the New and Old Testament theology is taught (*traditur*) by means of straightforward narrative (*per modum simplicis narrationis*) which simply states the truth. In the book of the *Sentences* it is taught *per modum scrutationis*, searching out the truth and discussing arguments for and against.'[47]

An example from the opening of the second Book (*Distinctio* I) will give the flavour of the collection. Peter Lombard begins with the first principle of creation: there was one first beginning, not several, as some have said. He quotes the text of Genesis 1.1, then cites Bede, the *Glossa Ordinaria* and Ambrose to explain and settle the difficulty. Ambrose gives him a convenient account of Plato's teaching that there are three first things, God, the exemplar to which he worked and the matter he used to make the world, and he is able to conclude by making the point that creation, in Christian teaching, is 'from nothing'.

He goes on to explain what is meant by 'creation', 'making', 'matter', so as to clarify the difference between a craftsman (*factor*) and a creator. Then he points out that in Scriptural usage the words *creator* and *creare* are often taken to mean *factor* and *facere*, without distinction of signification, although the strict meaning of *creator* is restricted to God alone, who makes things from nothing. Thus the same words are used in ways that may cause confusion unless we remember that they are not employed of God in the same way that they are employed in speaking of creatures. The discussion goes on in this way, portions of patristic (and more recent) material supporting each contention as far as possible, with clarificatory remarks and arguments from logic and the other liberal arts brought in where necessary to explain an obscurity in what the Fathers have said.

The difference between the *Sentences* and the *Summa* (also developing in the twelfth century and to come to its full unfolding in Thomas Aquinas's *Summa Theologiae* in the mid-thirteenth century), is not one of organisation or content, but one of emphasis. Peter Lombard thought of his work as a repository of patristic material arranged under topic headings. Aquinas set out to provide an orderly selection of questions and answers which would not have the faults of much contemporary teaching, which he sees as 'the multiplication of useless questions, articles and arguments' and a lack of 'order' in the 'subject-matter' (*Prologue*). There are ample selections from the Fathers in Aquinas's *Summa*, used to support arguments for and against under every heading. But the form and direction of the work is imposed on it by the considerations of systematic theology. It is first and foremost a work of a speculative and theological rather than an exegetical sort. Peter Lombard intended much the same blend of materials to be of use primarily in the study of the Bible. The shift of emphasis reflects the advent of an academic theology in the schools of the late twelfth century, developed out of the questions which arose from the study of the Sacred Page, but eventually taking on something of a life of its own, alongside Bible study and conceived of rather differently.

Alexander of Hales seems to have been one of the first of the friars to make use of the *Sentences*, as a textbook for Franciscan students in Paris in the 1220s. The two earliest Dominican Masters, Roland of Cremona and Hugh of St Cher, did the same between 1229 and 1235. (It was not until after 1231 that the task of commenting on the *Sentences* was regarded as a sufficiently mechanical and preliminary exercise to be left to the Bachelors). At Oxford the Dominican Richard Fishacre was perhaps the first mendicant Master to comment on the *Sentences* – though his doing so caused some bad feeling. Robert Grosseteste, at that time Bishop of Lincoln, who shared the reservation which had been voiced in the twelfth century about the orthodoxy of the Lombard's teaching, tried to prevent him and Papal intervention was necessary before he could continue.

Alexander of Hales certainly thought of the *Sentences* as a textbook of Bible study. The four books of the *Sentences* take their subject-matter from Scripture, he explains. The first book can be summed up as derived from the Lord's statement in Exodus 3.14–15:

Ego sum qui sum. It is concerned with the divine nature. The *materia subsequentium librorum* is taken from what immediately precedes this passage in the same chapter of Exodus (Exodus 3.7–8): 'I have seen the affliction of my people' who are 'in Egypt'. God says that he has heard their cry and come down to help them, and bring them to a land flowing with milk and honey. In other words, the remainder of the *Sentences* deals with the redemption of mankind and its aftermath.[48]

In the fifteenth century Gabriel Biel leads his students into the study of the *Sentences* by telling them 'It is our plan and intention to study theology' (*propositum nobis est atque intentio theologico vacare studio*). Since Scripture, by which we are led to a knowledge of God, is very broad (*latissima*), he continues, there is little to be gained by launching beginners on so wide a sea. It is for this reason that Peter Lombard wrote the *Sentences*, which brings together in an orderly way the source-materials the student needs, arranging them so as to settle each question as it arises, and there is no need to consult in the original all the books upon which he draws.[49] Here perhaps there is a certain shift of emphasis, away from regarding the *Sentences* as somehow constituting a part of the course of Bible study to looking on them as constituting a handbook of speculative theology; a hint of the same separation of purpose can be seen in Richard Fishacre's work. During his period of teaching at Oxford he produced a commentary on the first seventy Psalms and a commentary on the Lombard's *Sentences* which became very popular. He divides theology into a 'speculative' part, based on questions drawn out from the Bible and elsewhere, and considered in their own right, and moral instruction which was taken directly from exegesis. This was already common practice in Paris, but it seems to have been something rather newer and not uncontroversial at Oxford.[50]

Gabriel Biel's *Collectorium* of questions on Peter Lombard's *Sentences* illustrates how well the *Sentences* functioned by the mid-fifteenth century as a handbook of speculative theology at least as much as an aid to Bible study. Biel concentrated upon filling what he saw as gaps in the provision made by other commentators. He sums up Peter Lombard's account (with encouragement to the student to study the *Sentences* carefully for himself) and discusses the opinions of other Masters who have commented on the *Sentences*: notably Robert Holcot and William of Ockham. 'They have not made the nub of the question clear,' he explains. Then he applies the hardest, clearest and most respected method of proof available to mediaeval scholars, the demonstrative method (see pp. 142ff.), to the problem in hand. Proposition by proposition he sets out his case, building theorem upon theorem as Euclid does. Then he gives his *conclusiones*.[51]

But the *Sentences* continued to have a good deal to offer to the student of the Bible. 'Is the *cognitio supernaturalis* man needs in this life *sufficienter tradita* in Holy Scripture?' Duns Scotus explores several lines of thought on this. The human race has never lacked what it has needed to know, but in Old Testament times there was no New Testament. It seems, then, that the Bible contains more than is necessary to salvation. Again, he looks at the heresies which have arisen concerning the standing of various parts of Scripture. There are some who will accept no part of Scripture; some (the Manichees) accept only the New Testament; some (the Jews) only the Old Testament; some (the Moslems) only portions of both. There is talk of prophecy and of the harmony of Scripture.[52] There is a discussion of the authorship of Scripture[53] and of the notion that Scripture alone teaches all that is necessary to salvation.[54] All these matters Duns Scotus takes up in the light of contemporary debate, within the context of commentary on the *Sentences*.

Thus the *Sentences* made a bridge between lectures on the Sacred Text and questions arising from it, as they were bound to do as long as an aspiring Bachelor was obliged to lecture on the *Sentences* before he could reach the status of Master. Robert Holcot, for example, behaved just like his contemporaries, it seems, in carrying over questions of speculative theology from his *Sentences* lectures to the Bachelor lectures on the Bible he had to give afterwards.[55]

11

QUESTIONS

1 *Via antiqua, via moderna*

In October 1468 Stephan Hoest, Vice-Chancellor of the University of Heidelberg, delivered an address at the graduation ceremony for those who had studied the old syllabus (*via antiqua*), which kept largely to traditional textbooks and methods. In March 1469 he gave a second speech at a second graduation ceremony, for those who had followed the new syllabus (*via moderna*), involving the study of advanced logic and Aristotelian science. Hoest emphasises the advantages of each system for its own graduates. He himself was of the *via moderna* and he speaks warmly of the way in which by careful use of language (*dicendi proprietatem*) 'the modern way' is able to indicate ways of resolving the apparent contradictions in the Bible.[1] This was its great strength: making use of the technical skills of grammar and dialectic and the new Aristotelian science its practitioners could bring order and clarity to the most puzzling passages. The *via antiqua* preferred to keep for the most part to the help the Fathers could give, though it was far from untouched by modern methods.[2]

The arrival of the remainder of Aristotle's logical works in the West[3] had an enlarging effect upon the study of logic not only because there was now so much more textbook material to be worked on, but also because they suggested new emphases and brought to light new problems. The *Prior* and *Posterior Analytics*,[4] the *Topics* and the *Sophistici Elenchi* contain further discussions of aspects already covered in the textbooks of the Old Logic. In the *Prior Analytics*, for example, Aristotle looks further at predication and at the underlying metaphysical questions about the nature of things.[5] There is further talk of necessity and futurity, fuller analysis of the structure of arguments and the ways in which arguments may deceive – and a great deal that was entirely new to the students of the *logica vetus*. The result was a striking rise in the level of technical difficulty of the subject as taught in the schools.

Not only a degree of overlap but also some lack of consistency in Aristotle's arrangement and treatment made it necessary for commentators to review their courses and to write, in addition to commentaries and perhaps more urgently, a number of studies of their own, in which they examine individually some of the difficulties the new works of Aristotle have thrown up for them. These new topics ('obligations'; 'consequences'; *syncategoremata*) became an established part of the course and the need for them raised the important question whether Aristotle had perhaps handed down logic to his posterity *insufficienter* and incomplete.[6] Certainly something in addition came to be needed, and this extra material came to be known as the *Logica Moderna*.

Hand in glove with the new logic was the new science, providing examples and raising new questions about natural laws, and a respect for the demonstrative method which began in the late twelfth century[7] and runs as a steady current through the thought of the later Middle Ages. Wyclif, for example, falls naturally into talk of a 'mathematical principle' in his *De Christo et suo Antichristo*, where he attempts to marshal differences between the first principles of arithmetic (such as discrete quantity) and geometry (continuous quantity), in a discussion of the rule that every whole is greater than its quantitative parts.[8] We have already seen how Gabriel Biel uses Euclidean method in his commentary on the *Sentences*.

When the new Aristotelian material first began to arrive in the schools in the twelfth and thirteenth centuries there was at first a widespread confidence that it could be given a place in the syllabus and would simply serve to enlarge the resources of those who were studying the liberal arts in preparation for the study of the Sacred Page. Thomas Aquinas's master Albert the Great defended and covered the whole corpus, as far as he was able, and Aquinas himself uses the Philosopher's material with no reservations as to the advisability of doing so. But some always had disquieting glimpses of dangers. By the end of the thirteenth century there was bitter hostility between those who supported the use of the new logic and the new Aristotelian science, and those who thought it likely to prove a threat to orthodoxy. Melanchthon was still trying to find a judicious position in his Declamation *De Artibus Liberalibus* in 1517.

Like academics of later ages, the Masters were disputatious to the point where the discussion of certain topics led to high acrimony. The friars were often at the centre. They were great propagandists.[9] We find references to the contentions of the *fratres* on all sorts of subjects. In 1255–7 the mendicant orders were expelled from the University of Paris. In 1277 a dispute over the doctrines of Aquinas at Paris led to a row with echoes in Oxford and beyond. At a special congregation of all the Masters of Oxford, the Dominican Archbishop, Robert Kilwardby of Canterbury, condemned and prohibited the public teaching of thirty propositions, eleven days after the Archbishop of Paris had taken action to censure 219 propositions as heretical.[10]

This flair and enthusiasm for debate in the framework of formal disputation arising out of the study of Scripture were together highly conducive to the development of a literature of questions. The logicians developed a theory of *instantiae*, in which objections formed a branch of logic in their own right. Ockham cites several in his *Quodlibets*.[11]

Among logicians as among theologians there were strongly opposed schools. It is not easy to place either the leaders of the *via moderna* (Henry of Ghent; Duns Scotus; William of Ockham?), or their opponents (Bradwardine; Walter Burleigh?). The technical ramifications of their work as logicians are only now beginning to become clear.[12] But it was hard for any scholar of the late Middle Ages to avoid being drawn in to take a view on at least some part of the controversy.

2 Questioning the truth of Scripture

Thomas of Sutton, one of the Oxford Dominicans, is the author of a considerable body of works in which his dialectical interests are apparent. In his *Quaestiones Ordinarie* and in his *Quodlibets* problems of speculative theology are handled by logical procedures, and, in both cases, with rather fewer Biblical references than references to Augustine or to Aristotle: a number, in the case of the *Quodlibets*, roughly comparable to his borrowings from Averroes.[13] Among the *Quaestiones Ordinarie* all the commonplace devices of the dialectician are well to the fore. In considering the *nomina divina* in Question 33, for example, Sutton speaks of *univoca, aequivoca* and multiple signification.[14] The concentration of interest of many of these speculative theologians lay in the deep epistemological problems which lie behind any attempt to understand the language of the Bible: in the nature of the divine mind, the way God knows his creatures, differences of intellect between God and created rational beings, and so on.

The discussion consists mostly of logical analysis, but here and there a textual authority is brought in. In a question on the divine *intellectus*, for example, we have Romans 1.20 on the way in which the *invisibilia Dei* are understood by God's creatures through his works, with a comment taken from Peter Lombard on the word *invisibilia* and its possible meanings. This *glossa* and the Scriptural passage on which it is based have not prompted the question. Their function is to support and further a passage of argument. Meister Eckhardt makes a similar use of the beginning of John's Gospel in a question whether existence and understanding are the same in God.[15]

Robert Kilwardby was a Dominican contemporary of Aquinas and Regent Master at Oxford from 1256 to 1261. In a question among his 43 *Quaestiones* about angels and celestial motion which is mainly concerned with the mechanics of moving bodies, a Biblical text comes in briefly (Ecclesiastes 1.6): *In circuitu pergit spiritus*. What is meant by saying that a spirit goes in a circle? 'It can be expounded thus,' says Kilwardby: the spirit, for example an angel, moves, and by moving causes the heavens to move in a circle. A gloss from Jerome is noted. It is asked whether after the Day of Judgement the bodies of the wicked will be incorruptible by nature, since the motion of the heavens which is the cause of corruption will cease. The Bible has some evidence to contribute here. It is agreed that those who are damned suffer in the body. John says in the Apocalypse (14.10): *cruciabantur igne et sulphure* and the Psalm says: *Ignis, sulphur, spiritus [procellarum] pars eorum* (Psalm 10.7). This is the view of the *sancti expositores*, Kilwardby comments. But such Biblical matter is a small proportion of the whole.[16]

This tendency to use Biblical material not as the primary object of study but in support of proofs can be seen to develop in commentary itself. It is indeed of the very stuff of commentary from an early stage that texts should be brought in from elsewhere to clarify the passage under consideration and support the case that is being made for its meaning. The gloss, too, comes in as support or proof. Aquinas, writing on Galatians, mentions it again and again: 'as is mentioned in the Gloss'; 'to it is ascribed in the Gloss the remission of sins'; 'which in the Gloss is said to be a reconciliation with God'.[17] That authority, like reasoning, constitutes proof is a principle which goes back to the rhetorical textbooks. Reason and authority go hand in hand through mediaeval problem-solving. As late as the sixteenth century we find Johann Eck using terms of 'proof' in his description of the way in which Scriptural passages contribute to his argument: *ostenditur autoritate veteris testamenti*; *secundo probatur principaliter usu veteris testamenti*; *adducamus primo usum veteris testamenti*.[18] It is not a long step from using texts to prove points in commentary to employing them in arguments designed to resolve *quaestiones*. In a sense it is no step at all, since the *quaestiones* were originally part of the commentary.

But in another respect it is a major step. Biblical proofs have a minor place in many questions. The question-literature evolved its own system of organisation – a necessity since there was no single underlying text to provide a common link between the questions. The arrangement, which eventually became more or less universal, began with the first questions of theology: what kind of subject is theology? What is the nature of the divine being who is its object of study? In what manner is it possible for the God who is one also to be three? and so on: the scheme, in general, which Aquinas adopted for his *Summa Theologiae* and which had been arrived at in the experiments of the late twelfth and earlier thirteenth century. The systematic consideration of questions in order pushed Scriptural elements back.

Although, as we have seen, Aquinas considers Scripture's senses in the Questions of the *Summa Theologiae*, there is a comparative neglect of the subject in other questions. What is the Book of Life? The question here is whether the Book of Life is the book in which the names of the elect are written. That, Aquinas holds, is one of its meanings; or the expression may refer to what is written in the Old and New Testaments and leads us to life, as in Ecclesiasticus 24.32, according to the interpretation put upon it in the gloss.[19] In the discussion of the thirteen articles[20] which deal with the way in which God is known by us, there is no account of knowing God through the words of the Bible. The nearest Aquinas comes to that is in the thirteenth article, which considers whether a higher knowledge of God can be obtained by grace than by natural reason.[21] God, says Aquinas, has 'revealed to us by his Spirit' what 'none of the princes of this world knew' (I Corinthians 2.10).[22] It is as though, paradoxically, the focus of the endeavour in the *Quaestiones* and *Summae* was shifted by the demands of problem-solving away from the study of the Bible which generated many of the questions.

Scriptural proofs are used on both sides of an argument: John 14.6 to show that since God is truth the existence of God is self-evident; psalm 52.1 to show that it cannot be self-evident since the Fool was able to say in his heart that there is no God.[23]

This vigorous multiplication of the questions and question-literature and the habit of using Scriptural proofs both for and against had by a process of rebound a striking effect in encouraging some serious questioning of the Bible's truth. If on the whole the question-literature makes only modest use of Scripture as a prompter of questions or in supporting a proposition, the reverse is true for the use made of techniques of disputation in resolving textual diffi- culties. There questions about the text itself abound. Indeed Wyclif found certain scholars of his time 'in full cry against the unlogical, imprecise language of the Bible and the liturgy'.[24] The challenge was not in its essence a new one. It was an episode in the series of encounters which had taken place between secular learning and Christian learning from the beginning and was still going on with a new sophistication between supporters of the *via antiqua* and sup- porters of the *via moderna*. But it was perhaps new in degree, in what was claimed for the discoveries of grammar and logic in addressing the difficulties presented by the Bible's language. These aggressive critics of Wyclif's day, it seems, said that the Bible was not logical and found in that reason to question its truth, rather than to look to their logic for faults, as had been the traditional way.

Wyclif considered himself well placed to meet their objections. He had, he said, travelled the same road himself.[25] A sophist like them, he too had studied by the light of reason, and it had then seemed to him that the Bible did not speak logically.[26] He had come to think dif- ferently, and in the *De Veritate Sacrae Scripturae* and elsewhere he makes an original and vigorous case for Scripture's truth.

In looking to Wyclif for leadership in directions which were to lead to the thinking of the Reformation, modern studies have perhaps neglected to look closely at the implications of his early training in language and logic for the detailed working out of his own analysis of the Bible. His war was not with logic, but with the abuse of logic in exegesis. Wyclif had written his early textbook on logic[27] 'to sharpen the wits of the faithful', by teaching them those elements of logic which may be of help to them in their study of the Bible (*ponere probaciones proposicionum que debent elici ex Scripturis*). He has seen many taking up logic (*ad logicam transuentes*) in the belief that they will come to know God better (*per illam proposuerant legem Dei melius cognovisse*), and yet, by foolishly muddling technical terms as used by the secular authors on logic with terms used in Scrip- ture (*propter insipidam terminorum mixtionem gentilium*), they fail to come to any valid conclusion (*in omni probaciones propositionum propter vacuitatem operis eam deserentes*).[28]

The most obvious result of his early training in logic for Wyclif (as for his contemporaries) is the utter naturalness with which they think in logical terms when they are confronted by a textual difficulty; that is as true of followers of the *via antiqua* as of the *moderni*. Wyclif reads logicians' habits into Scripture. Scripture is seen to prove, to furnish material for arguments.[29] The student is encouraged to avoid sophistries.[30]

Bonaventure provides an earlier example of the sort of quibble Wyclif has in mind. John's Gospel says 'He who drinks of the water I shall give him, will not thirst for all eternity' (John 4.14). That, says the challenger, is either to be understood to refer to bodily thirst or to spiritual. If to bodily thirst, it is false, since those who have grace still get thirsty. If to spiritual thirst, it still seems to be false, because in Ecclesiasticus 24.29 we read: *Qui bibunt adhuc sitient*. Bonaventure settles the matter by explaining that it does indeed refer to spiritual thirst, but that we must further distinguish between the thirst felt by those who have not, and who thirst to have, and the thirst felt by those who have some but want more. The first is the thirst of desire; the second of grace. There is a third thirst, of those who have been satisfied, but who want that state of satisfied thirst to continue. That is glorious thirst. Even in a state of grace or in heaven, thirst may continue, but it will never be the thirst of emptiness, which Jesus says he satisfies for ever. Both passages of Scripture may be accommodated.[31]

Questions of this sort demanding the application of logic presented themselves everywhere. Preaching on Matthew 8.13 ('In that hour the boy was healed'), Wyclif notes a *triplex dubium*. The questions he answers are the sort to fuel the objections raised by those challengers of the Bible's truth to whom Wyclif addressed himself in the *De Veritate Sacrae Scripturae*. How can it be that Jesus, who knew everything from eternity, 'wondered' at something he foreknew even as a man (*eciam humanitus*)? The 'wonder', Wyclif explains, was a response of his power of feeling to the actual experience, for we know that he fully possessed *sensus* and *passiones* from his capacity to grieve and to grow in knowledge. How was it that Christ 'did not find such faith in Israel' when he found there the faith of his mother and his apostles? That, says Wyclif, is like someone who comes to London with his household and says that he does not find such gratitude among his contemporaries as he does in foreigners: we must understand 'except among his household and friends'. How is it that the darkness of Hell is an 'outer' darkness? That is because the darkness of ignorance in the inner man leads

rapidly to outer darkness.[32] These answers rest on common sense
and are implicitly tried against the text of Scripture which has raised
the difficulties. But they are also the answers of a logician. Terms
such as *supposita*; *signant*; *ponit*; *equivoce* occur naturally in the
course of discussion.[33]

The widespread discussion of such problems in the technical terms
of logic is apparent in the accounts which survive in the *Fasciculi
Zizaniorum*[34] of the attack the friar John Cunningham made on
Wyclif. John Cunningham takes the text of Amos 7.14: *non sum
propheta*. If we take it that a prophet understands what he
prophesies this has the same properties as the Cretan liar paradox,
and belongs among a considerable number of such items in
mediaeval debate (and a considerable number of solutions were
proposed: Paul of Venice lists fifteen).[35] Wyclif's arguments on
matters raised by this knotty problem are set out in the *Fasciculi*. He
makes a distinction between statements which are eternal (those of
the New Testament even before they were made) and statements
which are not ('I sit'; 'John speaks'). He insists on the literal meaning
of everything in Scripture: even, for example, that Christians have
the promised land already. He suggests that Amos did not say that he
was not a prophet, even though he said the words (*signa*) 'I am not a
prophet.'[36] John Cunningham points out that that 'contradicts'
(*repugnat*) Gregory in the *Moralia*. He speaks of antecedent and
consequent, *significatio termini*, being a prophet by genus and
species, or *communis intellectus*, *antiphrasis*, *accipiendo numerum*,
singularem pro plurali, *logicalis sententia terminorum*, *figura
locutionis*, some of them relatively commonplace technical terms,
some more advanced, as we shall see when we look at some aspects
of their use in detail.

Luther's table talk illustrates how persistent this sort of questioning proved to be even in the Reformation period, and even when it
took place outside the classroom:

In a letter which arrived on August 19th, Master Forster set before Luther several
questions that troubled him.

First he asked whether preachers should criticise publicly although the frater-
nal rebuke referred to in Matthew 18.[15] seems to speak only of personal sins.
Should not those who have sinned openly by their teaching be rebuked openly, as
Moses did to Korah, Dathan and Abiram, as Elijah did to the Baalites, as Paul did
to Peter and as we publicly oppose the Pope? Luther replied, 'A brother ought
first to be rebuked privately, especially if the fault is new and involves only a few
people. But if the error is firmly rooted among many people, so that it's not

possible to approach every individual and admonish him separately, the error must be rebuked and refuted publicly.'

The second question: The texts in Numbers 35.[6] and Deuteronomy 19.[3] seem to permit private revenge to a person who lays hold of the killer of a relative before he betakes himself to a city of refuge. These passages appear to be in conflict with the Scripture that forbids private revenge. He [Luther] replied, 'That precept in Moses is judicial and is abrogated, just as the usury of the Jews was permitted among the gentiles and only ceased when other judicial decisions were made.'

The third question: Why did Ruth act according to the law of propinquity when Boaz wasn't the brother of her deceased husband and the law in Deuteronomy 25.[5] clearly stipulates the brother of the deceased husband?

. . . The fifth question concerned the passage of the Scriptures in Joshua 24.[19]. 'You cannot serve the Lord, for he is a holy God, he is a jealous God; he will not forgive your transgression'. It seems plain that in these words an ungodly people is rejected, yet immediately after these words we read, 'If you forsake the Lord and serve foreign gods' (Joshua 24.20). These words refer to those who had hitherto been godly and had not yet fallen away. Luther replied, 'This was the farewell speech of Joshua. He admonishes the people with extraordinary feeling as if he would say, "I fear that you will provoke God's wrath again. If so, God will punish you, for he can't tolerate this. If you provoke him and fall away from him, God will be angry, etc." Another solution is that the earlier words were said of the ungodly and the later words of the godly, just as we have many psalms in which, here and there, people are praised and are lifted up to heaven, and immediately after are put down to hell; by synecdoche, in the former case, the godly in the whole people are spoken of and in the latter case the ungodly.'

. . . The eighth question: How is one to understand the passage in Joshua 5.9, which reads, 'This day God rolled away from us the reproach of Egypt'? Luther replied, 'The answer is easy, for after Moses had circumcised the people according to law, he said, now you are no longer Egyptians; now that you are circumcised you are no longer heathen.'[37]

3 Equivocation, fallacies and contradictions

Luther was confronted by an enquirer with the following difficulty: it seems that these texts are in conflict: God said to Abraham that he would spare Sodom if he found ten righteous men in it (Genesis 18.32); in Ezekiel (14.12–23) it is said that even if Noah, Daniel and Job prayed, God would not listen. Luther suggests that the apparent contradiction will disappear if we note that 'in the passage in Ezekiel, Noah and the others were forbidden to pray and Abraham was not'.[38]

Problems posed by words with two or more significations lie at the root of the majority of difficulties of interpretation which mediaeval scholars identified in the text of the Bible. The very hypothesis that Scripture has a multiplicity of senses rests on the assumption that it is a property of words to be capable of more than one signification. Wyclif's references to equivocation are legion, from simple notes that a word has two or more meanings (mercy; power)[39] to references to the logic of equivocation in the Fathers: in Jerome[40] or Augustine and Chrysostom.[41] He warns how deceptive equivocal usages are.[42] 'The scholastics labour upon such miserable expressions, confounding themselves vainly in equivocations.'[43] He puts the knowledge of the signification of terms and their equivocation (*terminorum significatio et eorum equivocatio*) high among the tasks of the commentator.[44] Scripture has its own modes of equivocation, and the critic should familiarise himself with them, and learn how to avoid equivocation himself, before he launches attacks on the truth of the Sacred Page.[45] Scripture's own equivocations are entirely good and helpful; it is simply a matter of studying them, to see, for example, in the case of Jesus's statement that John the Baptist was Elijah and John's own statement that he was not, how 'in this equivocation Christ and John the Baptist differed without contradiction' (*sine repugnantia variabant*).[46] Jesus was speaking 'figuratively', John 'personally'.

The commentators' scrutiny of equivocal usages normally begins with an analysis of the multiple significations involved. Bonaventure (*On Ecclesiastes* 1.1) separates *mutabilitas* which is *transmutatio* from change over time. He asks how mutability affects creatures and by a process of division distinguishes the changeableness in which there is 'vanity', which is the signification in question in this passage.[47]

In a not dissimilar manner, Wyclif defines 'law' in several ways in order to improve on Isidore's definition, which had become more or less standard, and avoid the ambiguity which he says resulted from its inadequacy. He wants to be sure that the ambiguity of the term (*equivocatio signi*) does not get in the way of proper understanding by causing confusion between law as created truth, justly exercised upon the subject (I Kings 8.11); law as taken to refer to divine power exercised in the world and law which is the uncreated truth (*veritas increata*) by which all things are made.[48] These distinctions of signification can always be used to clarify. There is a true mercy, appropriate to God and his angels, and there is the mercy we ourselves feel, which is a sensation of compassion compelling us to help the afflicted. The actual sensation cannot be felt by God and so the term in its usual sense cannot be applied to him except metaphorically (*nisi metaforice*); and thus the word is used *equivoce*, and we must be

clear which sense applies.[49] To 'deny' may mean to deny something
to be, as to deny that God exists, or to deny someone as when Peter
denied Christ, and to make sense of Luke 12 we must understand
which signification is intended.[50] 'Bread' may be a fruit of the earth,
or that bread which 'came down from heaven' (John 6.59), says
Wyclif, discussing the prayer of consecration used in the Eucharist.
In either case the meaning is *satis catholicus* and both the bread
which is substantially (*substantialiter*) the body of Christ and that
which is sacramentally (*sacramentaliter*) the body of Christ have
efficacy, depending on the faith of the recipient.[51]

So pervasive is this difficulty that it persists even in translation. A
similar awareness of the frequency of *equivocatio* finds its way into
the Prologue of the Wycliffite Bible:

> But in translating of wordis equivok, that is that hath manie significacions
> vndur oo lettre, mai lightli be pereil. For Austyn seith in the secounde book of
> *Cristene Teching* that, if equivok wordis be not translatid into the sense either
> vndurstanding of the autour, it is errour.
>
> Therfore a translatour hath greet nede to studie wel the sentence bothe bifore
> and aftir, and loke that suche equivok wordis acorde with the sentence . . . Also
> this word *ex* signifieth sumtyme of, and sumtyme it signifieth *bi*, as Ierom seith.
> And this word *enim* signifieth comynli forsothe, and, as Ierom seith, it signifieth
> cause *thus*, *forwhi* . . . Manie such adverbis, coniunccions and preposicions ben
> set ofte oon for another and at fre chois of autoris sumtyme; and now tho shulen
> be taken as it accordith best to the sentence.[52]

Equivocation was the focus of disputes over translation well into
the Reformation period, as we see in William Fulke's defence, in a
comment on 'your quarrels picked to words of one signification, as
"church" and "congregation", "justice" and "righteousness",
"elder" and "priest", "image" and "idol", "works" and "deeds"
and such like'.[53]

Wyclif draws the moral Peter the Chanter had drawn in the late
twelfth century: *in sensibus equivocis non est contradictio*.[54] There
can be no contradiction between statements where the same term is
used in different senses. In Bonaventure's writing on Scripture the
bulk of the *Quaestiones* turn on equivocation and he sets out systematically to show that, 'As Augustine says, equivocation does not
create contradiction; rather it differentiates for the sake of agreement' (*non facit contraria sed pro congruitate facit diversa*).[55]

The close connection between the study of equivocation and the
study of fallacies and contradictions was apparent to Wyclif, as it
had been to Bonaventure at an earlier stage of the development of the

technical skills necessary to resolve such puzzles. 'That contradiction is resolved' (*contradictio ista solvitur*), says Bonaventure confidently, 'according to Augustine's rule'. The rule involves asking whether what Christ does in a particular instance is done *secundum divinitatem* or 'as a man'.[56] 'It seems,' says Wyclif, that Chrysostom disagrees with Augustine, 'but these holy men are not in opposition here but in agreement' (*in isto contrarii sed in sensu concordes*) if we understand their use of terms correctly. Augustine is using *regnum* in a wide sense, Chrysostom more narrowly.[57] 'In this way are removed those objections (*instantia*) made against the truth of Scripture', by discovering the equivocation which takes away the contradiction.[58]

The *Sophistici Elenchi* arrived in the West in the first half of the twelfth century, and the treatment of fallacies was one of the earliest aspects of the New Logic to be taken up keenly.[59] It came with a commentary, which no doubt assisted its assimilation, and it met a need which had been only partly met in the *logica vetus*, for technical assistance in unravelling the fault in arguments with absurd or unacceptable conclusions which seem to follow from propositions set over against one another (or 'opposed') in what appears to be a straightforward manner. The problem with all these fallacies is that they appear to be perfectly satisfactory syllogisms, as the author of an early compensium comments: 'A sophistical syllogism is apparently a syllogism of contradiction, that is, which seems to be a syllogism when it is not.'[60]

Boethius had already explained in the *De Interpretatione* and in his treatise on categorical syllogisms, that fallacies arise when propositions which appear to do so do not in fact refer to the same subject or to the same predicate, or to the same time, and so on. He lists six cases where propositions appear to contradict one another, but where there is a hidden equivocation or univocation; or where a different part is referred to in each premiss (for example, *oculus albus est; oculus albus non est* are both true if in the first case 'eye' refers to the eyeball and in the second to the pupil). This was a particularly helpful principle to students of the Bible. In one of his diatribes against those scholastics who struggle and confuse themselves vainly in equivocations over words (*in talibus miseris locucionibus laborant, in equivocis sese confudendo*), Wyclif insists upon the importance of taking Scripture as a whole, not removing small pieces from their context or single words out of their sentences, for in that way confusion over the parts is bound to arise. Another common confusion is over a difference of relation or time (Socrates sits;

Socrates does not sit, both true at different times). Bonaventure gives an example of a Biblical 'contradiction' where both these principles are used to find a solution. Jesus said: 'You have followed me, not because you have seen signs . . . ' and in John 6.2 we read, 'There followed him a great multitude, because they had seen signs.' 'The *contrarietas* is resolved in two ways', says Bonaventure: it may be resolved by relating what is said to different times (*per relationem ad diversa tempora*); those who first followed Jesus because of the signs later, when they had been fed, followed him because they had been fed. Or it may be resolved by relating it to *diversas personas*. Some followed him *propter signa*, some for the sake of the food.[61]

These rules were much developed by the study of the *Sophistici Elenchi*, and other works of the new logic assisted. Aristotle explains in the *Prior Analytics*, for example, that just as the logician sometimes makes mistakes in setting out his terms, that is, in the form of his argument, so he sometimes errs in thinking about the application of the terms to the things they signify.[62] Bonaventure believes that somewhere in every fallacy and in every seeming contradiction in the Bible's pages there is a misconnection of this sort, and such mistakes presuppose the possibility that more than one connection can be made between a word and a concept or a thing.

The fact that fallacy and seeming-contradiction come together in this way led some to contend that the Bible is deliberately misleading. It was this kind of attack which lay behind John of Ragusa's insistence that Scripture is not deceptive. Wyclif, too, points out that if Scripture has ever deceived man, God himself is guilty of lying. It is impossible that it should be so.[63] Scripture has its own *logica subtilis* and we must understand its rules. Some want to defend their own logic and destroy the logic of Scripture in their pride.[64]

There was certainly much enthusiasm in the schools, even among the logicians themselves, for applying technical methods to the elimination of apparent fallacies in the Bible. Walter Burleigh gives an example: 'Every animal was in Noah's Ark.' This is proved by the following argument: Man was in Noah's Ark. Cattle were in Noah's Ark (and so on for each species of animal). Therefore every animal was in Noah's Ark. The confusion which leads to the false conclusion arises from a failure to distinguish distribution by species from distribution by number. So it is true to say that every species of animal was in Noah's Ark, but not that every specimen of every species was in Noah's Ark.[65] Bonaventure has another example, which turns on 'Whatever the Father does, the Son does likewise' (John 5.19). The

Father begets the Son; therefore the Son begets the Son. The 'doing' in John's Gospel is an *operatio*; the 'begetting' is a *relatio*; two different notions have been conflated under *quaecumque*.[66] Examples could be multiplied almost equally readily from logical and exegetical and theological works. The new logic stresses the role of 'opposing propositions' in the study of the theory of fallacy. In the study of the Bible, and in the long tradition of Gospel harmonies since Augustine, the test of sound interpretation is *consonantia*; Scripture is a whole and it is *unum et consonum*.[67] The intention behind the various Gospel harmonies which followed Augustine's *De Consensu Evangelistarum* was to demonstrate that unity. Thus when Wyclif examines the different versions of the parable of the talents in the Gospels he is able to content himself with saying that whether or not it is the same parable as told by Jesus, or more than one parable, the moral is the same (*concordat utrobique sententia*).[68] No gloss ought to be accepted unless it is in harmony with Scripture or with reason,[69] which Wyclif believes will always accord with the teaching of Scripture if it is properly handled. There are sometimes difficulties here, but if in doubt one must choose the rendering which is more harmonious with Scripture.[70]

A frequent and fundamental difficulty in the study of Scripture and the one most often a prompter of discussion, was that of contradiction or apparent contradiction between one passage and another. It is the first law of logic that two true statements cannot contradict one another. If the Bible does in fact contradict itself, it seemed to some commentators of Wyclif's day that parts at least of it must be false. Wyclif argues that evangelical truth (*veritas evangelica*) must be preserved (*servatur*), even if there seems some oddity or worse in the words (*licet in linguis disparibus fuerit promulgata*). The *sensus evangelii* is always true even if the words contradict one another (*licet evangelia in verbis aliqualiter discordarunt*). The contradiction is, for him, always apparent not real. The problem lies in false interpretation. A sense which is thus *male elicitum* is simply not true. The error of a man's belief does not falsify the true object of that belief (*nec error aliorum sensuum falsificat suum verum obiectum*). No argument can make what is true false or what is false true. The modern scholars who argue that Scripture contradicts itself and is therefore in part false begin from false premises. The contradictions are in their reading, not in Scripture.[71]

Alertness to contradiction is everywhere.[72] But again and again in the interpretation of Scripture, the contradiction is made to vanish by distinguishing the apparent contradiction in the form of words from the reality in which there proves to be no contradiction. A real contradiction must lie *in re* as well as in word (*contradictio enim non est nominis tantum, sed rei et nominis*), as Wyclif puts it.[73]

A typical example of an apparent contradiction in Scripture is Bonaventure's analysis of Jesus's statement in John 5.31, 'If I bear witness to myself, my witness is not true' and the statement in John 8.14, 'If I bear witness to myself my witness is true', taken together with Numbers 23.19, 'God is not a liar like man.'[74] Bonaventure provides several means of resolving the difficulty. We might consider the subject of the sentence. *Ego* may refer in one case to Jesus speaking as man (*secundum humanam naturam*) and in the other to his speaking as God (*secundum divinam*). Or 'My witness is not true' may mean that it will not be taken as true, even though it is true. Or we may be intended to understand Jesus as saying, 'If I bear witness to myself' as though he alone did so, although he is not alone but one with the Father, and so his testimony is in fact true because he does not bear witness to it alone. All these devices are familiar in logicians' exercises in resolving contradiction. In another example, Bonaventure identifies with technical exactitude a case where a contradictory pair of texts in John's Gospel is to be understood *per relationem ad diversa tempora*, by thinking of them as referring to different times, or else *per relationem ad diversas personas*, as referring to different persons, directly in the tradition of the *Sophistici Elenchi* commentaries.[75]

Wyclif does the same, and he even makes a little jest out of the notion of contradiction, so familiar is it. In one of his sermons he refers to those who 'contradict themselves' in their actions (*repugnant contradictorie sibi ipsis*).[76] The assumption which underlies these exercises is that since Scripture cannot contradict itself in reality, something has been misread or misunderstood if it appears to do so. The art of resolving contradictions is therefore close to the art of spotting the fault in a fallacious argument – not because Scripture is deceitful, as are the arguments of the sophists, but because human fallibility fails to see clearly what is being said.

4 Topics, consequences and obligations

From the end of the twelfth century demonstrative arguments were held in high respect because of the certainty of proof they offered, and attempts were made to use them beyond geometry, in theology,[77] political theory[78] and other subjects. They had a tightness and inevitability[79] which topical arguments were felt to lack. Nevertheless, topical arguments, consciously used and identified as such, are to be found widely in later mediaeval discussions of the text of the Bible. 'From this many take a topical argument.'[80] 'From this is gathered by a topical argument from the greater' (*per locum a maiori*).[81]

They pose difficulties. They had come to be thought an inferior method to that of demonstration (because the topic is a form of argument which produces opinion, not knowledge).[82] Moreover, it did not prove easy to define a topical argument. The mediaeval study of topics was complicated by the existence of two sets of textbooks, whose teaching cannot be satisfactorily married into one.[83] Cicero's *Topics*, with Boethius's commentary and the *De Differentiis Topicis* of Boethius was available long before Aristotle's *Topics* arrived in the West in the twelfth century.[84]

William of Sherwood talks in terms drawn from Cicero of topics as 'seats of argument' (*sedes argumenti*) from which the arguments are extracted, so that the probability of the argument is derived directly from the fact of its being taken out of or extracted from the general truth or maxim.[85] Boethius says that a topic may be one of two things: a self-evidently true, universal generalisation or maximal proposition, which is used to discover or confirm arguments (thus a 'seat of argument'), or a *differentia* which identifies the type of maximal proposition under consideration.[86]

The Ciceronian-Boethian *Topics* are principally concerned with the practical usefulness of ready-made arguments and commonplaces in a sequence of argumentation. Aristotle's *topics* provided some additional elements which bring the discussion of topics into the realm of metaphysics. Aristotle speaks of principles of inference (*rationes inferendi*) which are the means by which a topic is able to function as a source from which inferences may be drawn. These are general concepts, such as genus, species and definition.[87] Some argued that these general concepts or *intentiones* do not themselves form part of the arguments, but only the things which partake in them (*res subiectae intentionibus*).[88] That had the advantage of keeping metaphysical considerations and the actual running of the logical machinery separate. Thus the detailed application of the *loci* in argument involves the use of major premisses (*maximae propositiones*), which can be specified according to the subject-matter under debate, and the principle of inference itself stands apart and provides the point of reference which gives the argument force.

That force may not be great. It may be no more than probability. Aristotle himself claims for topics only the usefulness of making it possible to argue from commonly accepted opinions.[89] 'Extrinsic' topics can give only uncertain and weak conclusions because they are not taken from concepts which constitute features essential and proper to the things to which they are applied. Only intrinsic *loci* do that, and they deal with what is essential and proper to the things to which they are applied (*loci a definitione* and *a genere*).[90]

Garlandus Compotista, one of the earliest mediaeval logicians to write an original piece on topics, at the end of the twelfth century, says that the principal task of the topic is to provide and confirm the conditional premiss of a simple syllogism, consisting of the conditional premiss in question, a categorical premiss and a categorical conclusion. For example: a house is an integrated whole. If we say that it is white, then whiteness must be attributed in the consequent or conclusion to any integral part. If the whole house is white, the wall is also white. Topics 'from the whole', 'from a part', 'from an equal' are, says Garlandus, also uniquely important to the discussion of categorical syllogisms. He points here to a feature of topical arguments which was to be of considerable importance in later accounts. All topics have in this way a potential framework of antecedent and consequent, working from the affirmation of the antecedent to the affirmation of the consequent (*modus ponendo ponens*) or from the denial of the consequent back to the denial of the antecedent (*modus tollendo tollens*).[91] This was to be a principle of the first importance in the later development of the theory of 'consequences'. It is not hard to see how discussions of this sort came to focus on the types of inference (*illatio*) involved in arriving at a conclusion.

One type of topical argument is the form of condensed syllogism or enthymeme in which a relation between the terms leads directly from antecedent to consequent without a second intermediary premiss being stated. This relationship between antecedent and consequent terms (*habitudo terminorum*) can also be described as a *locus*, and so characteristic did this sort of topical argument appear that the *loci* are often seen as not syllogistic at all,[92] but as an alternative to syllogistic argumentation. A division which is to be found at least as early as Abelard separates the inferences which rest on the 'quantity and quality and order of the sentences' (that is, the syllogistic figures and moods) from the topical argument (which may not take the form of a syllogism at all).[93]

John Buridan (c. 1295/1300–after 1358) says that it is this *habitudo* or relation which makes the argument in question hold good, not the *maxim* or generally accepted truth as such. The *maxim* is there only in order to set out the relation in a statement.[94] It is, as Wyclif points out in the *De Veritate Sanctae Scripturae*, the nature of relatives (*natura relativorum*), that if one of them is known so is the other (*cognito uno cogniscitur et reliquum*).[95] This rule governing relation can itself be described as a maxim, for it is the 'seat of argument' from which topical arguments *a relativo oppositis* are drawn.[96]

This connection of the study of topics with discussion of the ways in which conclusions follow from what goes before, led in later mediaeval logic to the development of a new branch of the subject which came to be known as 'consequences'. The material on which it was built was drawn largely from Aristotle, by bringing together discussions scattered in various textbooks of the old and new logic.

When we begin to construct an argument, says Aristotle, we must set down first the subject of the argument, its definitions and all its properties, and secondly we must place the subject in its proper sequence of antecedents and consequents, working out what concepts are antecedents of the subject. We must also set aside attributes which cannot apply to the subject.

In looking at what follows from the subject, certain things must be borne in mind. Some consequents are implied in the very essence of the subject; others are predicated as properties; others are predicated as accidents, some really associated with the subject, some only apparently. We must look for those which really belong in it. Some consequents are consequents of only part of the subject and others of the whole subject. The latter are best for purposes of argument, for it is from universal premises that the syllogism proceeds.[97]

The *De Interpretatione* has a good deal to say about consequents when it comes to working them out in syllogistic form. Aristotle lists the things that follow from certain propositions of a modal sort: 'it may be' implies 'it is contingent'; 'it is not impossible'; 'it is not necessary'; 'it cannot be' implies 'it is necessary it should not be'; 'it is not impossible that it should not be'.[98]

The *Posterior Analytics*, too, contains material which refers to consequences. Some people argue fallaciously, for example, through

taking consequents of both terms: one says that fire spreads in geometrical progression, on the ground that both fire and geometrical
progression increase rapidly.[99]

What then, are consequences? No treatise on the subject has yet
been found which can be dated before 1300.[100] One of the earliest to
come to light gives a definition of a consequence as that which
'follows from' something else (*illud quod sequitur ex alio*). It can also
be described in terms of the emphasis on *habitudo* or relationship we
have already met in discussions of topics. A consequence is a
habitudo inter antecedens et consequens.[101] A consequent is a proposition which is inferred through the antecedent through the
mediation of an inferential sign.[102] The association with conditional
and hypothetical propositions is taken over from the study of topics,
too.[103]

Wyclif discusses consequences fully in the *Logica*. He calls a consequence a *habitudo*, a 'relationship' between antecedent and consequent which has an outcome in a consequent.[104] He gives twenty-two
rules by which it may be determined what the consequent will be in
different cases. These he applies in his own discussions, of *ius*, for
example, in the *De Mandatis Divinis*: 'although *ius ad rem* and *ius in
re* differ like antecedent and consequent, nevertheless, it is impossible
for anyone to have *ius ad rem* unless he has *ius in re* . . . and *vice
versa*'.[105] Every man ought to know that all human suffering,
whether of the just or the unjust, is just and *per consequens* pleasing
to God.[106] 'The soldier of Christ will not be crowned before he
finishes this fight and *per consequens* the great necessity [of putting
an end to it] urges him on in the midst of the battle.'[107] 'The everlasting crown infallibly follows (*infallibiliter consequitur*) the successful
end of the spiritual fight.'[108] 'It is obvious (*patet*) from this that
nothing is a greater security to a rational being, nothing more joyous
and *per consequens* nothing more perfect, than that the Lord should
deign to be with him.'[109] A more elaborately worked out example in
one sermon demonstrates the support which the major premiss of the
argument has, answers an objection and brings out the consequent in
that way.[110] But often Wyclif is confident enough of his listeners'
familiarity with the rules of consequences to make no more than a
passing reference to antecedent and consequent in a sermon, or in a
treatise. *Et per consequens* is frequently used on its own as an indication.[111]

Later mediaeval logicians handled antecedents and consequents
familiarly. In the sixteenth century, in Melanchthon's *Loci Com-*

munes, we find talk of the *necessitas consequentiae*, and in Luther's *De Servo Arbitrio* there is an extended discussion. In Bellarmine's *De Verbo Deo* one of the reformers' arguments is answered like this: 'The sum of the whole of Scripture, which consists in the Ten Commandments, the Creed, the Lord's Prayer and the sacraments, has the clearest testimony (*apertissima testimonia*) in Scripture. Therefore the whole of Scripture is *apertissima*. No, says Bellarmine. Both the consequent and the antecedent can be denied. The consequent is false because even if everything could be reduced in some way to these texts, yet they are very far from clear (*obscurissima*) in themselves. But it is even more certain (*certo certius est*) that the antecedent is false. For if there were such clear testimonies of all the articles of the Creed and all the sacraments, all controversies would be at an end.[112]

More than once in the treatises of the new logic Aristotle reflects on the need for the logician to develop a skill which will help him avoid being outwitted in argument. At the beginning of the *Topics* he says that he has two purposes: to teach his pupils 'to reason from generally accepted opinions' (or 'topics'), and to be able, when meeting an argument, to avoid saying anything which will weaken their own case.[113] In the *Prior Analytics* he gives more detail. If we are to avoid having a syllogism constructed against us when our opponent asks us to admit the grounds of his argument without disclosing his conclusions, we must be able to see ahead as in a game of chess. Conversely, when we are on the offensive, we should try to make our opponent concede the grounds of our argument and leave the conclusions obscure, so that he will not see where we are leading him, or ask him to concede points whose connection is not obvious – again so that he will not see where he is being led.[114]

A hint of the formal teaching of this sort of deliberate trickery is to be found in John of Salisbury's *Metalogicon*,[115] but systematic training in the game of 'obligations' seems to have become a recognised part of the teaching of logic in the thirteenth century;[116] first perhaps in a rather motley way, focussing on a few paradoxes, and then more systematically.[117]

The focal point of discussion is a place in the *Topics* where Aristotle is discussing contrariety hidden in the premises of an argument. The same obscuring of implications is at issue here.[118] Over and above the logical question there was the attraction of the 'game' of obligation.

Out of the study of 'consequences', then, came a further new topic of 'modern logic' which proved to be useful to theologians and exegetes. Wyclif gives his own account of 'obligations' in the *Logica*. Obligation, he says, is the art[119] which 'obliges' the 'respondent' to answer in the affirmative or the negative according to the 'proposer's' desire.[120] It is a logical game, with rules of play which are agreed beforehand – perhaps used to teach students to recognise what is relevant and what is irrelevant (*pertinens* and *impertinens*) in arguments and to think ahead.[121] Verbal pointers (*signa obligationis*) are used to identify the moves in the game. I posit (*pono*); I lay down (*depono*); I admit (*admitto*); I concede (*concedo*); I deny (*nego*); I doubt (*dubito*); I distinguish (*distinguo*); I propose (*propono*).[122]

Of Wyclif's two types of obligation, *positio* obliges the respondent to reply in the affirmative and *depositio* obliges him to reply in the negative. The rules are these:

1. During the exercise, a proposition which has once been admitted to be true must be considered indisputable, and all its formal implications admitted. For example, if 'Antichrist is in Rome' is admitted for purposes of argument, 'Antichrist is a man' must be admitted, too, because it follows from the first proposition. 'There is no Antichrist' must be denied, because that is incompatible with what has been agreed.[123]

2. Whatever follows when two propositions are brought together must be admitted, whatever the consequence may be; this will produce curious results when one proposition has been denied or admitted for purposes of argument and the other is denied or admitted in reality. For example if we take, 'Every man is in Rome' for purposes of argument and then I propose, 'You are in Rome', and you deny that because it is not true, if I then propose, 'You are a man', it must be denied, because it is not compatible with the truth (which has been agreed) of 'Every man is in Rome' and 'You are not in Rome'.[124]

3. If a proposition is irrelevant to the one proposed as obligatory, it must be admitted or denied or stated to be uncertain truthfully.[125]

4. What is absolutely impossible need not be admitted; what is absolutely necessary should not be denied; an obligation must be admitted only if it is possible.

5. Two contradictory propositions must not be admitted during the same exercise.[126]

The aim of the game on the opponent's part is to do everything he can to make the respondent reply badly (*male respondere*) and the respondent must do his best not to be put in a position where he is obliged to say anything absurd.[127]

Among the examples Wyclif gives in the *Logica* itself are two which suggest that the game of obligations was played with theological subjects and was therefore of far greater importance in its possible repercussions than the mere training of young men in a facility with logic. I posit *Deus sit homo*. That is admitted, because it is true that God became man. Then it is posited, 'God is immortal', and that is conceded. Then the argument runs like this: *Iste Deus* (that is, Christ) is mortal and the same is immortal. Therefore the same [God] is mortal and immortal. The respondent must be able to see that the difficulty can be got round by pointing out that 'mortal' and 'immortal' are not being used in the same way throughout (*isti duo termini non eodem modo significant per omnia*); 'immortal' is used of Christ as God and 'mortal' *secundam humanitatem.*[128]

Similarly, I posit that Peter grows in charity uniformly during this hour and Paul does the same. At the last instant of the hour, Peter dies, and Paul is still alive. Is Paul more perfect than Peter at that instant? Has he got an instant's more growth in perfection? No, because an instant is indivisible, the smallest unit of time, like a point in geometry, and if it is added to an hour it does not make it any longer.[129]

The game of obligations must have lent itself admirably to the purposes of those who wanted to catch the Bible out in misleading statements. Some of these 'adversaries' of Christian truth, says Wyclif, try to prove that Christ himself is a liar. They say that if a man deliberately says what is false, he is a liar. But Christ did so. Therefore he was a liar.[130] The intention here is to get the defendant to admit, just as in the formal game, an innocent-seeming proposition from which he will be led to accept far from innocent implications because he has not seen that they are entailed.

In these three areas of 'modern logic', then, as in others, Wyclif was obliged to maintain his own competence and to train his students if the truths of faith, and especially the truth of the text of Scripture, were to be defended. He was forced to be a man of his time in his approach to criticism and problem-solving in order to preserve ancient tradition.

The ways in which this same interplay of old and new in Wyclif's thinking led him into controversy towards the end of his life is another story, but we can surely see the beginning of it here, in the difficulty of maintaining a balance in the immensely difficult, refined and precisely technical application of a fourteenth century Oxford education to theology and also to law, politics, the Church, and the other subjects on which Wyclif came to speak. As for Wyclif, so for others.

5 The Bible's future tenses

Antichrist is a being whose future existence is guaranteed by Scripture, yet like any being not yet in existence he remains in some sense a future contingent. It can be argued that his future being is necessary and it can be argued that it is contingent.[131] This example was widely discussed in the thirteenth and fourteenth centuries. Robert Grosseteste takes it as a test case. If a sentence about the future ever was true, he argues, it will always be true. If 'The Antichrist will come' ever was true then (until the Antichrist comes) it will be true.[132] Peter Aureoli (c. 1280–1322) follows a similar line of thought. Wyclif chose the Antichrist of his own preoccupations as the subject of one of his polemical treatises, and considers, among other matters, the same paradox.[133] The case of Antichrist had a special usefulness because it introduced Christian theological considerations (of the absolute necessity of what God foretells in the Bible) into the long-running debates of the logicians about future contingencies. Whereas for Aristotle the matter had concerned logical and metaphysical difficulties (considerable enough in themselves) for mediaeval Christian thinkers it involved an attempt to account for a universe in which an omniscient and omnipotent God foresaw every future event while giving his rational creatures free choice to do what they wished; and, to compound the paradox, in which he himself had foretold a number of future events in a text which he had himself dictated. The Bible's prophecies had to be interpreted within the by now massive and involved framework of discussions (on the theological side) about predestination, divine foreknowledge, free will, and (on the logical side) about possibility, necessity, contingency and futurity. It was a formidable brief.

The subject is of immense complexity. We can do no more than sample it here.

Mediaeval thinking about necessity inherited from Aristotle a distinction between the ontologically necessary and the logically necessary,[134] between necessity *de re* and necessity *de sensu*. This created difficulties in several ways. A sentence such as 'A sitting man cannot walk' is true if we take it to mean that a man who is now sitting is not simultaneously also walking. It may be false if we take it to mean that a man who is now sitting cannot at some other time walk. In the first sense it is necessarily true that a man who is sitting is not walking. In the second sense no such necessity holds. Thus the surface appearance of the words may cover more than one reality.

When Ockham looks at the problem he shows a similar preoccupation with the difference between the necessity of things being as they are and the necessity of logical entailment. The way in which an accident may be predicated is affected by the nature of an accident: by what an accident is. An accident is a reality which is really distinct from its subject. It is able actually to inhere in it, or to be separated from it without the subject being destroyed. The whiteness of a white house may be lost without the house itself being demolished. We can only say of the house that it is possible that it is white or that it is white for the moment. Thus the contingency of the thing affects what may be said about it.[135] Walter Burleigh, too, remarks on the way in which the discussion of necessity and contingency by logicians is affected by the necessity or contingency of the things discussed. Certain things are themselves necessary (God) or contingent (the corruptible things of the created world) so that terms used to signify them may themselves be described as 'necessary' or 'contingent'.[136]

The consciousness of the importance of looking at both *res* and *verbum* was perhaps most fully exercised in discussions of the problems posed by the attempt to talk about things-in-the-future. If something will exist it will exist, for God does not change his mind. Can we then say that in some sense it always exists? The ontological status of future things remained a puzzle throughout the Middle Ages. But statements-about-future-things proved a more rewarding area of investigation. Aristotle raises the question of the difference between propositions in the past or present tense and propositions in the future tense, in the *De Interpretatione*. The difference he underlines is that in making statements in the past or present tense we can verify their truth, that is, their relation to reality; whereas in making a statement in the future tense we have no way of knowing whether it is true, and therefore no means of proceeding with its aid towards any conclusion. It seems that the logician simply cannot use statements in the future tense.

Aristotle arrives at this position in this way: if someone declares that a certain event will take place, and someone else denies it, one will be speaking the truth and the other will not. Both predicates cannot belong to one subject in reference to the future. If it is true to say that something is white, it must necessarily be white, and the reverse. All affirmations or denials must be either true or false, and Aristotle holds that that must in fact be the case for statements in the future tense, even though we cannot judge their truth or falsity.[137]

But mediaeval logicians were not satisfied; they wanted to be able to make use of statements in the future tense. Peter Abelard commented on this passage in the first half of the twelfth century by looking even more closely at the use of tenses and pointing out that we cannot treat the future as something quite distinct. In the case of a sentence which is now true, it was once the case that ' "P will be true" was true'.[138] Abelard wants to bring the rules governing propositions in any tense under the same rules by bringing the future into the past or present for purposes of discussion. Under the pressure of these difficulties even the principle that nothing can be both true and not true at the same time came to seem doubtful to some later mediaeval logicians as they wrestled with the problem of the necessity of future events.[139]

Aristotle makes an attempt to reason from his position in the *De Interpretatione* to the view that nothing happens by chance; there is no such thing as contingency. If at some point in the future it will be true to say that something is white, then it is necessary that it will be white.[140] But to say that something must be when it is, is not the same as to say that all things come about by necessity and Aristotle does not finally commit himself on the matter. Abelard, too, appears to have been left uncertain. In his gloss on the *De Interpretatione* he talks of 'determinacy' (we may say that a contingent sentence which is true in the event is *determinate*) and explains determinacy in terms of the way things actually turn out. A state of affairs is *determinate* if we know it because it actually occurs (*ex existentia sui*) or because of its nature (*ex natura rei*).[141] But in his *Logica Ingredientibus* he claims that future contingent sentences (true or false as they prove to be in the outcome) are only indeterminately true or false.[142] These apparently unresolvable difficulties present themselves as soon as the truth of a statement is tested against the event. That is to assume that the necessity of future events is in some way related to the truth of statements about them. Aristotle does not go so far as to say that predictions alter the course of events. But he does say that if at any point the nature of things is such that a certain prediction is true, that prediction must be fulfilled. He envisages a universe in which past, present and future are already finally set out.

For Christian scholars, who could add Augustine's discussions

(*De Civitate Dei* V.9) and Boethius's analysis in *Consolation* V, pr.
iii–iv to Aristotle, the question of causation in foreknowledge was a
pressing one. Boethius suggests that it is impossible to believe of God
that he can foresee and be mistaken. God cannot be of uncertain
opinion on matters of future happening. What sort of 'knowledge' is
it that can know that something either will or will not happen?[143] Yet
to say that he knows what will necessarily happen is to take away the
possibility of freedom of choice. Boethius wrestles unsuccessfully
with methods of stating the position which will not entail the implication that God causes what he foreknows. Anselm of Canterbury
tries to avoid this impasse by saying that it is possible to choose freely
even where what is chosen is the only available choice.[144] Abelard
tries to separate the two senses of 'It is possible for something other
than what God foreknows to happen.' In the first sense it is false, for
nothing other than what God foreknows does happen. In the second
sense it is true, for it is possible to claim that some event will not
happen and therefore is not foreknown, although it might have been
the case that it was going to happen (and would then have been
foreknown).[145] Anselm's argument is to do with *res*; Abelard's
largely to do with *verba*. Both are reluctant to let go of God's foreknowledge or of the liberty of human free choice.

Peter Lombard, in another unsuccessful attempt to resolve the
problem in the *Sentences*, tried to deny any causal connection
between divine knowledge and the objects of divine knowledge.[146]
Because his *Sentences* became the standard textbook of theology in
the Middle Ages (after the Bible), he set in train a long debate.
Aquinas turns to the idea of God's creative power for an explanation.
God makes things by knowing them, and thus in some sense he
causes them (*scientia Dei est causa rerum*).[147] Duns Scotus (c. 1265–
1308), in the next generation, placed the emphasis not upon God's
seeing the contingent future, but on his willing it; God looks at a possibility and then asserts or denies it by a 'determination' of his divine
will. The foreknowledge of God then sees how it will work out in the
event. Still commenting on the *Sentences* in 1509, Martin Luther in
his turn discusses the *scientia* and *praescientia* of God.[148]

Wyclif inherited the results of these enquiries as far as they had
proceeded up to his own day, and in his *Logice Continuatio* he comments (revealing some of his own underlying assumptions) that God
may, for example, prevent some men from reaching eternal bliss for
the sake of the working out of providence.[149] Or he notes that
'whatever God has made, he eternally foreordained . . .[150] for other-

wise his providence would disappear'.[151] For him, as for Augustine, God's providence is a stronger necessity than human free choice, and if one must be subordinated to the other in an account of the problem, he does not hesitate over which it shall be.

Before we go on to look, against this general background, at late mediaeval thinking on the way in which God may help to answer questions about the truth of future events by himself telling us in the Bible's prophecies that they will happen, we must pause for a moment over some further points in the logic of futurity.

If someone says, 'The man is running swiftly', remarks the logician William of Sherwood, he makes it clear what the action of the verb is, but that is all. But if one says, 'a man is necessarily an animal', something more is being determined: the way in which the predicate inheres in the subject. This pointing to 'the way in which' is characteristic of modal propositions. It is a feature of propositions containing 'possibly', 'impossibly' and 'contingently', as well as of propositions containing 'necessarily'.[152]

John Wyclif deals with propositions about what is 'necessary' and 'possible' and 'contingent' in Chapter II of his *Logice Continuatio*. The 'modal terms' (*termini modales*), *necessarium*, *impossibile*, *possibile*, *contingens* add, he says, something over and above the *significatum dicti*,[153] in various ways. 'Necessity', for example, has many meanings, some inappropriate to the logician's concerns (the 'necessities of life', such as bread or money), others closely his concern, when 'necessary' is used to describe the absolute truth, or an event which must take place if certain conditions are present, or when it is connected with the verb 'must'. Absolute truths themselves may be of various sorts: necessary *per se* (God exists); which never were nor will be untrue ($2 + 3 = 5$); accidentally necessary truths which cannot be untrue but which might have been (I exist); cases where the necessity depends on an antecedent necessity or a consequent necessity, or something which is concomitant.[154] These last are not necessarily true in themselves, but only contingent, depending as they do on a necessity other than themselves.[155]

Here again the logical tradition is Aristotelian (Aristotle gives a list of modal propositions and discusses their behaviour).[156] But the emphasis is upon the application of premises which include these 'modal' terms in discussing the realities of a universe governed by God. Aristotle talks of necessity in connection with demonstrative syllogisms which use premises which are not problematic;[157] Wyclif speaks of *conclusiones ex fide clara demonstrabiles*,[158] of what is 'agreed'.[159]

Wyclif, like his contemporaries, but with conclusions of his own, is making Aristotle work for him as a theologian. William of Ockham liked Aristotle's strictly logical approach and the idea of the high necessity of the divine. He tried to avoid the problem of the necessity which may inhere by derivation in created things, by confining necessity to God and logic.[160] For Christian thinkers only God himself is absolutely necessary. But because it derives from him, everything he creates comes to have a necessity, and that is where the difficulties arise. Indeed for Wyclif the demands of the subject-matter with which he is dealing are such that he is constantly thrown into arguments involving the possibility or necessity of created things. In the *Opus Evangelicum* he speaks of those who use the argument from necessity to support the Pope's power, and identifies the premiss on which their arguments rest, which has to do with the origin of power, in the context of the notion that all things which happen happen of necessity (*omnia que evenient de necessitate evenient*).[161] Or he identifies the *defectum* of the arguments of the *sophistae* who argue that God removes his laws sometimes, when he wants that they shall not be kept for a time. 'If it could come about that something could be kept for a time which God has not eternally defined, then the law might be [temporarily] removed, but that cannot happen' (*quod non potest contingere*).[162]

He gives a full and coherent early account of this complex of difficulties[163] in his *Logice Continuatio*, where he brings together both its logical and its theological aspects. His starting-point is the nature of time. Time, he believes, is made up of instants, which are of no duration in themselves but which behave like points in geometry and make up a 'line' of time just as they make up a line in space. The idea that time is a continuous quantity had been thoroughly developed in twelfth century discussions of Boethius and also in the thirteenth century on the basis of Aristotle's account of time in *Physics* VI and VIII.[164] Some contemporaries took this idea of an instant and argued that the present is simply 'this instant', that nothing 'is' except in this instant,[165] and that God can make this instant 'last' as 'long' as he likes before time moves on to the next instant. Many of the difficulties about futurity can be made to disappear in this way.[166] Wyclif does not like this device. If an instant can be prolonged so that all time may be a single instant, why did God make time, he asks?[167]

Wyclif prefers to emphasise the successiveness of time. In one of his early sermons, for example, he discusses the 'hours' mentioned in the parable of the labourers in the vineyard (Matthew 20.6), and draws parallels with the ages before Christ, in which God was bringing his labourers to the vineyard – patriarchs, kings, priests; the eleventh hour is the sixth age of the world, before the Day of Judgement, in which 'Christ calls the gentiles by an inward voice to build the Church with the Jews'. To these 'ages' correspond the ages of man in the individual. Consistently, in images of this sort and in his account of the matter in his *Logic*, Wyclif thinks of time as the duration of the created world as it changes along the line of successive instants.[168] Eternity was the first instant, and after it came the first instant of time, by which all the 'before' and 'after' of time is measured successively; 'from the beginning of the world to the end little by little' the human race is born, 'but the Word of God was always with the angels'.[169] This linear orderliness means that 'before' and 'after' can never change places. That is why it is absurd for the Pope to teach men that their prayers and alms can do any good to the dead, Wyclif argues, pursuing yet another ramification of the debate among his contemporaries.[170]

Created things exist within this temporal structure, all within time, but each thing does not necessarily exist at every instant of time.[171] Wyclif's insistence on dividing time into parts and then arranging those parts so that they occur one after the other, makes it a comparatively straightforward matter for him to account for the necessity of the future existence of created things, as something entailed by a prior necessity. Wyclif found himself in general sympathy here with the position of Anselm of Canterbury and Bradwardine, in thinking in terms of an antecedent and a consequent or subsequent necessity.[172] It also encourages him to take up a position in the current debate on 'beginning' and 'ending'.[173]

Here Wyclif argues, against those who maintain that the present instant is all that is, that if there is nothing but the present instant the rest of time must be somehow 'missing', as: in the middle instant of an hour both halves of it are missing; it is then not an hour but an instant. The instant is not a piece of time within which we may envisage things as being; rather it is a point of junction between parts of time. It begins, joins and unites (*iniciat, copulat, unit*) the parts of time.[174] This view had its difficulties, as contemporaries found, because the dividing point is both the end of one segment of time and the beginning of the next. If we divide time into two segments in one of which Socrates exists while in the next he does not exist, it is hard to see whether he exists in the dividing point or instant. It cannot be true, as it seems at first, that he both does and does not exist. That would be a contradiction.[175] But for Wyclif the advantages of the picture of an instant as a point of junction are great because it enables him to emphasise the successiveness of time and its irreversible linear flow.

It is this which distinguishes time from eternity. Eternity is not rigidly successive, and in it God sees everything (literally) at once.[176] Everything 'is', then, in eternal time (*in magno tempore eterno*); but it is not in every instant of time at once (*sed non in quolibet instanti vel qualibet parte temporis*).[177] God sees all these things (and events) at once, and thus in a sense simultaneously, but they remain consecutive in time.[178] Things before and after in time are eternally present to God.[179]

Created things come to be in time. If they were simultaneous in time as they are to God, they could not begin or end.[180] That my life and death take place in the same eternal 'time' does not prove that they are instantaneous in created time.[181] Their existence is, however, necessary in the sense that what God creates he has it in his mind to create. What is in his mind is eternally in his mind and ineradicably in his mind and therefore necessary; but that necessity must be thought of with some modifications in connection with created things. It is not necessarily the case that an eternal antecedent (God's intention to create) causes its consequent eternally, or everything would be eternal, since God is the cause of all and his will is external.[182] God never knew that I did not exist, but he knew that I did not exist at such and such a time.[183] All things which were once or will be, are (in eternal time) but not necessarily.[184] If God knows anything, it is, and necessarily. He always knows all things which were or will be, but it is his knowing which is necessary and not the existence of the thing.[185] If God determines (*determinat*) to do anything he does it, and he knows if I have determined to do anything.[186] Necessity again lies in God's knowledge before it can lie in the thing known. Thus things past, which now cannot not have been, and things which will be but are not now,[187] all lie within the sphere of God's present knowledge.

This tension between a futurity which is in some sense contingent and a futurity which is necessary because known to God is one of which Wyclif is much aware.[188] It is of a piece with Wyclif's thinking about the tension between divine power and necessity in their relation to human free will. Wyclif finds a divinely appointed lesson in the duality of force and restraint in the world. In the *De mandatis Divinis* he explains that God did not want his rational creatures to be proud. He therefore established the two parts of a contradiction in their freedom of will, so that they would feel the force of tension and be humble (*ponit in libertate arbitrii utramque partem contradiccionis*).[189] On a larger scale (but with the same purpose) God allows there to be a law in the world which is *contra Deum*. This *lex* shows his providence more clearly than would have been the case if he had created the whole universe without *repugnantia*; there is no danger of this opposition resisting or impeding his ultimate end and purpose for the universe.[190] Human action is free, yet contingent upon God's will.[191] We know that some are predestined for heaven, but God hides from us the knowledge of who they are, so that there will be no temptation to try to buy their prayers as being potent to help us.[192] In all these ways, God is in charge of, or overseeing, events which occur in time. If men are upset by what happens to them and complain, they are grumbling at the unalterable justice of God,[193] for these 'happenings' occur within an orderly and good providential scheme (it is not possible for sin or evil to happen except when someone is idle (*nisi occasione ociositas*), and we may even say that idleness is in itself the cause of all wickedness).[194] Wyclif came to place an increased emphasis on the *determinatio* of divine necessity.[195] But he never rules out the possibility of contingency of some sort existing within it and creating with it that necessary tension which men must feel for their souls' good.

In an attempt to explain how this duality works in the universe, Wyclif distinguishes between two sorts of necessity: *absolute* and *ex suppositione*. The first is that which cannot be, whether God himself, the *prima veritas*, or such created things as the fact that two and three make five. The second is a form of hypothetical necessity. It is true for a certain time (*pro aliquod tempore*) and it has a cause from which it follows that it is. The fact that it is for a time gives it a necessary existence, 'for if anything was or will be, then it is true in the "great time" or eternity' (*in magno tempore vel eternitate*). In God's sight all time is one and God's will about it is eternal, and therefore it is necessary because it is the effect of the First Cause which produces it.[196]

There are three sorts of hypothetical necessity in Wyclif's analysis. Eternal truths are above all time: God wills the Antichrist to be and the Antichrist actually comes to be. Some truths are of a sort which necessarily always must be (*necesse super est*), such as the existence of the world (in time). Thirdly, some truths are contingent, necessary for a shorter or longer period of time.[197] There is no reason why such a *necessarium ex suppositione* should not be contingent, if Wyclif defines contingent as he does: *contingens sit illus quod pro aliqua mensura non est modo*. It does not follow from its not being for a time (*pro ista mensura*) that it does not exist, for it is impossible for anything which was or will be simply not to be. Wyclif confesses that he himself once found this difficult to grasp and he says that it requires some logical training to understand it.[198] But it is important to do so, for error on this point causes many to go astray in their thinking about the necessity of future things.[199] Some think that every future thing is *absolute necessarium* because God foreknows, fore-ordains or determines it.[200] The world is utterly contingent in its hypothetical necessity, says Wyclif; that hypothetical necessity does not exclude contingency. God is in eternity. He still can, as he once could, not-produce or produce the world, as he wills (*non producere vel produxisse hunc mundum*). Although for us, in time, what has been has become a necessity, God could cause time never to have been.[201] The importance of Wyclif's assertion lies in this: if necessity of this hypothetical sort does not exclude contingency, free will may remain.[202]

There has been much talk of tenses. Wyclif, like his contemporaries and immediate predecessors writing on the problem, but again in his own way, approaches it with that logician's training he recommends to everyone who would think clearly in this area. Aristotle makes the point that a modal sentence is ambiguous if it does not make it clear what time is spoken of and includes mutually exclusive predicates. It is not apparent whether the predicates are to be envisaged as being actual at the same time (*in sensu composito*) or at different times (*in sensu diviso*). This can give rise to fallacies *secundum diversum tempus*, which can be resolved very simply if it can be shown that two different times are referred to.[203] Wyclif, as we have seen, developed Augustine's notion of the simultaneous presence of all temporal things to God in eternity, so that the problem of correct use of tenses in statements which cause difficulties vanishes into this infinitely larger concept, and everything can be made to make sense. William of Ockham's view, which became the common opinion of the early fourteenth century, was that it was essential to distinguish between sentences which are verbally (i.e. in their use of tenses) about past, present or future, and those which are really about past, present or future. For example, the statement, 'To say "The Antichrist will come" is true' is in the present tense and seems to be about the present. But it is really, Ockham believes, about the future, and so it is just as contingent as 'The Antichrist will come'. This principle runs into difficulties when God is being talked of. 'God knew that the Antichrist will come' cannot be resolved out of its tenses in this way. Ockham's device is intended to preserve the principle Aristotle insists on, that two statements which contradict one another cannot both be true and also to hold onto the absolute necessity of the past.[204] But it does so at the expense of the flexibility Wyclif is looking for in his own account.

Wyclif would like to extend the word *est* to a universal tense, which refers to 'every possible time', past, present and future.[205] It then refers to an eternal 'time'. This usage enables a number of classic difficulties in Scripture to be resolved, where the tense causes confusion or creates an apparent contradiction with some other passage. He would also like to believe that there is a detachable connection between the verb 'to be' and what it signifies, such that we may talk of it as signifying *pure presens tempus* without any connotation of succession or any sort of accident attaching to it, as in the case with verbs like 'move', 'run', 'become'.[206] He explores every means of freeing the verb from its tenses for purposes of discussion of the problem of future contingent statements; in eternity, *esse* has that freedom; it is not formally either *fore* or *fuisse*.[207] As the grammarians say, a verb is not then being used in the normal way.[208] But Wyclif's point is that it cannot be so used. Time is not eternity and tenses have to do with time. We can see how this works in a small way when we try to use a verb to speak of 'this instant', which, it can be argued, is past, present and future, because it is the terminus of the past and the first instant of the future as well as being the present instant, 'which it is most confusing to express because then there would be no difference between the times of the verbs'.[209]

Again and again in these attempts to unravel the paradoxes presented by the existence of God in eternity alongside his creation in time, the tenses of verbs in the Bible come into question. Wyclif himself brackets divine foreknowledge and revelation at one point in the *Logica*.[210] If God is the author of Scripture his use of tenses may well reflect considerations beyond the purely temporal purposes for which they are normally employed in human language. That is a commonplace of mediaeval exegesis. Robert Holcot, one of Ockham's followers in this, discusses in his commentary on the

Sentences whether God is able to reveal a future contingent. He distinguishes two senses of 'reveal'. To 'reveal' is to cause, he says, a fresh assent in the mind of a creature, either to something true or to something whether it is true or not. This device has some advantages, but it does not allow him to give a satisfactory account of prophecy.[211]

Ockham himself sometimes sees prophecies as disguised conditionals, which say what God would do under certain conditions, and sometimes as revelations which commit God, as it were, to the necessity of the things in the created world which he has used as instruments to reveal them, but which are not themselves thereafter necessary.[212] God's statement of future things is not, by this account, causative.

All this must be seen against the background of contemporary thinking about prophecy in a much wider framework of assumptions, and primarily concerned with the interpretation of Biblical prophecies.[213] It is within this broader range of thinking that Wyclif's discussion of prophecy belongs. In the *De Veritate Sacrae Scripturae*, for example, he asks whether God is the author of falsehood in those prophets whose prophecies have not been fulfilled. Certain things are sure: the prophets were *plene illuminati* in those things which concern the Christian faith; and Scripture is wholly true in everything it says, 'without the possibility of fallacy or falsehood'.[214] He therefore sets about distinguishing different types of prophecy: those which simply state what is to come are only one sort; others warn or threaten or have some figurative meaning.[215] He is aware that it is objected that prophecies can have no certitude because they are conditional.[216] He holds that a prophet is a creature, rational and having the spirit of prophecy. Both men and angels can therefore be prophets. But Christ himself was the *propheta maximus* and therefore we cannot exclude from the definition the possibility that prophecy sees ahead perfectly.[217] Yet the human prophet may fail to understand his own prophecy. God tells him the truths he speaks and their certitude, literal or figurative, lies in that and not in his capacities as a human speaker.[218]

6 The reaction against scholasticism

In the reformers' determination to get clear of these intricacies 'scholasticism' became a term of opprobrium. Calvin made a point of avoiding 'the refutation of others' in his commentary. He has men-

tioned opinions opposed to his own only where not to do so would
leave his readers puzzled, he explains in the dedication of his commentary on the Psalms. Disputatious commentary merely provides
an opportunity for showing off.[219] The idea, as Luther puts it, is that
'Our Lord did well to leave many things unwritten so as to avoid
tempting men to speculation.'[220] He deliberately turns his back upon
the scholastic method. The marks of that method are still visible in
the early writings of the reformers who had been trained in it. In
Luther's early notes on Peter Lombard's *Sentences* he turns naturally
to syllogisms and talk of corollaries. One syllogism seems to have
had the status of a familiar mnemonic; it should, says Luther, 'always
be borne in mind'.[221]

But the reaction, when it came, was vigorous. 'To students of our
time the sophisticated terminology of that age is altogether unfam-
iliar and seems barbarous . . . Scotus, Bonaventure, Gabriel [Biel] and
Thomas [Aquinas] had to embroider their thoughts with fantasies
because they had no serious tasks to perform.'[222]

Luther describes for us the process of his disillusionment. He
realised that these earlier scholars did not share his conception of the
Bible. 'Gabriel [Biel] wrote a book on the canon of the Mass which I
once thought was the best [but] the authority of the Scriptures meant
nothing to Gabriel.'[223]

Scholastic theology agrees on this point, that man can merit grace . . . by his
purely natural powers . . . But Ockham, though he was superior to all the others
in mental acumen and refuted all the rest of the positions, expressly said and
taught that it isn't to be found in the Scriptures that the Holy Spirit is necessary
for good works.

These men had talent and leisure and grew old as they lectured, but they had
no understanding at all of Christ because they despised the Bible and because
nobody read the Bible for the sake of meditation but only for the sake of knowledge as one would read a historical writing.[224]

The attraction which seduced the scholastics from a proper
concentration on Scripture was, as he saw it, the temptations of
Aristotelian method. 'Scotus had abbreviated Thomas [Aquinas] . . .
When I was a young theologian and was required to prepare nine
corollaries from one question, I took these two words: "God
created". Thomas gave me about a hundred questions on them. This
is the procedure of Thomas: First he takes statements from Paul,
Peter, John, Isaiah, etc. Afterwards he concludes that Aristotle says
so and so and he interprets Scripture according to Aristotle.'[225]
'Occam was very clever in his devotion to method; he had a fondness

for enlarging upon and amplifying things into infinity. But Thomas was very loquacious because he was seduced by metaphysics.'[226] There was often misunderstanding behind this hostility: 'In the sacrament of the altar Thomas [Aquinas] invented transubstantiation.'[227] Luther also enjoyed scoring points for wit. 'Peter Lombard was adequate as a theologian. None has been his equal. He read Hilary, Augustine, Ambrose, Gregory, and also all the Councils. He was a great man. If he had by chance come upon the Bible he would no doubt have been the greatest.'[228]

Meanwhile the mediaeval tradition was undergoing an assault from humanist scholars, who had a distaste for it for a different reason: that in its contorted efforts to express ideas and truths with logical exactitude, scholastic Latin had lost all grace and elegance and even comprehensibility. Reuchlin speaks in the Prologue to his commentary *In Septem Psalmas* (printed 1512) of how he himself had turned both from logic and from eloquence to the study of the Bible.

In France and Spain and Italy, where the mediaeval Church continued to hold sway in the sixteenth century, the study of logic went on for a time along scholastic lines. In Germany and northern Europe it gave way to other studies, to the point where English textbooks on logic of the sixteenth century represent often only a small advance in difficulty on the sixth/seventh century *Etymologiae* or encyclopaedia of Isidore of Seville. Or textbooks written in the early fifteenth century were reprinted, reproducing fourteenth century work: the *Libellus Sophistarum Cantabrigiensium* was reprinted four times between 1497 and 1524 and seven times between 1497 and 1530.[229] The *Logica Magna* of Paul of Venice (d. 1429) proved to be the last – and definitive – major textbook of mediaeval logic. It brings together in its attempted resolutions the debates of the later Middle Ages on a vast range of technical and procedural matters.

Already in the fifteenth century there was a move towards simplification. Rudolph Agricola (1444–85) wrote a *De Inventione Dialectica* which was popular during his lifetime and was published in 1515. He influenced Melanchthon, who himself composed several logic texts suitable for use in schools.[230] With a similar urge to take a fresh look at the subject, Peter Ramus proposed revolutionary modifications which had some popularity in the sixteenth century. At the same time, scholastic logic was being by-passed in favour of new studies of Aristotle, now being read in the Greek and prompting the writing of new commentaries (Agostino Nifo, J. F. Burana,

Jacopo Zabarella).[231] One last development has gone relatively unmarked, but it was most important for early Reformation theology: the *loci communes*, whose authors made an attempt to put all Christian truth in the form of self-evident or readily proved 'truths' which resemble Euclidean geometry in their use of demonstrative method.[232] We shall come to these in a moment.

The technical explorations of mediaeval logic did not cease abruptly. There were still some developments.[233] But there seems to have been some running out of steam even before humanism can have had any appreciable effect in capturing the interest of the best minds of the day.[234] New pioneering textbooks ceased to be produced and such teaching as went on along the old lines was more or less mechanical, although it persisted, in Italy especially.[235] Bellarmine was able to use a scheme of *disputatio* familiarly, setting out the issues for and against, and then in a separate section resolving the objections against his preferred view. Stillingfleet (1635–99) was able to speak dismissively of 'school points' in his 'disproving' of the statements of the Council of Trent, as though the very use of scholastic method were an argument against a contention's being true.[236]

7 Commonplaces

Late mediaeval logic showed one last burst of life. In his Preface to Cicero's *De Officiis* Melanchthon notes that Cicero's treatise contains many commonplaces (*loci communes*). His conception of a 'commonplace' owes a good deal to the classical rhetoricians, who collected them for use in speeches. He speaks of a variety of 'figures' and examples,[237] or of commonplaces as 'definitions'.[238] But for dialecticians, topics (*loci*) had, as we have seen, a narrower technical sense in their use in formal argument. There seems, in the sixteenth century, to have been a further and still more exact sense in which the term *locus* could be understood, as a *communis animi conceptio* (as Boethius puts it),[239] a common conception of the mind. This might be a self-evident truth of an absolute sort, or something closer to a commonly-accepted opinion in ethics.[240] The latter sense seems to be the one Luther has in mind in the *Conclusiones* of his Disputations of 1517, where he notes that statements are *contra dictum commune*; *contra communem*; *contra usum multorum*, or against the opinion of a particular group or groups: *contra Scotum* [Duns Scotus]; *contra Gabrielem* [Biel]; *contra scholasticos*.[241]

The search for self-evident truths which could be built up into demonstrative arguments had gone on sporadically throughout the later Middle Ages. One or two attempts had already been made to establish the whole body of systematic theology in that way. Pico della Mirandola had made a list of such axioms, drawn from Latin, Arabic, Greek and other authorities in his *Conclusiones*.[242] Melanchthon explains that in philosophy there are not only opinions but things known for certain, which are *demonstrationes* or their building-blocks (*membra*), that is, first principles (*principia*) or *conclusiones*. 'Just as in the other arts there are *principia* and *demonstrationes* which cannot be evaded, so in moral philosophy there are firm practical principles (*sunt certa principia practica*) from which demonstrations may be made out'.[243] The same thing might be aspired to for theology.

The first half of the fifteenth century saw something of a fashion for attempting such exercises. Luther's *Heidelberg Disputations* were conducted within the traditional framework of scholastic disputation. Luther stated the *conclusiones*, or theses, and his opponent Master Leonhard Beyer had to defend them. There are 28 theological and 12 philosophical ones. The theological ones already show a heavy emphasis on questions of sin, human action, merit: 'Free will after sin exists in name only (*de solo titulo*) and when a man does what is in him, he sins mortally' (13). Free will after sin is potential for good, actual for evil (14).[244] The proofs (*probationes*) consist largely of the adducing of support authorities.[245]

Melanchthon's *Loci Communes* were far from being merely a young man's work. He revised them over decades. He clearly did not regard them as scholastic trivia of which he came to disapprove.[246] He turns back to the *Posterior Analytics* for a warrant for what he is doing.[247] But he conceives of his purpose as primarily exegetical. He says that he does not want to draw men away from the study of the Bible, but to lead them back to it.[248] Nevertheless, the work is not a commentary.[249] Rather, it is to be seen as an attempt at a complete *summa* of systematic theology,[250] and this is the light perhaps in which we should see this genre: as a latter-day version of what Aquinas and his predecessors had been working for – a means of setting out the faith systematically side by side with Scripture's treatment.

12

PREACHING THE WORD

1 Preachers' keys to the Bible

In a treatise on the art of preaching devised by a Dominican in the late Middle Ages nine methods of expanding the subject-matter of a sermon are suggested: concordance of authorities, discussion of words, explanation of the properties of things, multiplication of senses, the use of analogies with things in the natural world, pointing out opposites, making comparisons, interpretation of names, multiplication of synonyms.[1] These are all, as we have seen, techniques in common use in exegesis and their adaptation for the purposes of preaching underlines the exegetical nature of preaching as it had developed on patristic models in the earlier Middle Ages.[2] The homilies of Augustine and Gregory the Great were systematic, if highly varied, commentaries on selected books of the Bible. Guibert of Nogent and Bernard of Clairvaux took the book of Genesis or the Song of Songs in a similar way and interpreted it for their listeners piece by piece. Gregory the Great had made much of the comparison of one text with another drawn from elsewhere in Scripture, the examination of the variety of meanings a word may have, the use of analogies with the natural world, the multiplication of senses – many of the devices our Dominican author recommends, but used freely as they seemed to be needed.

A glance at the advice given by Humbert of Romans earlier in the history of the Order on the materials with which the preacher should familiarise himself, gives a picture of the variety of matter which proved to be relevant and at the same time the academic pressure which the preaching purpose of their studies put on mendicant students of the Bible: Humbert lists Bibles, commentaries on the *Sentences* of Peter Lombard, glosses, collections of decretals, chronicles, Peter Comestor's *Historia Scholastica*, lives of the saints, the acts of martyrs, works of the Fathers.[3] All these are to be found widespread in the manuscripts on which the preachers drew.

144

As aids specifically designed for the use of preachers, concordances, dictionaries, annotated lectures and collections of illustrations (*exempla*) provided the raw material, collections of model sermons a standard and a notion of what was needed, and manuals on preaching a set of instructions for putting a sermon together with the help of all these. Often, in a single manuscript, extra helps are gathered together with, for example, a concordance. Ms Canon pat. lat. 7 in the Bodleian Library has an additional table of topics for sermons (vainglory, gluttony, etc., with a list of aspects of each under the headings and detailed suggestions for texts which may be used in expounding each theme, fo. 257ff).

The first of these aids to be developed was the dictionary of terms, the collection of *distinctiones*. Several such collections were put together before the end of the twelfth century. For each entry Biblical texts in which a given word was used were brought together so as to show how many different senses – principally figurative senses – it carried in the Bible.[4] Although these came to be chiefly helps for preachers as they look for material to develop a theme, their genesis in exegesis is plain. They owe a great deal to Gregory the Great's habit of *distinctio*, especially in the *Moralia in Job*. Practically speaking, perhaps their most important contribution was the development of the practice of using alphabetical order.

The first verbal concordance[5] to the Scriptures seems to have been produced at the Dominican house of St Jacques in Paris, in the middle of the thirteenth century. It had its precedents. It had been common practice for the Masters of Paris to give lists of references to parallel passages in their glosses for some decades: Stephen Langton's lists were long and were sometimes called *concordantia*. Some independent efforts survive in the form of more comprehensive lists of parallel passages.[6] But the grand enterprise required the massive organisation which the Dominicans were able to bring to it by mid-century.

The mechanical aspects proved manageable. Stephen Langton is credited with the chapter divisions which are still (by and large) in use as he arranged them, and which already had currency in the 1230s in Paris. Finer divisions were achieved by making each chapter notionally into seven parts, labelled, a, b, c, d, e, f, g.[7] There is some evidence that the words and their references were first collected and then arranged on loose quires in alphabetical order, roughly at first, and then with a rearrangement to bring them into exact order. The finished concordance gave reference only, and was therefore of limited usefulness, although it included some phrases: *natus caecus*; *natus est stultus*; *natus filius*; *natus furor*; *natus populus*, as well as *natus*, for example, and for prepositions such subdivisions as *ab abgelis*; *ab aquilone*; *de angustia de arca* (MS Canon pat. lat. 7, fo. 1, fo. 43, Bodleian Library, cf. MS Corpus Christi College, Oxford, fo. 485).

There followed an attempt by the English Dominicans, among whom the name of Richard of Stavensby seems undoubtedly associated with the concordance, to make a concordance with a full sentence of context for each entry. The compilers probably worked at St Jacques and took advantage of the work already done there. Despite an attempt to compress the result by giving only the initial letter of the *lemma*, with a number-code to indicate whether it is in the nominative, genitive, dative and so on, or in the case of a verb how it is to end, the result was impossibly lengthy and cumbersome, if made more manageable by the use of columns. (See, for example, Oxford, New College, MS 70, fos. 1–317, a typically small, portable volume, and for a specimen of the columns, Oxford, Bodleian Library, MS Selden Supra 102, fos. 3–4).

The last and most successful experiment seems to have been at least in some measure an independent effort, derived directly neither from the St Jacques concordance nor from the English one. A briefer context is given, and the seven-part chapter division is modified so that in the case of short chapters only four parts are used. The concordance appears to have been made at Paris between about 1280 and 1330. The surviving copies are numerous (at least 80) but they are frequently expensively produced handsome volumes, and although by the 1340s Thomas Waleys takes it for granted that the preacher will be able to use a concordance for preparing his sermons, it seems unlikely that he can have had a copy of his own.[8]

The lecture-commentary itself, copied and circulated beyond the schools, became, with some modification and adaptation, a source of material for preachers. It was often annotated for the purpose. Marginal notes and headings were put in to point to passages especially suitable for certain days; tables and indexes were added; the whole commentary might be broken up and copied in sections so as to provide material for sermons running through the liturgical year and following, for example, the Gospels or Epistles of the day.[9] (The term *postill*, originally used for the comment, came to refer to such collections). Alexander of Hales's *Commentary on the Apocalypse* survives in one particularly beautiful thirteenth century manuscript (Cambridge, University Library, MS Mm.v.31), profusely illustrated with pictures and with marginal notes in a later hand picking out topics useful to a preacher (for example, ff. 6ᵛ–7 has *facies, sol, pedes, dextera*). Less splendid but equally practical is Simon of Hinton's collection of excerpts from the gloss, arranged in a condensed form to make them easier to handle than was possible with large volumes containing the full text and the gloss together.[10] Indexes became common. Simon's *Moralia sive Postilla* on the minor prophets has tables and an alphabetical index at the end in New College, Oxford, MS 45, fo. 235ff. There are indexes of the beginnings of the chapters of several of Augustine's treatises and a full index to the *De Genesi ad Litteram*, for example, in Cambridge, University Library, MS Ff.III.29ff. 1–10ᵛ. All these commentary materials were thus made available to the preacher in need of a reference, together with Gospel harmonies, and, at another level, more fanciful interpretative matter such as the popular *Lives* of Jesus,[11] and Peter Comestor's summary of Biblical history with additional information about such characters as Herod, Archelaus, Augustus.[12] Material which provided an overview or organisation of a mass of facts was popular: Peter Aureoli's *Compendium Sensus Litteralis Totius Divinae Scripturae* divided the Bible helpfully into eight parts. There were compendia of Bible history in verse and verse harmonies of the Gospels, designed to make their subject-matter easier to remember. Equally popular were good stories, even if apocryphal, such as the *Acts of Pilate*, which made their point without necessarily keeping close to the facts (we hear of the raising of Jairus's son).[13]

Model sermons were also found to be helpful. Jordan of Saxony, author of a *Liber Vitasfratrum*, made a collection of 460 sermons on the Sunday Gospels, etc.[14] Bodleian Library Oxford, MS Laud. Misc. 511 contains a compilation of sermons made probably at the Dominican house at Oxford soon after 1279, and including sermons by a variety of authors, notably Richard Fishacre and Simon of Hinton. The compiler gives several models for the Sundays and Feast Days, and he notes from which book in the library he has taken each example (*De Libro Rubeo Maiori*, for example, fo. 49ᵛ). In the margin are divisions of topics and sometimes further sub-divisions, arranged in the standard way, like fingers spreading out:

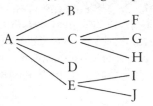

MS Hatton 107, also in the Bodleian Library, includes more than a hundred sermons for various occasions, of the second half of the thirteenth century, with a subject-index (fo. 3) giving such topics as: *De abstinentia et quid sit*; *de actione honesta*; *de ortu accidie vel secularis tristitie*; *contra accusatores*; *qare est triplici adventus*; *de affectione animi*. These are linked to the texts by means of a reference system of numbers and dots which take the reader to a precise passage. In a later hand, there is, fo. 270ff, a table of sermons proper for Sundays and Feast Days. MS Auct D. 4.12 (4) is a small volume of abbreviated sermons on the Epistles and Gospels.[15]

Actual examples of the formal university sermon display the advantages of the use of such preachers' aids. Thomas Agni of Lentini (d. 1277) preached a sermon on St Dominic in which he took as his theme-text 'He who practises and teaches, he is the one who will be called great in the kingdom of heaven' (Matthew 5.19). He divides his theme. There are, he says, three things to be learned from this text which recommend someone to us as a saint: his life, his teaching and his glorification. Dominic practised holy living, taught and has the reward of glory. If we take first the merit of his life, he continues, developing his divisions of the theme, we can find five things to consider laid down in II Timothy 4 (verse 5): 'Keep vigil, toil in everything, do the work of an evangelist, fulfil your ministry, and be sober'. Taking the first, 'Keep vigil', we can find three ways in which Dominic did this when he was a student. He directed his study to three things: wisdom, abstinence, compassion. The first is given authority by Proverbs (8.17): 'Those who keep vigil for me from early morning will find me'; the second by Ecclesiasticus (31.1): 'Keeping vigil for an honourable life will reduce your flesh'; the third by Psalm 40 (verse 2): 'Blessed is the man who shows understanding towards the poor.' There is room for an aside on those who failed to keep vigil: Peter, when he was threatened with death (Acts 12.6); Jonah when he was in danger of drowning (Jonah 1.5); Abner when he was supposed to be guarding his lord (I Samuel 26.25); the apostles immediately before the Passion (Matthew 26.40). And so we proceed, division by division, and Thomas always has an appropriate Biblical quotation to illustrate and support his point and to help him link it with the next. The result is an impressive display of Biblical erudition behind which is likely to stand the assistance of a concordance – and no doubt some texts became particular favourites in this way and correspondingly well known.[16]

The same pattern is still in use at the beginning of the fourteenth century. Simon of Cascina (d. c. 1420) preached for a formal academic occasion – a *sermo licentie* for graduation – taking the Epistle for the day: *Vocati estis ut benedictionem hereditate possideatis* (I Peter 3.9). He addresses himself to his distinguished audience: *Benignissime archiepiscope, commendandi canonici, facundi doctores, periti scolares, laudandi capellani, cives providi et discreti*, calls on the grace of God to assist him, and then bends to the task of dividing his theme and developing the subdivisions. In the sixteenth century Johann Eck was still making outline plans along the same lines, and consulting volumes of sermons for material to support and enrich his own.[17]

For a short span, from about 1200 to the end of the Middle Ages, preaching was regarded, formally speaking, as a branch of rhetoric. In the sixteenth century classical notions of rhetoric came to the fore again, and rhetoric is divided by Thomas Wilson, for example, into demonstrative, deliberative and judicial, as Cicero would have divided it. Rhetoric had sunk so low in England that it was no longer a subject to which all his education ultimately fitted a man, as it had been for the Romans; it had become a school rather than a university subject.[18]

From the mid-thirteenth century a large number of preaching manuals were produced. They frequently contained material for preaching in the form of condensed sermons, but their primary purpose was to explain how to put a sermon together. They are practical above all. As Robert of Basevorn puts it, they are designed to teach the preacher how to lead many to be good in the shortest possible time (*pluribus facere persuasio ad merendum, moderatum tempus retinens*).[19] Reuchlin's *De Arte Praedicandi* (printed 1508) still follows the pattern of *inventio, memoria* and *pronuntiatio*, with recommendations on how to begin, how to present the Biblical text which is the theme, how to divide up the subject and set out the argument and bring it to a conclusion.

The form of the sermon is almost always fundamentally the same: a theme is taken in the form of a text, and the subject it suggests is divided and subdivided for consideration. But that allowed a good deal of variation, and it was possible, as Ranulph Higden indicates, for a preacher to adopt one of the other 'types' of *expositio*: that which is really exegesis (*postillatio*), the homiletic of the Fathers (which he regards as the ancient form of sermon) or a mixture of the latter and the modern thematic method. Within the 'modern' method itself there were many ways of introducing a theme: by a syllogism, by a consequent, by an induction, by example, by using an authority from philosophy, by division, by distinction, by a figure, by a question.[20]

The most substantial borrowing from the art of rhetoric (in terms of the widespread use that was made of it), was the illustrative story or parallel or analogy, the *exemplum*. Luther was happy to use examples in his early sermons. To take a typical instance from a Dominican sermon:

The first living creature was like a lion, the second like an ox, the third like a man, the fourth like a flying eagle.   (Revelation 4.7)

A moral interpretation can take these four living creatures to mean the four kinds of people there are in our Order, says Peter of Rheims (d. after 1247). The lion is the superior. If we look at the behaviour and the natural history of lions it is easy see why this is a proper meaning. Lions guard and protect the animals which are subject to them. Peter gives several Scriptural illustrations (Ecclesiasticus 7.6; Luke 2.8; Proverbs 30.30); lions are kind to those who humble themselves and cruel to those who rebel against them. Similarly, it belongs to the superior's position to behave with mercy to those who acknowledge his rule and fight down those who raise themselves up against it (II Timothy 4.2 and a large number of other texts are cited here). Lions rouse their cubs by roaring just as a superior brings those who are subject to him back to life by his exhortations. Lions wipe out their tracks with their tails to avoid being caught by hunters; similarly, a superior should hide his good works.[21] The lion and his attributes are used here as pegs on which to hang Scriptural texts, but the morals could be drawn without Scriptural support.

The example alone would suffice, if the audience for the sermon consisted of laymen without a detailed knowledge of the Bible but standing in need of instruction in terms they could understand. In his *Treatise on the Formation of Preachers* another early Dominican, Humbert of Romans, lists the kinds of knowledge a preacher needs. He puts 'a knowledge of Scripture' first, 'because all preaching ought to be taken from Scripture', as it says in Psalm 103.12 'From the middle of the rocks they will give utterance.' But he adds a knowledge of created things and the natural world, of historical stories, as well as of the Church's teaching and experience in dealing with men's spiritual problems, and common sense in adapting the preaching to the audience.[22] The use of material such as stories and pictures of animal behaviour became the staple of preaching to the laity. From the beginning,[23] collections of examples and anecdotes[24] were made to help preachers find appropriate stuff for their sermons, over and above the Biblical texts they could discover in dictionaries and concordances.

One *Liber Exemplorum* for the use of preachers, probably put together by an English Franciscan in the thirteenth century, separated 'things above' (Christ, the Blessed Virgin, angels, St James, arranged in order of precedence) from 'things below' (arranged in alphabetical order) and includes anecdotes from the Fathers and various history books, with a clear sense that material from outside the Bible was necessary and useful in preaching to the laity.[25] There is a marked lack of reference to the Bible itself, although references to 'something I have found written in certain famous postills on John' or to 'the Master of the Histories' (Peter Comestor's *Historia Scholastica*)[26] indicate the scholarship which lies, at whatever remove, behind such collections and which is itself ultimately Biblical scholarship. Preaching to the laity was not wholly divorced from the biblical endeavour, but it withheld the text of the Bible from the laity nevertheless.[27] The mediaeval female mystics came to their knowledge of the motifs of Christian mysticism through their spiritual directors.

This withholding led in time to a curiosity about the text of the Bible among the laity, as we shall see.

2 The friars and the laity

Those friars who reached the standard of learning and holiness the order required in them if they were to be licensed as preachers, were examined before they began their preaching work. Their academic record was looked into and an unsatisfactory candidate might be sent back for further studies.[28]

When the licensed Dominican friar went out to preach he took a companion (*socius*) with him, a junior friar who was under obedience to him as he would be to the prior, and who was often a preacher in his own right, learning from his senior as he watched him and even preaching himself. The *socius* gave support and companionship and the pair kept one another up to the standards of behaviour and sound preaching the Order expected, speaking, it was intended, only with God in prayer and of God to their neighbours.[29] Their behaviour was governed by strict rules: they were forbidden to ask for money for any purpose because that would damage the reputation of the Order. They were to remain on amicable terms with the local clergy, going to see the bishop when they arrived in a diocese and obeying his instructions as they worked. Bishops were generally glad enough to have their help, though other local clergy were sometimes resentful of their popularity and the loss of the revenue they themselves might have got out of the work the friars did. The friars kept their masses short to make more time for the sermon, and the people preferred to come to them rather than to the parish church. There was also an attraction in being buried in a mendicant churchyard where one could enjoy the benefit of the prayers the friars offered.[30]

From the beginning there were both preachers-general (older, perhaps more able preachers, experienced men who had a licence to preach anywhere within their own province) and preachers-in-ordinary who were licensed only within the territory of their own prior and under instruction from the prior. The preachers-general had a higher level of learning: three years' study of theology at least.[31]

Of all the friars' extensions of the preaching task, their work as confessors brought them perhaps most familiarly into contact with the laity, especially the nobility and among them, well-born women. It was a natural extension: to move a man's heart to repentance is to create a need for confession and penance. The development of the confessors' manual kept pace with that of the *Art of Preaching*.[32] The constitutions of the Orders envisaged the two functions together.[33]

It was in their intimate work with the laity that the friars were challenged hardest when the laity began to demand, not only to read the *Lives* and stories and extracts from the Fathers in the vernacular with which the friars gladly furnished them, but to read the Scriptures for themselves. The friars' emphasis had always been upon the learning of local languages, and although sermons were often written in Latin (but see MS Trinity College, Cambridge 43 and 323, for collections of sermons in the vernacular), they were given in the vernacular.[34] But that did not go as far as the laity began to want; the Bible was being kept from them in its bare completeness.

3 Preaching against the heretics

A curiosity about the Bible among the laity had long been a feature of certain sects which the Church identified as heretical, both those which were setting out on the road to Reformation and those which taught plain error in any Christian's eyes. Twelfth and early thirteenth century authors of treatises against the dualist Cathars claim that they are only too ready to produce texts to support their views; the same phenomenon occurred among the Waldensians, who wanted to live lives of apostolic poverty. It became a commonplace to speak of theology as involving not only the setting-out of the truth, but also its defence against attack by heretics: 'The heretics provoke us to search the Scriptures', says Luther. 'Heretics are useful. We don't realise how good it is for us to have opponents.'[35] Aquinas prefaced his *Catena Aurea*, a collection of patristic quotations for exegesis, with the comment that it was his intention to provide not only an interpretation of the literal and mystical sense of the Gospels, but also a destruction of errors against the faith.[36] The 'heretics' to whom Aquinas refers are ancient or more recent examples of holders of opinions the Church has come to condemn, who have persisted in those opinions knowing them to be unorthodox. That is the sense in which Bellarmine uses the term, too. But Luther can speak of 'heretics', too, and mean those who are out of step with the true Church as he identifies it. In the sixteenth century 'heretic' came to be freely used by reformers and counter-reformers alike as a term of abuse for the other side.

Certain authors addressed themselves directly to the misrepresentations of the heretics of their day: Roland of Cremona, for example, in his commentary on Job,[37] and Raynerius Sacconi, in his *Summa* of Cathar and Waldensian teaching[38] of the mid-thirteenth century. Durandus of Huesca makes much of the right use of Scripture for proof of sound doctrine against the heretic's misuse. 'I know,' he says, 'that the Cathars' who use the Bible's witness, 'neither believe nor understand' its witness. They alter the text. From *Deum, qui fecit hunc mundum* they remove *hunc* so that they can read the Bible as saying that God made not this visible world but only the invisible world. This Durandus can show to be a false reading, because he has looked up the passage in various manuscripts in Rome and elsewhere and found that *hunc* is always present – and indeed it is sometimes found even in copies belonging to the heretics themselves.[39]

Durandus's own procedures are not above reproach if we take them on his own terms. He uses the spiritual senses as a basis for proof. When we read that Joseph and Mary could not find Jesus anywhere but in the Temple in Jerusalem in the midst of the doctors, Durandus wants us to understand that 'true salvation' is to be found nowhere but in 'Jerusalem', that is, in the catholic Church. The heretics object that this is a proof from tropology.[40] Much of Durandus's attack is outright fulmination. The Cathars are demented, he says; they abuse the authorities.[41] But there is much, too, that is intended to convince by its reasonableness. He promises that if sane judgement is applied to the texts they cite, along the lines he proposes, it will be clear that in fact they oppose the case the Cathars are trying to make them prove.[42] Durandus's way of dealing with the heretics' use of Scripture is, then, to deploy the resources of academic commentary against them. He explains to them that words in Scripture may have many meanings and shows them that they have, at key points, chosen one which is wrong for its context.[43] Underneath his bluster is a sound base of traditional exegetical method.

The limitations of this procedure are that it requires a degree of Latinity and a fair competence in academic theology on the part of those who are to be converted from their wrong views. The real challenge came in the end not from these Bible-twisting dualists, but from those who were in some sense heirs of the Waldensians: honest articulate laymen who wanted to read the Bible for themselves.

It was a vigorous challenge. William of Ockham comments in 1337–8 that 'laymen and old women' will tackle trained theologians on the question of free will and contingency, and Chaucer's Chanticleer could entertain a lay readership which knew about the contemporary debate concerning pelagianism.[44] Robert Holcot complains that laymen insist on being given reasons for their faith.[45] Robert Bellarmine speaks with feeling of the result of their having such access to Scripture. He consistently calls the reformers 'heretics'.

4 The new preaching to the laity

Wyclif saw preaching as the most important duty of a priest: not such preaching as he says the friars gave, full of comedies and tragedies and fables and amusing stories, but preaching on the Bible.[46] After the Holy Spirit had come upon them the apostles were turned into preachers.[47] The preacher's words ought to come from above, and in that sense to be the Word of God. Luther has some comments which rest on the same assumptions:

> Somebody asked, 'Doctor, is the word that Christ spoke when he was on earth the same in fact and effect as the Word preached by a minister?'
> Luther replied, 'Yes, because he said, "He who hears you hears me" (Luke 10.16). And Paul calls the Word "the power of God" ' (Romans 1.16).

Then the inquirer asked, 'Doctor isn't there a difference between the Word that became flesh (John 1.14) and the Word that is proclaimed by Christ or by a minister?'

'By all means!' he replied. 'The former is the incarnate Word, who was true God from the beginning, and the latter is the Word that's proclaimed. The former Word is in substance God; the latter Word is in its effect the power of God, but it isn't God in substance, for it has a man's nature, whether it's spoken by Christ or by a minister.'[48]

Preachers follow in the tradition of the prophets and are enlightened by Christ himself.[49] Both priests and deacons should preach, and not only in their own parishes.[50] Wyclif's own published sermons are, he says, intended as helps and guides for other preachers. He suggests ways in which a point or topic may be developed. 'Interpreting truths, we should collect from Scripture excerpts with which to feed the faithful and impress the Word of God upon them as fully as we can.'[51] The spirit is Tyndale's: 'For when the evangelion is preached, the Spirit of God entereth into them which God hath ordained and appointed to eternal life; and openeth their inward eyes, and worketh such belief in them.'[52]

Wyclif's followers put together a cycle of sermons in which his principles were put into practice.[53] In a sermon on Luke 15.11–32 a parallel is drawn between the two sons, the elder brother and the prodigal, and God's 'two sons', the Jews and the gentiles.[54] In a sermon on John 10.11–18 we learn how a good Shepherd should behave and how the people of God stand in need of a good shepherd to 'brynge men to hevene', the office filled perfectly by Christ, who is both God and man.[55] There is frequently a contemporary application, but the stuff of the interpretation is conventional and familiar, with the modification that it is often expressed in terms which will make it easier to grasp and remember for a lay audience to which it is not familiar. A sermon for the first Sunday after Trinity on the story in Luke 16 about the rich man explains that 'Crist telluth in this parable how richessus ben perilows.' The word 'parable' is explained as 'a word of story that by that huydyth a spiritual wit'. The rich man in the story 'disusede hys richessys in pruyde and in glotenye'. This Gospel gives the priest an opportunity to 'telle of false pruyde of ryche men' and of the 'longe peynes of helle and of ioyful blisse in hevene' – and to develop the theme 'as the tyme askith'.[56] A sermon on the Epistle for the first Sunday in Advent considers the status of the Epistles as 'gospelis of Crist, for he spac hem alle in hem, and Crist may not erre; . . . And, all if the Hooly Goost speketh eche word of hooly write, ne eles Crist spac in Poule more plenteously and sutelly.'[57] Everything is patient and helpful; no question of critical method or theology is barred. The vernacular sermon proved a fit vehicle for exegesis as the Latin had long done.

There was, however, a new sense of freshness and directness and challenge in the vernacular sermons. The air of challenge in particular encouraged the spread of copies of Wyclif's *sermones rudes* for the people among the religious reformers on the Continent as well as in England itself.[58] Jean Gerson (1363–1429), reformer and mystic, is conscious of a difference between the way in which he would be obliged to preach if he were engaging in a scholastic exercise (*in scholastico exercitio*) or if he were preaching to unbelievers (*apud incredulos*), and the manner in which he is free to speak 'in a house of prayer and a school of devotion' where he can rely upon his listeners.[59] In his vernacular sermons this freedom and ease is clearly visible. 'Rejoice, Christian people! I bring you good news . . . written by God's secretary (*le divin secrétaire*) St John the Evangelist.' He encourages the congregation to see the Word of God as something they ought to hear for themselves and keep close. 'But how will you keep the Word of God if you do not know it? And how can you know it better than by hearing it?'[60] In practice, Gerson does not do a great deal to familiarise his listeners with the text. He quotes Scripture rather sparingly and in Latin: 'Cry with the Apostle Paul: *O altitudo diviciarum sapiencie*, etc.'[61] He uses miracles, historical *example* and legends as well as biblical material,[62] much as the friars were doing when the Lollards challenged them. But Gerson has something of the reformers' sense of the necessity for preaching if God is to make himself known to men through the Word. He insists on it in every sermon.[63] It is through 'the words of Holy Scripture . . . that one can know God's will and his promises', he explains. His messengers, heralds and secretaries are all preachers and publicisers of the Word.[64]

The new powerful urge to communicate the Bible in full to the laity which moved Wyclif's followers persists in the preaching of the sixteenth century reformers. Luther exclaims at the hugeness of the task: 'What does it amount to that we have the gospel in this little corner [of the world]? Just reckon that there is no gospel in all of Asia and Africa and that the gospel isn't preached in many parts of Europe, in Greece, Italy, Hungary, Spain, France, England, Poland.'[65]

But the work was painfully controversial and even dangerous in the first strivings of the Reformation:

> On July 1 news arrived in writing from Italy that recently in Bologna forty-two monks preached the gospel in public with freedom and clarity, that they spoke with as much boldness as it could have been done in Wittenberg, and that their numerous audience received them with great applause, and yet the bishops and the Pope resorted to force against them. When advised to flee, they took care of themselves, but one of them, who had books by Luther and books in translation under the name of Erasmus of Rotterdam, was seized and imprisoned while the books were burned.[66]

There is nothing like warfare for making it necessary to pick sides. In the charged atmosphere of the conflict Protestants and Catholics began to think that nothing the enemy said could be other than part of a plot against the truth. And so the benefits of common labour were lost sight of, and with them an appreciation of how much of the labour had been common.

CONCLUSION

The scholastic education of a John Wyclif or a Martin Luther had this in common with Augustine's education in the schools of rhetoric of the late Roman world, that both involved a most thorough and vigorous training of the mind in sophisticated verbal skills and abstract conceptions which were held in high respect by their contemporaries. The Bible surprised and stirred each of them. To Augustine it seemed at first crudely-written and lacking in the eloquence he would have expected of the compositions of the divine mind. His own exegetical endeavour was to show that it had an *eloquentia* of its own, obeying its own rules and far superior to anything the mind of man could devise. Wyclif discovered the force of the Bible's truth after a long theological training which had made him conscious of the degree to which its veracity was being attacked in the course of school disputations. Once he had hit upon this notion it proved to be the key to all that made him uncomfortable or angry in contemporary scholarship or polemic. Luther discovered the Bible as a whole after a training which had introduced it to him in parts. For each of them something in the training which had formed his mind had obscured the Bible for him or made it appear less than itself until a shift of perspective showed him its importance with great simplicity. Once he had a grasp of his particular insight, each of them felt the Bible's power.

Why did the same powerful sense of the Bible not come to others? The answer must be that it did, and we can see plentiful evidence of the fact in the evocative language of the late mediaeval mystics and even in the enormous care the scholastics took to find the right interpretation of fine points in the text. But a few individuals succeeded in conveying to others the impact the Bible had had on them, with results which altered the way in which it was perceived significantly, and for a long time.

Perhaps the essential difference between the sixteenth century view and that of the late mediaeval centuries is the bringing together

158

again of speculative theology and exegesis, which had become separated for purposes of study into two parallel tracks in the late twelfth century. After some practice Luther could use the Bible directly as a source-book for theological discussion, without reference to *Sentences* or *summa*.

This new complexion of exegesis undoubtedly contributed to the polarisation of protestant and Roman Catholic views of the nature of the enterprise which took place in the sixteenth century. Polemical treatises from either side reflect upon the assumptions and principles of the other; there is much talk of 'our tenets' and of 'the heretics', much enquiring into the arguments of the other side, much consciousness of what is implied in the choice of a particular method. Yet this awareness of differences covers, as we have seen, a vast bulk of common endeavour and hides from view the preponderance of common assumptions about the nature and purpose of Scripture on which apologists for both sides were in fact proceeding.

There was, too, a good deal of talk of the need for fresh appraisals in the light of new insights: that notion that the present age has made advances which cause us to regard old ideas as out of date which is a commonplace of the theology of every century, including our own:

The circumstances of the present age demand a wholesale reassessment of the Christian faith . . .

The entirely new perspectives forced upon any thinking Christian by the arrival of biblical criticism . . . and the resolutions of thought brought about by the Renaissance, the Enlightenment and the rise of science have made a new interpretation of the Christian faith an imperative necessity . . .

The old doctrine of original sin cannot be perpetuated once we have ceased to believe that the first three chapters of Genesis give us an historically reliable account of the origin of mankind.

Many would regard it as our plain duty . . . to frame our belief in the Incarnation so as to take account of the fact that St John's Gospel in the greater part of its record of what Jesus said is not giving us his actual words or teaching, but is interpreting his significance by means of discourses written in his name.

Richard Hanson, *The Times*, 25 February 1984

The arrogance of the seemingly new insight obscures a solid body of continuing work and unrejected assumptions. We might let George Bull have the last word. In his *Harmonia Apostolica* of 1669–70 (2nd ed., Oxford, 1844, Introduction), he tried to show that James and Paul taught alike about justification. In his introduction he runs an eye over the problems posed by the interpretation of Scripture. There is very little in what he says that could not be put into the mouth of Augustine or any of our mediaeval scholars, or of a reformer or counter-reformer in the sixteenth century. The continuity of effort is the most significant feature of the exegetical endeavour throughout the period of self-conscious change with which we have been concerned:

Although all, who are truly Christians, fully allow both the infallible authority of Scripture and the most perfect harmony of its parts; still, unhappily, it too often occurs that no few apparent contradictions and almost inextricable difficulties are found in that sacred Volume. Whether this be owing to the sublimity of the subject, or the singularity of its style, to our own ignorance of the opinions and customs of those to whom no small part of Scripture was necessarily addressed (customs which by so very long an interval are almost entirely obliterated), to our own dulness in understanding, or negligence in studying the Holy Scriptures, or, in short, to all these taken together, or whatever other . . . cause . . . the fact and its consequences we are obliged to perceive and lament.

NOTES

Introduction

1 *Opus Epistolarum*, ed. P. S. Allen, H. M. Allen and H. W. Garrod (Oxford, 1906–1958), 12 vols., II.90–114, tr. J. C. Olin in *Christian Humanism in the Reformation: Selected Writings of Erasmus* (New York, 1965).

2 *Ibid.*, IV.96–107.

3 *Ibid.*, II.90–114. See *The Collected Works of Erasmus* (Toronto, 1974).

4 Compare Matthew Poole, *A Commentary on the Holy Bible* (repr. London, 1962), III.477 and Aquinas, *Lecturae super Epistolas S. Pauli*, ed. P. Raphael (Rome, 1953), Prologue, 12.

5 For the story up to 1200, see my *Language and Logic* I.

1 'Scripture hath for its author God himself'

1 Thomas Stapleton, *A Fortresse of the Faith first Planted among us Englishmen* (St Omer, 1625), p. 223.

2 J. Mathesius, *Historien von des ehrwürdigen in Gottseligen teuren Manns Gottes D. Martini Lutheri: Anfang, Lehr, Lebe und Sterben* (Nürnberg, 1566), ed. G. Loesche (Prague, 1906), p. 1.

3 See A. Hudson's remark that the component ideas of Wyclif's heresy 'show little that was completely original'. It is the system that he made of them, centred upon the Bible, that is his own. *Selections from English Wycliffite Writings* (Cambridge, 1978), p. 4.

4 Luther, WA, 54, 183ff.

5 Luther, Letter to Staupitz his friend and superior, in *Briefwechsel*, ed. E. L. Enders (Stuttgart, 1884).

6 William Whitaker, *A Disputation on Holy Scripture*, ed. W. Fitzgerald (Cambridge, 1849), p. 289.

7 See A. B. Collins, *The Secular is Sacred: Platonism and Thomism in Marsilio Ficino's 'Platonic Theology'* (The Hague, 1974), pp. 5–6.

8 Marsilio Ficino, *The Philebus Commentary*, Chapter 12, ed. and tr. J. B. Allen (California, 1975), p. 141.

9 Alexander of Hales, *Glossa in Quatuor Libros Sententiarum Petri Lombardi*, Dist. II.6 (Florence, 1951), p. 29.

10 M. Colish, *The Mirror of Language*, revised ed. (Nebraska, 1983), discusses the mediaeval theory of signs.

11 Aquinas, *Commentary on Thessalonians*, I.i.

12 *Selections from English Wycliffite Writings*, ed. A. Hudson (Cambridge, 1978), no. 16, p. 83.

13 *Heresy Trials in the Diocese of Norwich, 1428–31*, ed. N. P. Tanner,

Camden Series, 4, 20 (London, 1977), p. 49, and see W. R. Jones, 'Lollards and Images: the Defence of Religious Art in Later Mediaeval England', *Journal of the History of Ideas*, 34 (1973), 31.

14 Melanchthon, *Loci Communes*, ed. and tr. C. L. Manschreck, Oxford, 1965, xix.

15 Zwingli, *Of the Clarity and Certainty of the Word of God*, tr. G. W. Bromily, *Library of Christian Classics*, 24 (London, 1953), pp. 60–95.

16 Calvin, *Commentaries*, tr. J. Haroutinian and L. P. Smith (London, 1958), p. 59. The commentaries are printed in full in *Corpus Reformatorum*, vols. 28–69, Brunswick, Berlin, Zurich, 1859–1900.

17 On the historical aspect of prophecy, see M. Reeves, *The Influence of Prophecy in the Later Middle Ages* (Oxford, 1968). On the revival of Pelagianism, see G. Leff, *Bradwardine and the Pelagians* (Cambridge, 1957).

18 Calvin, *Commentaries*, tr. cit., pp. 41–2.

19 *Ibid.*, p. 39, on Acts 20.32.

20 B. Smalley, 'William of Auvergne, John of la Rochelle and St. Thomas Aquinas on the Old Law', *Studies*, p. 127, and K. Hagen, *A Theology of Testament in the Young Luther* (Leiden, 1974), pp. 63–5.

21 Melanchthon, *Loci Communes*, XVI and see P. Fraenkel, '*Testimonia Patrum*: the Function of the Patristic Argument in the Theology of Philip Melanchthon', *Travaux d'humanisme et renaissance* (Geneva, 1961), pp. 70–4.

22 William Tyndale, *Prologue to Romans*, *Prologues*, ed. H. Walter (Cambridge, 1848), p. 417.

23 For an example, see J. P. Gilson, 'Friar Alexander and his Historical Interpretation of the Apocalypse', *Coll. Franc.* 2 (1922), 20–36. Alexander of Hales himself makes a common distinction between Old and New Covenant, that the old teaches only how to turn from evil, the new how to do good: *Glossa in Quatuor Libros Sententiarum*, p. 8.8–11.

24 Aquinas, *Commentary on Romans*, II.

25 Bonaventure, *Commentary on John*, I.35, *Opera Omnia*, VI.254.

26 Matthew Poole, *On Revelation* (reprinted London, 1963), p. 947.

2 The human authors of Scripture

1 Gabriel Biel, *Defensorium Obedientiae Apostolicae*, ed. H. A. Oberman, D. E. Zerfoss and W. J. Courtenay (Cambridge, Mass., 1968), pp. 114.10–11.

2 See pp. 70ff. and A. J. Minnis, *Medieval Theory of Authorship* (London, 1984).

3 Duns Scotus on Peter Lombard's *Sentences*, ed. P. M. F. Garcia (Florence, 1912), Prologue, Q, II.36.

4 J. P. Torrell, *Théorie de la prophétie et la connaissance aux environs de 1230*, SSL, 40 (1977), p. 93, pp. 154–5.

5 *Ibid.*, article I, obj. 7, pp. 3–5 (*Prophetica est inspiratio vel revelatio divina rerum eventus immobili veritati denoncians*). Cf. Peter Lombard on the Psalms, PL 191.58 and Cassiodorus on the Psalms, CCSL, 97, p. 7.

6 Torrell, *op. cit.*, p. 6.9–13.

7 *Ibid.*, p. 80.

8 *Ibid.*, pp. 45.9–16. See *Fasciculi Zizaniorum*, pp. 48–9 on Amos 7.14.

9 *Ibid.*, pp. 52.18–19.

10 Albertus Magnus, *Postilla super Isaiam*, ed. F. Siepmann (Aschendorff, 1952), Prologue, pp. 1–4, especially p. 4.86ff.

11 Wyclif, *Sermones*, I.18–20 and see the later chapter on 'The Bible's Future Tenses'.
12 Calvin, *A Harmony of the Gospels*, tr. A. W. Morrison (Edinburgh, 1972), I.xii–xiii.
13 Luther, *Table Talk*, no. 475, pp. 79–80.
14 *Ibid.*, no. 663, p. 121.
15 *Ibid.*, no. 396, p. 62.
16 On this, see *Cambridge History Bible*, III.12–13.
17 Stapleton, *Relectio Scholastica*, in *Opera* (Paris, 1620), I.508–9.

3 Handing on and explanations

1 William Fulke, *Defence of the English Translation of the Holy Scriptures*, ed. C. H. Hartshorne (Cambridge, 1843), p. 47.
2 Marsilius of Padua, *Defensor Pacis*, ed. C. W. Prévité-Orton (Cambridge, 1928), II.vi.1.
3 *Ibid.*, II.xix.2–3. On *sola scriptura*, see pp. 31ff.
4 H. A. Oberman, *Forerunners of the Reformation* (London, 1967), pp. 288–9.
5 Chrysostom's large popularity may owe something to Aquinas. Some Chrysostom had been translated from the Greek in the early fifth century, but a new translation was made by Burgundio of Pisa (d. 1194) in the twelfth century. See J. A. Weisheipl, *Friar Thomas d'Aquino* (Oxford, 1974), pp. 121–2.
6 Gabriel Biel, *Defensorium*, *ed. cit.*, p. 119.
7 Luther, *Table Talk*, no. 584, pp. 104–5.
8 G. Leff, *Bradwardine and the Pelagians* (Cambridge, 1957), and see H. A. Oberman, *Masters of the Reformation*, tr. D. Martin (Cambridge, 1981), p. 65 on the Augustinian renaissance in the later Middle Ages.
9 See P. Fraenkel, *Testimonia Patrum*, pp. 86–100 for discussion and references.
10 *Johann Ecks Predigttätigkeit*, ed. A. Brandt (Munster, 1914), for example, Sermon II.21 Sunday after Trinity.
11 K. Hagen, *A Theology of Testament in the Young Luther* (Leiden, 1974), pp. 15–18.
12 Luther, *Table Talk*, no. 347, p. 49.
13 *Ibid.*, no. 347, p. 49.
14 *Ibid.*, no. 3975, p. 304.
15 *Ibid.*, no. 316, p. 44.
16 *Ibid.*, no. 252, p. 33.
17 *Ibid.*, no. 445, p. 72. Compare Luther on Galatians 1.17 (1535), WA, vol. 40, p. 142, Luther's *Works*, vol. 26, p. 74, and Galatians 1.20, WA, vol. 40, p. 148, Luther's *Works*, vol. 26, p. 77.
18 Luther on Deuteronomy 16.21. WA, vol. 14, p. 667, Luther's *Works*, vol. 9, p. 164.
19 Brevicoxa, *Tractatus de Fide et Ecclesia, Romano Pontifice et Concilio Generali*, in J. Gerson, *Opera Omnia*, ed. L. E. du Pin (Antwerp, 1706), I. cols. 805–904, Part III. Q. i–iii.
20 Robert Bellarmine, *De Verbo Dei* IV.i–ii.
21 William Fulke, *Defence*, pp. 88–9.
22 Bellarmine, *De Verbo Dei*, IV.ii.
23 *Ibid.*, IV.iii–iv.
24 *Ibid.*, IV.v–viii.

25 Aquinas, Prologue to *Lecturae super Epistolas S. Pauli*, ed. P. Raphael (Rome, 1953), 4.
26 Stillingfleet, *The Council of Trent Examin'd*, 2nd ed., corrected with an Appendix concerning the Prohibiting of Scripture in Vulgar Languages (London, 1688), p. 1.
27 Matthew Poole on Revelation, 1685 (repr. London, 1962), p. 947. On the idea that more recent authority is less, see *Fasciculi Zizaniorum*, pp. 1–6 for John Cunningham's account of Wyclif's views.
28 Gabriel Biel, *Defensorium*, ed. cit., p. 7423–5, p. 79.20–3.
29 Whitaker, *Disputation*, ed. cit., pp. 53–4.
30 Gabriel Biel, *Defensorium*, p. 114.1–3.
31 Aquinas, *Commentary on Galatians*, I. Lectura 2.
32 *Ibid.*, Lectura 3.
33 M. O'Rourke Boyle, *Rhetoric and Reform: Erasmus' Civil Dispute with Luther* (Harvard, 1983), p. 49, and the notion is found in the debates in *Fasciculi Zizaniorum*.
34 Bellarmine, *De Verbo Dei*, IV.ix.
35 *Fasciculi Zizaniorum*, p. 481.
36 Tyndale, *Answer to Sir Thomas More's Dialogue*, ed. H. Walter (Cambridge, 1850), p. 48.
37 Marsilius of Padua, *Defensor Pacis*, II.iv.2.
38 *Ibid.*, II.i.1, Whitaker, *Disputation*, p. 29.
39 Marsilius of Padua, *Defensor Pacis*, II.i.3.
40 *Ibid.*, II.ii.2.
41 Tyndale, *Answer to Sir Thomas More's Dialogue*, p. 9.
42 *Ibid.*, p. 11.
43 Marsilius of Padua, *Defensor Pacis*, II.xx.1.
44 *Ibid.*, II.xx.2–6.
45 Tyndale, *Expositions*, ed. H. Walter (Cambridge, 1848).
46 Bellarmine, *The Use and Great Moment of the Notes of the Church* (tr. London, 1687), pp. 2–5, and see R. M. Kingdon, 'Peter Martyr Vermigli and the Marks of the True Church' in *Continuity and Discontinuity in Church History*, ed. F. Forrester Church and T. George (Leiden, 1979).
47 Tyndale, *Expositions*, p. 24. A notable contribution to this debate was the controversy over Luther in which John Fisher, Bishop of Rochester (1469–1535) involved himself. See his *Assertionis Lutheranae Confutatio*, in *Opera Omnia* (Wurzburg, 1697, facsimile reprint 1967), col. 272ff. Fisher proceeds by listing *veritates* and *articuli* in an attempt to prove his case by demonstrative method, and thus to give it the utmost force of rational conviction.

4 Sola scriptura

1 Tyndale, *Expositions*, pp. 183–4.
2 Calvin, *Commentaries*, tr. cit., p. 104.
3 *Ibid.*, pp. 66–70.
4 Whitaker, *Disputation*, p. 25.
5 *Ibid.*, pp. 280, 288. Origen, On Numbers 16.9, *Opera*, ed. Baehrens, VII.153; Jerome, In Gal. 5.19–21, PL 26.417A and see J. P. Torrell in *Revue Thomiste*, 66 (1966), 81 n. 2.
6 Duns Scotus on Peter Lombard's *Sentences*, *Commentaria Oxoniensia*, ed. P. Marianus and P. Garcia (Florence, 1912), 2 vols., Prologue, Q.II.44–5.

7 H. Østerrgaard-Nielsen, 'Scriptura sacra et viva vox', *Forschungen zur Geschichte und Lehre des Protestantismus*, 10 (Munich, 1957), 11–19.
8 William Fulke, *Defence*, p. 77.
9 *Ibid.*, p. 76.
10 Bellarmine, *De Verbo Dei*, I.1.iii.
11 *Ibid.*, III.iii–ix.
12 *Article*, VI.

5 Towards private judgement: 'The children of God spy out their Father'

1 Tyndale, *Answer to Sir Thomas More's Dialogue*, p. 51.
2 On this view of the laity, see Smalley, *Studies*, p. 130; for Simon of Tournai's comment, see A. Landgraf, *Dogmengeschichte der Frühscholastik*, 3, 1 (Regensburg, 1954), p. 32.
3 For Hildegard's visions, see *Analecta Sanctae Hildegardis*, ed. J. B. Pitra, *Spicilegium Solesmensis* (1880), 2nd ed. M. Böckeler (Salzburg, 1975).
4 Calvin, *Commentaries*, tr. cit., p. 85.
5 Bellarmine, *De Verbo Dei*, I.i.
6 Luther on Galatians (1535), WA, vol. 40, p. 134, *Luther's Works*, vol. 36, p. 67.
7 Calvin, *Commentaries*, tr. cit., p. 85.
8 *Ibid.*
9 *Ibid.*, p. 88.
10 Tyndale, *Expositions*, p. 138, Prologue to the Exposition of I John.
11 *Ibid.*, p. 140.
12 *Ibid.*, p. 36, on Matthew 5.14–16.
13 Cranmer, *Remains*, ed. H. Jenkins (Oxford, 1833), vol. 4, p. 272.
14 Martin Bucer, *Commonplaces*, tr. D. F. Wright (Abingdon, 1972), p. 76.
15 Calvin, *Commentaries*, tr. cit., p. 78, on Psalm 1.2.
16 Luther on the Psalms, WA, vol. 3, p. 20.

6 The ground rules

1 John of Ragusa's Oration at the Council of Basel, *Concilia*, N. Coleti, 17 (Venice, 1781), 832–4.
2 See my *Language and Logic I* for an account of these ideas.
3 On the history of the four senses, see H. de Lubac, *Exégèse médiévale* (Paris, 1959), 2 vols.
4 For twelfth century work on the Hebrew text, see B. Smalley, 'Andrew of St. Victor, a twelfth century Hebraist', RTAM, 10 (1938), 358–73 and 'The School of Andrew of St. Victor', RTAM, 11 (1939), 145–67.
5 See E. Jeauneau, '*Nani gigantum humeris insidentes*', *Vivarium*, 5 (1967), 94–5, and Adelard of Bath, *Quaestiones Naturales*, ed. M. Müller, *Beiträge zur Geschichte der Philosophie*, 31, 2 (1934), 12: Omnis quippe litera meretrix est, nunc ad hos, nunc ad illos affectus exposita.
6 See *Language and Logic I*, pp. 133–63.
7 R. B. C. Huygens, *Accessus ad Auctores* (Leiden, 1970).
8 *Fasciculi Zizaniorum*, p. 7, and see pp. 108ff. for Wyclif's battle against the challengers of the Bible's truth.

7 The literal sense

1　On this verse, see Smalley, *Studies*, p. 285.
2　On the architectural metaphor, see Lubac, *Exégèse médiévale*.
3　Smalley, 'William of Auvergne, John of la Rochelle and St. Thomas Aquinas on the Old Law', *Studies*, pp. 121–6.
4　Smalley, *Studies*, pp. 137–43.
5　Tyndale, *Prologues*, ed. H. Walter (Cambridge, 1848), p. 421, on Leviticus.
6　Smalley, 'Which William of Nottingham?', *Studies*, p. 285.
7　On Nicholas of Lyra's account, see H. A. Oberman, *Forerunners of the Reformation* (London, 1967), p. 286.
8　The text of the key passage of William of.Auvergne's *De Legibus* is given in Smalley, *Studies*, pp. 179–81. On William of Auvergne, see C. Ottaviano, *Guglielmo d'Auxerre, Biblioteca di Filosofia e Scienza*, 12 (Rome, 1950).
9　Aquinas, *Summa Theologiae*, I^a, Q.I.a.10, obj. 3 and reply.
10　*Ibid.*. On words and things, see my *Language and Logic I*, pp. 51–8.
11　Aquinas, *Summa Theologiae*, I^a, Q.29 a.4, reply obj. 1.
12　Smalley, *Studies*, pp. 179–81.
13　Bonaventure, *Quaestiones Disputatae de Scientia Christi*, Q.2, *Opera Omnia*, V.9.
14　Aquinas, *Summa Theologiae*, 1^a, Q.5, a.3.
15　See Part I.i.
16　Aquinas, *Summa Theologiae*, I^a, Q.1. a.9, obj. 1. Cf. C. Fierville, *Une grammaire latine inédite du xiiie siècle* (Paris, 1886), p. 166 and Sir John Harington, *A Preface or rather a Briefe Apologie of Poetrie*, Preface to translation of *Orlando Furioso*, 159a, in *Elizabethan Critical Essays*, ed. G. Gregory Smith (Oxford, 1904), II.201–2.
17　*Magistri Echardi: Liber Parabolarum Genesis*, Prologue, *Lateinischen Werke*, vol. I (Stuttgart, 1964), pp. 447, 451–2, 454–5.
18　See J. A. Weisheipl, *Friar Thomas d'Aquino*, p. 106 and Smalley, *Studies*, p. 162. On the academic framework within which Aquinas came to his inception, see G. Leff, *The Universities of Oxford and Paris in the Thirteenth and Fourteenth Centuries* (New York, 1968).
19　Ockham, *Quodlibet* VII.Q.6.a.1, *Quaestiones Disputatae*, ed. R. Spiazzi (Rome, Turin, 1928), pp. 145–8.
20　John Quidort, *De Potestate Regia et Papali*, ed. F. Bleienstein (Stuttgart, 1969), Nicholas of Lyre Prologue, II, cf. note 29.
21　*Quaestiones Disputatae*, *loc. cit.*, cf. *Summa Theologiae* I^a Q.1.a.10.
22　Sermon on John 3, *Luthers Werke*, ed. E. Vogelsang, vol. V (Berlin, 1955), p. 26.16.
23　Bellarmine, *De Verbo Dei*, III.iii.
24　S. Ozment, *The Age of Reform, 1250–1550* (Yale, 1980), pp. 69–72.
25　Sermon for the 23rd Sunday after Trinity, *Johann Ecks Predigtätigkeit*, ed. A. Brandt, p. 186.
26　*Ibid.*, pp. 172–3, On Job 19.21, All Saints' Day, 1525.
27　*Ibid.*, p. 184. On typology, see U. Krewitt, *Metaphor und tropische Rede in der Auffassung des Mittelalters*, Supplement to *Mittellateinisches Jahrbuch*, 7 (Ratingen, 1971); E. Auerbach, *Typologische Motive in der Mittelalterlichen Literatur* (Krefeld, 1964); E. Curtius, *Europäische Literatur und Lateinisches Mittelalter* (Bern, 1948) and tr. W. R. Trask (London, 1953); M. Henschel, 'Figuralbedeutung und Geschichtlichkeit', *Kerygma und Dogma*, 5 (1959), 306–17.

28 Calvin, *Commentaries, tr. cit.*, p. 107 and for Bellarmine's reposte, *De Verbo Dei*, I.iii.
29 Tyndale, *The Obedience of a Christian Man*, ed. H. Walter (Cambridge, 1848), p. 303.
30 Luther, *Table Talk*, no. 5285, p. 406.
31 *Ibid.*, no. 335, p. 46.
32 Tyndale, *The Obedience of a Christian Man*, pp. 304–5 and p. 307.
33 *Ibid.*, p. 305. On allegory's inability to prove, see p. 46.
34 *Ibid.*, p. 307, and p. 425.
35 *Ibid.*, p. 310.
36 *Ibid.*, p. 312.
37 *Ibid.*, p. 411.
38 *Ibid.*, p. 449.

8 Vis vocis

1 I hope to discuss this further in a future study.
2 Smalley, *Studies*, p. 179 and pp. 152–4.
3 Augustine, *Soliloquies*, I.i.4, PL 32.871.
4 Alexander of Hales, *Glossa in Quatuor Libros Sententiarum* (Florence, 1951), p. 30.
5 Albertus Magnus, *Postilla super Isaiam*, p. 136.72–86.
6 V. Law, 'Normative Grammar in the Thirteenth Century', *Proceedings of the Convegno Internazionale di Studi: Aspetti della letteratura latina nel secolo 13* (Perugia, forthcoming).
7 V. Law gives an example from Paris, Bibliothèque nationale, MS lat. 16670, where, after giving both Donatus's and Priscian's definitions of the noun, the author asks 'Why was the noun invented?' (*ut significat suppositum in locutione*), then the further question 'What is the *suppositum*? What is the *appositum*?' Later '*nominative unde regitur*?' See, too, Thomas of Erfurt, *Grammatica Speculativa*, ed. and tr. G. L. Bursill-Hall (London, 1972) and J. Pinborg, 'Die Entwicklung der Sprachtheorie im Mittelalter', *Beiträge zur Geschichte der Philosophie und Theologie des Mittelalters*, 42, 2 (Münster, Copenhagen, 1967).
8 G. A. Padley, *Grammatical Theory in Western Europe, 1500–1700* (Cambridge, 1976).
9 *Ibid.*, p. 56.
10 Wyclif, *Logica*, ed. M. H. Dziewicki (London, 1893–9), 3 vols., I.1.3–8.
11 On *usus loquendi* in early mediaeval logic, see D. P. Henry, *The Logic of St. Anselm* (Oxford, 1967).
12 Wyclif, *De Mandatis Divinis*, ed. F. D. Matthew (London, 1896), p. 49.12–14.
13 *Ibid.*, p. 63.28ff.
14 *Ibid.*, p. 72.31.
15 *Melanchthons Werke*, III.83–4 (*Praefatio in Officia Ciceronis*); Bellarmine *De Verbo Dei*, I.i; on the metaphysical aspects, see L. M. de Rijk, 'On Buridan's Doctrine of Connotation', *The Logic of John Buridan*, ed. J. Pinborg (Copenhagen, 1976), pp. 91–101.
16 Bonaventure, *In John*, I.86, Q.5, *Opera Omnia*, VI.264. The second example is from Wyclif, *Sermones*, II.166 (Sermon 23).
17 *Godfrey of Fontaine's Abridgement of Boethius of Dacia's 'Modi Significandi' sive 'Quaestiones super Priscianum Maiorem'*, ed. A. C. Senape

McDermott, *Studies in the History of Linguistics*, 22 (Amsterdam, 1980), Q.2, p. 28 and Q.14, p. 50. On twelfth century work on universal grammar, see Gilbert of Poitiers, *Commentaries on Boethius*, ed. N. M. Häring (Toronto, 1966), pp. 189–90, where Gilbert says that grammar is unique among the *artes* in lacking self-evident first principles.

18 That does not necessarily make him a 'terminist'. On 'terminism', see *Cambridge History LMP*, pp. 161–97.

19 Wyclif, *Logica*, I.2.1–5.

20 *Ibid.*, p. 2.6–10.

21 *Ibid.*, p. 76.21ff and p. 77.5ff.

22 *Cambridge History LMP*, p. 405.

23 P. V. Spade, 'Ockham on Terms of First and Second Imposition and Intention, with Remarks on the Liar Paradox', *Vivarium*, 19 (1981), 47–55.

24 Wyclif, *Logica*, I.77.

25 On William, see the introduction to William of Sherwood's *Introduction to Logic*, tr. N. Kretzmann (Minneapolis, 1966), p. 19. On the description of *suppositio, appellatio, copulatio* as 'functions' of *significatio*, see L. M. de Rijk, *Logica Modernorum* (Assen, 1967), 2 vols., II^i.514.

26 Paul of Venice, *Logica Magna: De Suppositionibus*, ed. A. R. Perreiah (New York, 1971), pp. xi–xii.

27 *Ibid.*, p. xii.

28 Walter Burleigh, *De Puritate Artis Logicae*, ed. P. Boehner (New York, 1955), p. 54.

29 See A. Maierù, *Terminologia logica della tarda scholastica* (Rome, 1972), on *appellatio* among other terms. On *appellatio*, see, too, William of Sherwood, *Introductiones in Logicam*, ed. M. Grabmann (Munich, 1937), p. 82 and Chapter V *passim*; Walter Burleigh, *De Puritate*, p. 47ff, *Cambridge History LMP*, pp. 174–87.

30 W. and M. Kneale, *The Development of Logic* (Oxford, 1962), p. 249; William of Sherwood, *Introductiones*, p. 82.

31 William of Sherwood, *loc. cit.*

32 Walter Burleigh, *De Puritate*, p. 47.26–33.

33 See Wyclif, *Logica*, I.39.7–9 and 25–30. On the grammatical origin of the notion, see de Rijk, *Logica Modernorum*, II^{ii}.521.

34 See Kneale and Kneale, p. 249, but on the technical terminology, note that *supponere* is often used by Wyclif for *ponere*, e.g. *De Statu Innocentiae*, I, ed. J. Loserth and F. D. Matthew (London, 1922), p. 475.12, p. 477.30; *De Differentia inter Peccatum Mortale et Veniale*, ed. *ibid.*, p. 532.41ff, *Sermones*, II.57 (Sermon 8).

35 Walter Burleigh, *De Puritate*, p. 2.12–13.

36 Bonaventure, *In John*, VIII.42, Q.2, *Opera Omnia*, V, 362.

37 S. F. Brown, 'Gerard Odon's *De Suppositionibus*', *Franciscan Studies*, 35 (1975).6; see, too, G. B. Matthews, 'Supposition and Quantification in Ockham', *Nous*, 7 (1973), 13–24.

38 Ockham, *Quodlibeta Septem*, ed. J. C. Wey (New York, 1980), Quod. V, Q.11, p. 524ff.

39 Paul of Venice, *Logica Magna: De Suppositionibus*, ed. A. R. Perreiah (New York, 1971), p. vii ff.

40 Wyclif, *Logica*, I.39.17–20.

41 Walter Burleigh, *De Puritate*, p. 2.

42 Paul of Venice, *Logica Magna, ed. cit.*, p. 2.

43 S. F. Brown, *Gerard Odon, ed. cit.*, p. 44.
44 Walter Burleigh, *De Puritate*, p. 2.
45 Wyclif, *Sermones*, III.48–9 (Sermon 7).
46 Wyclif, *Sermones*, II.125 (Sermon 17).
47 Wyclif, *Sermones*, IV.262.1ff (Sermon 31).
48 Wyclif, *Sermones*, IV.199 (Sermon 23).
49 Wyclif, *Sermones*, IV.200.31ff (Sermon 23).
50 John Hus, *Super IV Sententiarum*, ed. W. J. Flajšhans and M. Komínková, *Opera Omnia* (Prague, 1903), II.5.14, *Inceptio* I.5.
51 William of Sherwood, *Syncategoremata*, ed. J. R. O'Donnell, *Mediaeval Studies*, 3 (1941), 46–93, Chapter XVII.1.
52 Bonaventure, *In Ecclesiasten*, I.i, Q.II, *Opera Omnia*, VI.14ff. On the terminology, see de Rijk, *Logica Modernorum*, II^i.513.
53 Bonaventure, *loc. cit.*, Q.1, p. 14.
54 Bonaventure, *In John*, I.1, *Opera Omnia*, V.247–8.
55 Peter of Spain, *Tractatus Syncategorematum*, tr. J. P. Mullaly (Milwaukee, 1964), p. 17.
56 William of Sherwood, *Syncategoremata*, p. 46.
57 *Ibid.*
58 For a convenient summary of the classification, see E. J. Ashworth, 'The Structure of Mental Language: Some Problems Discussed by Early Sixteenth Century Logicians', *Vivarium*, 20 (1982), 59–82.
59 Walter Burleigh, *De Puritate*.
60 On these, see N. Kretzmann in *Cambridge History LMP*, p. 17.
61 Wyclif, *Sermones*, III.262 (Sermon 32).
62 F. Giusberti, 'A Treatise on Implicit Propositions from around the Turn of the Twelfth Century', *Cahiers*, 21 (1977), 45–115.
63 Wyclif, *Logica*, I.61.2–4.
64 *De Veritate Sacrae Scripturae*, 19, ed. R. Buddensieg (London, 1905), 2 vols., II.115.4.
65 *Ibid.*, 18, II.75.3.
66 Martin of Alnwick, *De Veritate et Falsitate Propositionis*, p. 7.
67 L. M. de Rijk, 'Some Fourteenth Century Tracts on the *Probationes Terminorum*', *Artistarium*, 3 (1982), p. 4.
68 Bonaventure, *In John*, VI.80, Q.1, *Opera Omnia*, V.318.
69 *Ibid.*, VIII.69, Q.2, p. 368.
70 *Ibid.*, I.14.

9 The text

1 C. Spicq, *Esquisse d'une histoire de l'exégèse latine du moyen âge* (Paris, 1944), p. 144.
2 See *ibid.*, p. 145ff on the discussion of the content of the canon. This, of course, was an ancient debate and it was to continue into the sixteenth century.
3 Bellarmine, *De Verbo Dei*, I.iv.
4 Spicq, *Esquisse*, p. 156.
5 *Ibid.*, pp. 144 and 152.
6 PL 192.1299.
7 Luther, *Table Talk*, no. 311, p. 42.

8 *Ibid.*, no. 46, p. 7.
9 Calvin, *Commentaries*, *tr. cit.*, Preface to Olivétan's New Testament, p. 65.
10 G. Bull, *Harmonia Apostolica* (1670), *Dissertation* I.i.2.
11 *Cambridge History Bible*, II, pp. 140–2, and see E. Nestlé, 'Scotus Erigena on Greek Manuscripts of the Fourth Gospel', *Journal of Theological Studies*, 13 (Oxford, 1912), 596. See, too, Alexander Neckham's *Correctiones super Genesim*, British Library, London, MS Harley 6, fo 158–158ᵛ *et passim.*
12 Text quoted by B. Smalley, *Friars*, from Thomas Waleys, *Moralitates*, Oxford, New College, MS 30, fo. 68ᵛ.
13 Aquinas, *Commentary on Galatians*, Chapter 2, Lecture 2.
14 Roger Bacon comments on this, *Opus Maius*, III, *Linguarum Cognitio*, ed. J. H. Bridges (Oxford, 1897), pp. 66–81.
15 *Cambridge History Bible*, II, pp. 150–2 and Spicq, *Esquisse*, p. 167.
16 B. Smalley, 'John Russel, O.F.M.', *Studies*, p. 240–1.
17 Spicq, *Esquisse*, p. 196.
18 Jacobus Faber Stapulensis, *Commentarii in Epistolas Pauli* (Cologne, 1531), *Apologia.*
19 Bellarmine, *De Verbo Dei*, II.i.
20 *Ibid.*, II.vii.
21 *Ibid.*, II.viii–xi. This work will be discussed in a later study.
22 On these friars, see Smalley, *Friars*. Miss Smalley points to seven in particular (p. 1): Thomas Waleys, John Ridevall, Robert Holcot, William d'Eynecourt, Thomas Hopeman, Thomas Ringstead, John Lathbury.
23 Text in Appendix to Smalley, *Friars*, p. 320. John Ridevall on *De Civitate Dei.*
24 Text *ibid.*, p. 321, Robert Holcot on Ecclesiasticus.
25 Text *ibid.*, p. 329, Robert Holcot, Sermon, 45.
26 Text, *ibid.*, p. 341, John of Lathbury on Lamentations.
27 B. Smalley, 'John Baconthorpe's Postill on St. Matthew', *Studies*, pp. 306–7.
28 Melanchthon, *Declamationes*, Preface *In Officia Ciceronis*, ed. R. Nürnberger, *Werke* (Tübingen, 1961), III.86.13–14.
29 Melanchthon, *De Corrigendis Adolescentiae Studiis*, *Werke*, III.40.315.
30 Preface *In Officia Ciceronis*, pp. 83–4.
31 *De Philosophie Oratio, 1536, Werke*, III.92.4–7.
32 Preface *In Officia Ciceronis*, p. 84.23.
33 *De Corrigendis Adolescentiae Studiis*, p. 45.19–25.
34 *Ibid.*, p. 45.14.
35 *Ibid.*, p. 45.33–9.
36 *Ibid.*, p. 38.31–2.
37 *Ibid.*, p. 31.6–9.
38 On *Eloquentia*, see C. Mohrmann, *Etudes sur le latin des chrétiens*, 1 (Paris, 1961).
39 Smalley, *Friars*, pp. 288–9 and B. L. Ullmann, *Studies in the Italian Renaissance* (Rome, 1955), 27–53. Smalley, *Friars*, Chapters 10 and 11, looks at France and Italy.
40 Melanchthon, *De Corrigendis Adolescentiae Studiis* (Yale, 1967).
41 M. U. Chrisman, *Strasbourg and the Reform* (Yale, 1967).
42 S. Ozment, 'Humanism, Scholasticism and the Intellectual Origins of the Reformation', *Continuity and Discontinuity in Church History*, ed. F.

Forrester Church and T. George (Leiden, 1979), pp. 133–49 on the search for a 'German national culture'.
43 Melanchthon, *In Laudem Novae Scholae, Werke*, III.67.6ff.
44 On Andrew of St Victor, see B. Smalley, 'Andrew of St. Victor, Abbot of Wigmore', RTAM, 10 (1938), 358–73.
45 Johannes Reuchlin, *Lexicon Hebraicum* (Basle, 1537), Prefatory Letter.
46 *Ibid.*, p. 11.
47 *Ibid.*, p. 63.
48 On Reuchlin, see further M. Brod, *Johannes Reuchlin und sein Kampf* (Stuttgart, 1965), pp. 46, 73, 174ff.
49 Erasmus, *Opus Epistolarum*, ed. P. S. Allen, II.90–114. See, in general, H. Holeczek, *Humanistische Bibelphilologie als Reformproblem bei Erasmus von Rotterdam, Thomas More und William Tyndale* (Leiden, 1975).
50 J. H. Bentley, 'Erasmus', *Annotationes in Novum Testamentum* and the Textual Criticism of the Gospels', *Archiv für Reformationsgeschichte*, 67 (1976), 37.
51 Bentley, p. 39.
52 Bentley, p. 39.
53 Bentley, p. 46.
54 Bentley, p. 36. Whitaker, *Disputation*, p. 36.
55 J. B. Payne, 'Erasmus and Lefèvre d'Etaples as Interpreters of Paul', *Archiv für Reformationsgeschichte*, 65 (1974), 60.
56 Melanchthon, *Oratio de Studiis Linguae Graecae, Werke*, III.135.5.
57 *Ibid.*, p. 137.25–139.18.
58 *Ibid.*, p. 139.18–21.
59 *Ibid.*, p. 139.27–30.
60 *Ibid.*, p. 139.38.
61 *Ibid.*, p. 142.15–143.21.
62 *Ibid.*, p. 140.9–16.
63 *Ibid.*, p. 140.18–27.
64 *Ibid.*, p. 140.27–30.
65 *Ibid.*, p. 143.31–40.
66 *Ibid.*, p. 145.24–146.20.
67 *Ibid.*, p. 146.26–31.
68 Calvin, *Commentaries, tr. cit.*, p. 17.
69 Luther, *Table Talk*, no. 439, p. 71.
70 *Ibid.*, no. 2808, p. 171. A study of this work awaits a future vol.
71 Calvin, *Commentaries, tr. cit.*, p. 63. New trans. awaited.
72 Stillingfleet, *The Council of Trent Examin'd*, Appendix, p. 150.
73 Bellarmine, *De Verbo Dei*, II.xv.
74 M. Coverdale, *Remains*, ed. G. Pearson (Cambridge, 1846), Dedication of his translation of the Bible to Henry VIII.
75 Tyndale, *Answer to Sir Thomas More*.
76 M. Deanesley, *The Lollard Bible* (Cambridge, 1920), pp. 25–7. Jean Gerson, *Oeuvres Complètes*, I.106.
77 *The Lollard Bible*, p. 21.
78 M. Deanesley, 'The Gospel Harmony of John de Caulibus', *Collectanae Franciscana*, 2, ed. C. L. Kingsford *et al.* (Manchester, 1922), pp. 10–20.
79 *The Lollard Bible*, p. 21.
80 'John de Caulibus', pp. 15–19.
81 *Four English Political Tracts of the Later Middle Ages*, ed. J. P. Genet (London, 1977), p. 5 and note 29, on the commonness of this assertion.

82 *The Lollard Bible*, p. 12.
83 F. Bühler, 'A Lollard Tract: On Translating the Bible into English', *Medium Aevum*, 7 (1938), 167–83.
84 A. Hudson, *Selections from English Wycliffite Writings* (Cambridge, 1979), Prologue to the Wycliffite Bible, Chapter 15, pp. 67–8.
85 Hudson, *Selections*, pp. 69 and 71. On Bede and Alfred, cf. *The Lollard Bible*, p. 132.
86 Hudson, *Selections*, pp. 6–7.
87 *The Lollard Bible*, pp. 132–5, cf. *Cambridge History Bible*, II, pp. 367–79.
88 *The Lollard Bible*, pp. 147, 153.
89 *Ibid.*, pp. 185–205 and 298–9.
90 *Ibid.*, pp. 19 and 299.
91 *Ibid.*, p. 41.
92 *Ibid.*, p. 43.
93 *Ibid.*, p. 55.
94 *Ibid.*, pp. 59–83.
95 Hudson, *Selections*, p. 48.
96 *Ibid.*, p. 51.
97 *Ibid.*, pp. 67–8.
98 *The Lollard Bible*, pp. 427–9 from Cambridge, Trinity College, MS. 347, fo. 44^{v}, col. 2.
99 Hudson, *Selections*, pp. 68–9, cf. Tyndale, *Prologues*, p. 468.
100 Hudson, *Selections*, pp. 68–9.
101 Tyndale, *Expositions*, Prologue to I John.
102 Tyndale, *Prologues* (Cambridge, 1848), p. 468.
103 Luther, *Table Talk*, no. 312, p. 42.
104 *Ibid.*, no. 5533, pp. 445–6.
105 Luther on Psalm 45 (1532), Luther's *Works*, vol. 12, p. 199.

10 Lecturing

1 On the dispute at Oxford, see W. A. Hinnebusch, *The Early English Friars Preachers* (Rome, 1951), p. 342.
2 Hinnebusch, p. 337. On the effect of the changes brought about by the advent of the friars, see B. Smalley, 'The Gospels in the Paris Schools in the Late Twelfth and Early Thirteenth Centuries', *Franciscan Studies*, 39 (1979), 230–55, especially p. 230. On the use of natural science, see B. Smalley, 'Some Thirteenth Century Commentaries on the Sapiential Books', *Dominican Studies*, 2 (1949), 325.
3 Hinnebusch, pp. 335–6 and J. A. Robson, *Wyclif and the Oxford Schools* (Cambridge, 1961); p. 10ff, and M. O'Carroll, 'The Educational Organisation of the Dominicans in England and Wales 1221–1348', *Arch Frat. Pred.*, 50 (1980), 23–61.
4 B. Smalley, 'John Baconthorpe's Postill on St. Matthew', *Studies*, pp. 289–343.
5 G. Leff, *The Universities of Oxford and Paris* (New York, 1968), p. 11 gives a convenient account.
6 Robson, *op. cit.*, pp. 15–16.
7 *Statuta*, pp. cix–cxii, 51, 195.
8 Robson, p. 16.
9 On Luther's *Sentence*-commentaries, see P. Vignaux, 'Luther, Com-

mentateur des *Sentences*, Livre I, Distinction XVII', *Etudes de philosophie médiévale* (Paris, 1935). The question of the reformers' debt to scholastic training must wait for further treatment in a future volume. See section iv following on the *Sentences*.

10 For a list of surviving commentaries, see F. Stegmüller, *Repertorium Biblicum Medii Aevi* (Madrid, 1940–), vols. 1– .

11 On the forming of the *Glossa Ordinaria*, see B. Smalley, *The Study of the Bible in the Middle Ages*, 2nd ed. (Oxford, 1952).

12 D. M. Solomon, 'The Sentence Commentary of Richard Fishacre and the Apocalypse Commentary of Hugh of St. Cher', *Arch. Frat. Pred.*, 46 (1976), 367–77.

13 Meister Eckhardt, *Prologue to the Book of Commentaries*, in *Parisian Questions and Prologues*, tr. A. A. Maurer (Toronto, 1974), p. 104.

14 See my *Language and Logic I*, pp. 37–50 and PL 192.1297.

15 PL 192.1299.

16 On Grosseteste's early life and his study at Oxford, see R. W. Southern's forthcoming study, Oxford, 1985, Grosseteste, *Hexameron*, ed. R. C. Dales and S. Gieben (London, 1983), Proemium, p. 18.7–9.

17 *Ibid.*, para. 10, p. 20.2–18 and PL 192.1302.

18 *Hexameron*, para. 4, p. 18.16ff.

19 *Ibid.*, *Particula Prima*, XIX.2, p. 79.14–19, cf. I.ix.1, p. 62.28–30.

20 *Ibid.*, *passim*, but especially *Particula Tertia*, III.6, p. 105.4–5.

21 *Ibid.*, *Particula Prima*, XXIII.1, p. 82.17–18.

22 *Ibid.*, *Particula Prima*, III.1, p. 52.

23 *Ibid.*, *Particula Prima*, V.i, p. 54.29–31.

24 Luther WA, V, p. 2.

25 Calvin, *Commentaries, tr. cit.*, on John 3.12, and see my *The Language and Logic of the Bible* I, Introduction.

26 Calvin, *Commentaries, tr. cit.*, on I Corinthians 10.11.

27 Tyndale, *Expositions*, p. 41.48–9.

28 Luther, *Table Talk*, no. 2894A, p. 179; on *lectio divina* see *Language and Logic I*, pp. 13ff.

29 Tyndale, *A Pathway into the Holy Scripture* (Cambridge, 1848), pp. 398, 400, 404, 441.

30 Melanchthon, *Annotationes in Epistulas Pauli ad Corinthios*, ed. P. F. Barton, *Werke*, IV (Gütersloh, 1963), p. 16.12–13.

31 *Ibid.*, p. 16.26ff.

32 *Ibid.*, p. 24.34–25.1, p. 29.29.–30.

33 *Ibid.*, p. 17.18–24.

34 *Ibid.*, p. 17.25ff.

35 D. C. Steinmetz, 'Hermeneutic and Old Testament Interpretation in Staupitz and the Young Martin Luther', *Archiv für Reformationsgeschichte*, 70 (1979), 24–58.

36 Luther, *Table Talk*, no. 3033[b], p. 189.

37 *Ibid.*, no. 116, p. 13.

38 Tyndale, *Exposition*, p. 16.

39 *Ibid.*, p. 3.

40 *Ibid.*, p. 5.

41 Luther, *Scholia on the Psalms*, ed. E. Vogelsang, *Werke* (Berlin, 1955), V.85.6–8.

42 Luther, *Table Talk*, no. 81, p. 9.

43 *Ibid.*, no. 674, p. 121, cf. no. 1877, p. 165, where this image is repeated and Luther also says that he has read the Bible twice every year.
44 *Ibid.*, no. 352, p. 51.
45 *Ibid.*, no. 1317, pp. 135–6.
46 Calvin, *Commentaries*, *tr. cit.*, p. 73.
47 Henry of Ghent quoting Nicholas Gorran in Oxford, Bodleian Library, MS Laud. Misc., 161, fo. 2vb, in B. Smalley, 'A Commentary on the Hexameron by Henry of Ghent', RTAM, 20 (1953), 60–101. On the first lectures on the *Sentences*, see Alexander of Hales, *Glossa in Quatuor Libros Sententiarum Petri Lombardi* (Florence, 1951), Introitus, p. 1.1–10.
48 J. A. Weisheipl, *Friar Thomas d'Aquino*, p. 68.
49 Gabriel Biel, *Collectorium circa Quattuor Libros Sententiarum*, ed. W. Werbeck (Tübingen, 1973), p. 6.1–8.
50 D. M. Solomon, 'The Sentence Commentary of Richard Fishacre and the Apocalypse Commentary of Hugh of St. Cher', *Arch. Frat. Pred.*, 46 (1976), 367.
51 Gabriel Biel, *Collectorium*, pp. 387–93 has all these features.
52 Duns Scotus, Commentary on Peter Lombard's *Sentences*, Prologue, Q.II.29–34.
53 *Ibid.*, Prologue, Q.II.36.
54 *Ibid.*, Prologue, Q.II.44.
55 W. J. Courtenay, 'The Lost Matthew Commentary of Robert Holcot, O.P.', *Arch. Frat. Pred.*, 50 (1980), 103.

11 Questions

1 See G. Ritter, *Studien zur Spätscholastik*, 2 (Heidelberg, 1922, repr. 1975), and *Reden und Briefe*, ed. F. Baron (Munich, 1971), pp. 168–76, discussed in H. A. Oberman, *Masters of the Reformation*, tr. D. Martin (Cambridge, 1981), p. 34.
2 Stephan Hoest, *Reden und Briefe*, p. 154.133–49, cited in Oberman, *Masters of the Reformation*, p. 189, on the conflict.
3 *Cambridge History LMP*, Chapter IV.
4 Commentaries on the *Posterior Analytics* seem to have been made only rather slowly.
5 *Prior Analytics*, ed. H. Tredennick (London, 1973), I.xxvii.43^a.
6 De Rijk, *Logica Modernorum*, I.15.
7 See my *Alan of Lille* (Cambridge, 1983), pp. 64–80.
8 Wyclif, *De Christo et suo Adversario Antichristo*, *Polemical Works*, II, ed. R. Buddensieg (London, 1883).
9 B. Smalley, 'Oxford University Sermons, 1290–3', *Studies*, pp. 183–203.
10 Hinnebusch, *The Early English Friars Preachers*, p. 342, Wyclif, *De Solutione Sathane*, *Polemical Works*, II, p. 392.1–3.
11 William of Ockham, *Quodlibeta Septem*, ed. J. C. Wey (New York, 1980), p. 320 (*Quodlibet* IV.5).
12 For a list of texts now in print, see *Cambridge History LMP*, Bibliography and add the new series *Artistarium*.
13 Thomas of Sutton, *Quodlibeta*, ed. M. Schmaus and M. González-Haba (Munich, 1969), *indices*.
14 *Quaestiones Ordinarie*, ed. J. Schneider (Munich, 1977), p. 909ff.
15 *Quodlibeta*, *ed. cit.*, II.Q.3, p. 184.

16 H. F. Dondaine, O.P., 'Le *De 43 Quaestionibus* de Robert Kilwardby', *Arch. Frat. Pred.*, 47 (1977), Q.XIX, p. 25, Q.XXVI, p. 30.
17 Meister Eckhardt, *Parisian Questions and Prologues*, tr. A. A. Maurer (Toronto, 1974), Q.1. Aquinas on Galatians I.i.
18 *Johann Ecks Predigttätigkeit* (Munster, 1914), pp. 175–6.
19 *Summa Theologiae* Iᵃ Q.24.a.1, obj. 1 and reply.
20 *Ibid.*, Q.12.
21 *Ibid.*, Q.12.a.13.
22 *Ibid.*
23 *Ibid.*, Q.2.a.1.
24 B. Smalley, 'The Bible and Eternity: John Wyclif's Dilemma', *Studies*, p. 408.
25 On Wyclif as a Biblical scholar and theologian, see S. H. Thompson, 'The Philosophical Basis of Wyclif's Theology', *Journal of Religion*, 11 (1931), 86–116; S. Smalley, 'John Wyclif's Postilla super Totam Bibliam', *Bodleian Library Record*, 4 (1953), 186–205; 'The Biblical Scholar', *Robert Grosseteste*, ed. D. A. Callus (Oxford, 1955), pp. 70–97. On the lack of commentaries carrying the kind of criticism to which Wyclif refers, see Smalley, 'The Bible and Eternity', p. 403.
26 Smalley, 'The Bible and Eternity', p. 403.
27 On the date of the *Logica*, see *Logica, ed. cit.*, p. vi ff. Peter the Chanter seems to have been one of the first to make a systematic collection of problems. See my *Alan of Lille*, pp. 23–9 and Appendix II, and 'A Work of Terminist Theology? Peter the Chanter's *De Tropis Loquendi* and some *Fallacie*', *Vivarium*, 20 (1982), 40–57.
28 Wyclif, *Logica*, I.1.3–8.
29 Wyclif, *Sermones*, II.40 (Sermon 6); II.47 (Sermon 7); III.179 (Sermon 23).
30 *Sermones*, I.218.19 (Sermon 32).
31 Bonaventure, In John, 4.27, Q.5, *Opera Omnia*, VI.293.
32 *Sermones*, IV.236 (Sermon 28).
33 *Sermones*, II.453–7 (Sermon 61).
34 *Fasciculi Zizaniorum*.
35 See 'Scripture's Divine Warrant', ii, on the idea that a true prophet must understand the meaning of his own prophecies. On *sophismata* of this sort in the Middle Ages, see W. and M. Kneale, *The Development of Logic* (Oxford, 1962), pp. 227–9. See, too, the list in P. V. Spade, *The Mediaeval Liar: a Catalogue of the Insolubilia-Literature* (Toronto, 1975).
36 *Fasciculi Zizaniorum*, pp. 44–8.
37 Luther, *Table Talk*, no. 3967, p. 300.
38 Luther, *Table Talk*, no. 5510, p. 439. De Rijk, *Logica Modernorum*, I, pp. 94–6 summarises the debate on these classifications, which are by no means hard and fast for all our authors.
39 Wyclif, *Opus Evangelicum*, ed. J. Loserth (London, 1895), 2 vols., I.41.21–36, Chapter 13; *ibid.*, I.96.35–7, Chapter 28.
40 *Ibid.*, II.20–22, Chapter 16.
41 *Ibid.*, I.276.22–3, Book II.10.
42 *Ibid.*, I.281.35, Book II.11.
43 Wyclif, *De Veritate Sacrae Scripturae*, II.126. Chapter 19.
44 *Opus Evangelicum*, I.281.4, Book II.11.
45 *Sermones*, III.189 (Sermon 24).
46 *Sermones*, I.399 (Sermon 60).

47 Bonaventure, *In Ecclesiasten*, I.i, *Opera Omnia*, V.11.
48 Wyclif, *De Mandatis Divinis*, ed. F. D. Matthew (London, 1896), p. 1.7–10, Chapter 1.
49 *Opus Evangelicum*, I.41, Chapter 13.
50 *De Veritate Sacrae Scripturae*.
51 Wyclif, *Sermones*, II.453 (Sermon 61).
52 A. Hudson, *Selections from English Wycliffite Writings*, p. 71.
53 Fulke, *Defence*, p. 65.
54 Wyclif, *Sermones*, III.84 (Sermon 11).
55 Bonaventure, *In John*, 12, Q.1, *Opera Omnia*, VI.415.
56 *Ibid.*, *In John*, 6.84–8, *Opera Omnia*, VI.333.
57 Wyclif, *Opus Evangelicum*, II.10, p. 276.22–3.
58 Wyclif, *Sermones*, III.189 (Sermon 24).
59 See S. Ebbesen, 'The *Summulae, Tractatus VII, De Fallaciis*', in J. Pinborg (ed.), *The Logic of John of Buridan*, pp. 139–40.
60 See de Rijk, *Logica Modernorum*, I.27, on the passages in Boethius's Commentary on the *De Interpretatione* and in his treatise on categorical syllogisms which touch on fallacies, and S. Ebbesen, 'Paris 4720A, a Twelfth Century Compendium of Aristotle's *Sophistici Elenchi*', *Cahiers*, 10 (1973), p. 2.20–2 and p. 3.31ff and cf. 'Anonymi Bodleiani in Sophisticos Elenchos Aristotelis Commentarii Fragmentum', *Cahiers*, 8 (1972), 3–72.
61 De Rijk, *Logica Modernorum* (Assen, 1967), I.27 and 39, cf. Wyclif, *De Veritate Sacrae Scripturae*, II.126 (Chapter 19) and Bonaventure, *In John*, VI.50, Q.1, *Opera Omnia*, VI.326.
62 Aristotle, *Prior Analytics*, II.xxi.66[b].
63 Wyclif, *De Veritate Sacrae Scripturae*, II.18, p. 67.13ff.
64 *Ibid.*, p. 69.21ff.
65 Walter Burleigh, *De Puritate*, p. 253.26–254.5.
66 Bonaventure, *In John* 5.45, Q.III, *Opera Omnia*, VI.310.
67 Wyclif, *Sermones*, III.217 (Sermon 38).
68 *Sermones*, II.37 (Sermon 6).
69 *Sermones*, III.1 (Sermon 1).
70 *Sermones*, I.4.16ff and 7.27–30 (Sermon 1).
71 *De Veritate Sacrae Scripturae*, *passim*.
72 For example, Wyclif deals in his treatise *De Christo et Suo Adversario Antichristo* with the *contrarietas* of the two lords.
73 Wyclif, *Logica*, II.203.
74 Bonaventure, *In John*, 5.68, Q.1, *Opera Omnia*, VI.316.
75 *In John*, 6.50, Q.1, *Opera Omnia*, VI.
76 *Sermones*, p. 45.
77 See my article, 'Boethian and Euclidean Axiomatic Method in the Theology of the Later Twelfth Century', *Archives internationales d'histoire des sciences*, 30.105 (1980), 36–52.
78 *Ibid.*
79 Wyclif, *De Trinitate*, ed. A. du Pont Brech (Colorado, 1972), I.4.
80 *Opus Evangelicum*, I.53.18, Chapter 16.
81 *De Veritate Sacrae Scripturae*, II.201.14, Chapter 22.
82 *Cambridge History LMP*, p. 281.
83 N. Green-Pedersen, 'Discussions about the Status of *loci dialectici* in Works from the Middle of the Thirteenth Century', *Cahiers*, 20 (1976), 37–78.

84 Cicero, *Topics*, ed. H. M. Hubbell (London, 1968), II.8.
85 William of Sherwood, *Introductiones in Logicam*, M. Grabmann (Munich, 1937), IV.1–2.
86 *Cambridge History LMP*, p. 274.
87 Green-Pedersen, *op. cit.*, pp. 43–4.
88 *Ibid.*, p. 49.
89 *Ibid.*, pp. 43–4.
90 *Ibid.*, p. 45.
91 *Cambridge History LMP*, pp. 275–7.
92 Green-Pedersen, *op. cit.*, pp. 42, 46.
93 *Ibid.*, p. 42.
94 *Ibid.*
95 Wyclif, *De Veritate Sacrae Scripturae*, II.100, Chapter 19.
96 William of Sherwood, *Introductiones in Logicam*, p. 71.21.
97 *Prior Analytics*, I.xxvii.43b.
98 *De Interpretatione*, xiii, 22a.
99 *Posterior Analytics*, I.xi.78a *et al.*
100 N. J. Green-Pedersen, 'Two Early Anonymous Tracts on Consequences', *Cahiers*, 35 (1980), 2.
101 *Ibid.*, citied British Library MS Royal F.XIX, fo. 11ra–112rb.
102 Peter of Spain, *Tractatus Syncategorematum*, tr. J. P. Mullaly (Milwaukee, 1964), p. 135.
103 W. and M. Kneale, *The Development of Logic*, pp. 274–5.
104 Wyclif, *Logica*, I.43.2–3.
105 *De Mandatis Divinis*, p. 15.18, Chapter 3.
106 *Sermones*, IV.213.29–31 (Sermon 25).
107 *Ibid.*, p. 209.30–3 (Sermon 24).
108 *Ibid.*, p. 209.22.
109 *Sermones*, IV.511.13–15 (Sermon 24, preached for a degree day).
110 *Sermones*, IV.197–8 (Sermon 23).
111 *Opus Evangelicum*, I.6.11–16.
112 Melanchthon, *Loci Communes*, p. 233.12; Luther, *De Servo Arbitrio*, WA, vol. 18, pp. 609–17; Bellarmine, *De Verbo Dei*, III.2.
113 *Topics*, I.i.100a.
114 *Prior Analytics*, II.xix.66a.
115 John of Salisbury refers to a game of this sort in the *Metalogicon*. See A. Drew, *John of Salisbury's 'Metalogicon'*, Cambridge University Ph.D. thesis, forthcoming.
116 *Cambridge History LMP*, pp. 315ff.
117 *Ibid.*, p. 332.
118 *Topics*, VIII.13.163a$^{14–28}$.
119 Wyclif, *Logica*, I.69.4–8.
120 *Ibid.*
121 M. A. Brown, 'The Role of the *Tractatus de Obligationibus* in Mediaeval Logic', *Franciscan Studies*, 25 (1966), 26–35.
122 *Ibid.*, p. 28.
123 *Logica*, I.69.16–70.8.
124 *Ibid.*, p. 70.9–19.
125 *Ibid.*, p. 70.20–5.
126 *Ibid.*, p. 71.1–12.
127 *Ibid.*, p. 71.19–20.

128 *Ibid.*, p. 73.18–20.
129 *Ibid.*, p. 74.5–22.
130 *De Veritate Sacrae Scripturae*, II.1.
131 William of Sherwood, *Syncategoremata*, ed. J. R. O'Donnell, *Mediaeval Studies*, 3 (1941), Chapter xv, cf. *Cambridge History LMP*, p. 364 and G. Leff, *Bradwardine and the Pelagians* (Cambridge, 1957), p. 10, on aspects of the general problem of the relationship between divine foreknowledge and the openness of the future to the influence of human free will. See, too, on the difficulty of referring to things which do not exist, John Buridan, *Quaestiones Longe super Librum Periermeneias*, ed. R. van der Lecq, *Artistarium* (Nijmegen, 1983), p. xii ff.
132 R. Grosseteste, *De Libero Arbitrio*, Chapter 6, ed. L. Baur (Aschendorff, 1919), p. 170.23–8.
133 See *Cambridge History LMP*, pp. 369–70. Wyclif's *De Christo et suo Adversario Antichristo*, p. 678.20 and p. 653.1–2 *et al.*
134 *Sophistici Elenchi*, 166a.22–30, and see *Cambridge History LMP*, p. 347.
135 G. Leff, *William of Ockham* (Manchester, 1975), p. 193.
136 Walter Burleigh, *De Puritate*, p. 234.17–28.
137 *De Interpretatione*, IX.18ᵃ–19ᵃ. The problem is also discussed in *Metaphysics*, VI.3, but the text came on the scene late, and mediaeval writers came to think it referred to 'causal' rather than 'logical' determinism. See *Cambridge History LMP*, p. 358, n. 1.
138 Abelard, Gloss on *De Interpretatione*, ed. M. dal Pra in *Pietro Abelardo: Scritti di Logica* (Rome, 1969), p. 103.
139 For example, Peter Aureoli, *Cambridge History LMP*, p. 370.
140 See note 137.
141 *Loc. cit.*
142 Abelard, *Dialectica*, ed. L. M. de Rijk, 2nd ed. (Assen, 1970), p. 211.5ff.
143 Cf. Horace, *Saturae*, ii.5.59 and Cicero, *De Natura Deorum*, 1.70.
144 *Cambridge History LMP*, p. 360.
145 *Ibid.*, p. 363.
146 Peter Lombard, *Sentences*, I. Dist. 38–40.
147 Aquinas, *Summa Theologiae*, I.Q.14.a.8.
148 Duns Scotus on the *Sentences*, I. Dist. 39, a.1–5, n. 44.
149 Wyclif, *Logica*, II.128.33–4.
150 *Ibid.*, III.225.11–14.
151 William of Sherwood, *Introductiones*, I.22.
152 *Ibid.*, I.23, but cf. I.24 on the cases where the modal adverb merely determines the action of the verb and the proposition is not itself modal.
153 Wyclif, *Logica*, I.156.
154 *Ibid.*, p. 157.
155 *Ibid.*, p. 158.
156 *Prior Analytics*, I.xiii.32b ff, II.xxvii.69b, etc.; *De Interpretatione*, XII.22a.11–13; xiii.22a.32–8.
157 *Prior Analytics*, I.xiv.33b.
158 *Sermones*, IV.253.15 (Sermon 19).
159 *Ibid.*, p. 253.23: *Constat quidem*; p. 206.22 (Sermon 24): *Constat ab experientia*; p. 206.32: *Constat . . . ex sermone septimo*; p. 208.23: *Necessitas pugnandi patet ex . . .*
160 G. Leff, *William of Ockham*, p. 277. For a view of other contemporary opinions and the general climate of debate, see R. A. Robson, *Wyclif and the Oxford Schools* (Cambridge, 1961), pp. 101–4.

161 Wyclif, *Opus Evangelicum*, I.101.10ff, Chapter 29.
162 *Ibid.*, p. 118.1, Chapter 23.
163 Robson, *op. cit.*
164 Aristotle, *Physics*, VI and VIII and O. L. Nielsen, 'Thomas Bradwardine's Treatise on *Incipit* and *Desinit*: Edition and Introduction', *Cahiers*, 42 (1982), 1–83.
165 *Logica*, III.168.31ff.
166 *Ibid.*, p. 170.24ff.
167 *Ibid.*, p. 171.1ff.
168 *Ibid.*, pp. 171–2; cf. p. 175.13–17, p. 184.8–24, and *Sermones*, IV.149.8–10.
169 *Logica*, III.174.28–34, and *Sermones*, IV.149.8–10 and 186.24–7.
170 *Logica*, III.174.30ff.
171 *Ibid.*
172 Cf. *Cambridge History LMP*, p. 360 for Anselm of Canterbury, p. 374 for Bradwardine. Cf. Robson, *op. cit.*, p. 198.
173 Nielsen, *loc. cit.*
174 Wyclif, *Logica*, III.167.37–8.
175 See Nielsen, *loc. cit.*, p. 8 and p. 11 on William of Sherwood's account of his contemporaries' views on how to think of past, present and future in relation to these instants.
176 Wyclif, *Logica*, III.174.15–23. Cf. Robson, p. 196.
177 Wyclif, *Logica*, III.173.30ff.
178 Cf. Anselm, *Opera Omnia*, ed. F. S. Schmitt (Rome, Edinburgh, 1938–69), 6 vols., II, *Cur Deus Homo*, ii.17 and *De Casu Diaboli*, xxi and Aquinas, *Summa Theologiae*, I, Q.14.13, reply obj. 3.
179 Cf. Wyclif's discussion of predestination in *De Volucione Dei*, *De Universalibus*, 14, and *Summa de Ente*, ed. S. H. Thompson (Oxford, 1930).
180 Wyclif discusses this problem in *Logica*, III.177ff.
181 *Ibid.*, p. 183.26ff.
182 *Ibid.*, p. 191.35ff.
183 *Ibid.*, p. 191.10–13.
184 *Ibid.*, p. 185.1–2.
185 *Ibid.*, p. 168.31ff.
186 *Ibid.*, p. 168.39–40.
187 *Logica*, II, Chapter 7.
188 *Logica*, III, p. 182.18–21 and cf. *Fasciculi Zizaniorum*, p. 8 and *Summa de Ente*, p. 100.
189 *De Mandatis Divinis*, p. 36.26, Chapter v.
190 *Ibid.*, p. 40.23–6.
191 *Sermones*, IV.130.24–8 (Sermon 16).
192 *Ibid.*, p. 76.6ff (Sermon 9).
193 *Ibid.*, p. 223.10 (Sermon 26).
194 *Ibid.*, p. 249.20 (Sermon 29).
195 *Ibid.*, p. 45.31ff (Sermon 5).
196 *Logica*, III.179.17.
197 *Ibid.*, p. 180.
198 *Ibid.*, p. 181.5–8.
199 *Ibid.*, p. 181.10–17.
200 *Ibid.*, p. 181.18–21.
201 *Ibid.*, p. 181.25–8.

202 *Ibid.*, p. 181.35–40.
203 *Sophistici Elenchi*, 166a.22–30, *Cambridge History LMP*, p. 347.
204 Ockham, *De Praedestinatione*, ed. P. Boehner and S. Brown (Franciscan Institute, 1978), p. 534.36–52, and cf. *Cambridge History LMP*, pp. 371–2.
205 *Logica*, III.173.30ff.
206 On this complex of discussion, see *ibid.*, p. 175ff.
207 *Ibid.*, p. 187.38.
208 *Ibid.*, p. 188.1.
209 *Ibid.*, p. 187.21ff.
210 *Ibid.*, p. 181.30–33.
211 *Cambridge History LMP*, p. 373, *Commentary on the Sentences* II.ii.
212 *Cambridge History LMP*, pp. 372–3.
213 See J. P. Torrell, 'Théorie de la prophétie', *op. cit.*
214 *De Veritate Sacrae Scripturae*, p. 77.23–8, Chapter 18.
215 *Ibid.*, p. 110ff, Chapter 19.
216 *Ibid.*, p. 111.17.
217 *Sermones*, I.18 (Sermon 2).
218 *Ibid.*, and see further on Wyclif on prophecy, *Summa Insolubilium*, ed. P. V. Spade and G. A. Wilson, Introduction (forthcoming).
219 Calvin, *Commentaries*, *tr. cit.*, p. 57.
220 Luther, *Table Talk*, no. 319, p. 44.
221 *Luthers Works*, V.11 and p. 15.33. See, too, P. Vignaux, 'Luther Commentateur des *Sentences*, Livre I, Distinction XVII', *Etudes de philosophie médiévale* (Paris, 1935).
222 Luther, *Table Talk*, no. 3722, p. 263.
223 *Ibid.*
224 *Ibid.*, no. 5135, p. 391.
225 *Ibid.*, no. 280, p. 38.
226 *Ibid.*, no. 3722, p. 263.
227 *Ibid.*, no. 96, p. 12.
228 *Ibid.*, no. 192, p. 26.
229 *Cambridge History LMP*, p. 788.
230 *Ibid.*, p. 791.
231 *Ibid.*
232 On demonstrative method, see next section.
233 *Cambridge History LMP*, pp. 793–4.
234 *Ibid.*, p. 795.
235 *Ibid.*
236 Stillingfleet, *The Council of Trent Examin'd and Disproved by Catholic Tradition.*
237 Melanchthon, *Declamationes*, *Werke*, III, 84.11–14.
238 *Ibid.*, p. 87.4–5.
239 Boethius, *De Hebdomadibus*, in *Theological Tractates*, ed. H. F. Stewart, E. K. Rand and S. J. Tester (London, 1973), p. 40.
240 Gilbert of Poitiers, *Commentaries on Boethius*, ed. N. M. Häring (Toronto, 1966), pp. 189–90.
241 *Luthers Works*, IV, *Disputationes*. John Fisher, *Assertionis Lutheranae Confutatio*, *Opera Omnia* (Wurzburg, 1697, facsimile reprint 1967), cols. 272ff.
242 See my *Alan of Lille*, pp. 64–80, and Pico della Mirandola, *Conclusiones*,

ed. B. Kieszkowski (Geneva, 1973). For an example of the use of *regulae* in the interpretation of Scripture (with political applications), see Matthew of Janova, *Regulae Veteris et Novi Testamenti*, ed. V. Kybal and O. Odložilík (Innsbruck and Prague, 1908–26), 5 vols.
243 Melanchthon, *Philosophiae Moralis Epitomes*, *Werke*, III. 158.32–8.
244 *Luther's Works*, V.378–80.
245 *Ibid.*, pp. 385–6.
246 Melanchthon, *Werke*, ed. H. Engelland (Tübingen, 1952), II.5.3–6.
247 *Ibid.*, p. 5.23–5.
248 *Ibid.*, p. 3.10–13, p. 4.19–28.
249 *Ibid.*, p. 66.4–5.
250 *Ibid.*, p. 6.1–13.

12 Preaching the Word

1 H. Caplan, 'The Four Senses of Scriptural Interpretation and the Mediaeval Theory of Preaching', *Speculum*, 4 (1929), 282, from *Tractatulus Solemnis de Arte et Vero Modo Praedicandi*, Cornell University Library, 2964 E 51 (Hain, no. 1354).
2 See J. J. Murphy, *Mediaeval Rhetoric* (Toronto, 1972).
3 See Humbert of Romans, *Opera*, ed. J. J. Berthier (Rome, 1888–9), 2 vols., II.265.
4 R. H. and M. A. Rouse, 'Biblical *Distinctiones* in the Thirteenth Century', AHDLMA, 41 (1974), 27–37.
5 A. and M. Rouse, 'The Verbal Concordance to the Scriptures', *Arch. Frat. Pred.* 44 (1974), 5–30 covers the developments sketched here.
6 Rouse and Rouse, 'The Verbal Concordance', give an example in Paris, Bibliothèque nationale, MS lat. 393, which contains glosses, interpretations of Hebrew names and concordances in the form of lists of parallel passages, and an allegorical concordance.
7 See C. Spicq, *Esquisse*, pp. 173–4 for the claims of Thomas of Vercelli to have invented this system; it is perhaps more likely that it·is a device of the Dominicans of St Jacques.
8 Thomas Waleys, *Artes Praedicandi*, ed. M. T. Charland, *Artes Praedicandi* (Paris, 1936), p. 390.
9 See, for example, such a series on the Gospels taken from Aquinas's *Catena Aurea*, G. Meersseman, 'La bibliothèque de la Minerve au xv siècle', *Mélanges A. Pelzer* (Louvain, 1947), 613. On the formation of the lecturing system, see Spicq, *Esquisses*, p. 142ff, J. A. Weisheipl, *Friar Thomas d'Aquino*, pp. 45–50 and 116–17, B. Smalley, *Friars*, p. 34ff, *Cambridge History Bible*, II, p. 198ff.
10 B. Smalley, 'The *Quaestiones* of Simon of Hinton', p. 210.
11 M. Deanesley, *The Lollard Bible*, p. 174 on Bible Harmonies, and p. 177 on Lives of Jesus. See also B. Smalley, 'Which William of Nottingham?', *Studies*.
12 Peter Comestor's *Historia Scholastica* is printed in PL 198.1050, summaries in Oxford, Bodleian Library, MS Laud. lat. 109, University College MS 42, Magdalene College, Oxford, and see Deanesley, *op. cit.*, p. 177.
13 Deanesley, pp. 178–9.
14 Jordan of Saxony, *Liber Vitasfratrum*, ed. R. Arbesmann and W. Hümpfner (New York, 1943), p. xxxi.

15 On this manuscript, see A. Pelster, 'An Oxford Collection of Sermons of the End of the Thirteenth Century', *Bodleian Quarterly Record*, 6, 67 (1930), 168–74.

16 Text from Vatican, MS lat. 4691, tr. S. Tugwell, *Early Dominicans* (London, 1982), p. 61.

17 Ed. T. Käppeli, 'La raccolta di discorsi e di alti scolastici di Simone da Cascina, O.P. (d. c. 1420)', *Arch. Frat. Pred.*, 12 (1942), 235, cf. *Johann Ecks Predigttätigkeit*, pp. 17–18.

18 Thomas Wilson, *The Arte of Rhetorique* (1553), facsimile with introduction by R. H. Bowers (Florida, 1962), p. viii.

19 Ed. Charland, *Artes Praedicandi*, p. 238.

20 For a discussion of these manuals and an example see M. Jennings, 'The *Ars Componendi Sermonis* of Ranulph Higden', *Mediaeval Eloquence*, ed. J. J. Murphy (California, 1978), 112–27.

21 Peter of Rheims, *Sermon on the Evangelists*, tr. S. Tugwell, *Early Dominicans*, pp. 146–8.

22 Humbert of Romans, *Treatise on the Formation of Preachers*, II.ix, *Early Dominicans*, pp. 106–12.

23 Etienne of Bourbon (d. 1261), the French Preacher-General, was the first Dominican to make a compilation of sermon-tables. He includes examples from the sermons of early Dominicans such as Matthew of France and Henry of Cologne (Hinnebusch, *The Early English Friars Preachers*, p. 300).

24 See B. Smalley, 'The *Quaestiones* of Simon of Hinton', pp. 209–10 on Simon's use of anecdote even as a lecturer. At least two *exampla* derived from his lectures were remembered and recorded.

25 *Liber Exemplorum ad Usum Praedicantium*, ed. A. G. Little (Aberdeen, 1908). On *exampla*, see J. T. Welter, *L'Exemplum dans la littérature religieuse et didactique du moyen âge* (Paris, 1927), Z. Zafarana, 'La predicazione ai laici dal secolo xiii al xiv', *Studi Medievali*, 24 (1983), 265–74.

26 E.g. *Liber Exemplorum, ed. cit.*, pp. 2, 4, 5.

27 See W. Riehle, *Studien zur englischen Mystik des Mittelalters unter besonderer Berücksichtigung ihrer Metaphorik* (Heidelberg, 1977), tr. B. Standring (London, 1981), p. 29.

28 Hinnebusch, *Friars Preachers*, p. 287.

29 *Ibid.*, pp. 283–4.

30 *Ibid.*, pp. 314–21.

31 *Ibid.*, pp. 286–9.

32 We meet both in the last decades of the twelfth century.

33 *Monumenta Historica S. Dominici*, I, 12, ed. M. H. Laurent, *Monumenta Ordinis Fratrum Praedicatorum Historica*, 15 (Paris, 1933), I.149.

34 Hinnebusch, *Friars Preachers*, p. 308, and see D. W. Robertson, 'Frequency of Preaching in Thirteenth Century England', *Speculum*, 24 (1949), p. 378, n. 15.

35 Luther, *Table Talk*, no. 626, p. 111; no. 5525, p. 444.

36 Aquinas, *Catena Aurea*, ed. P. Angelici Guarentini (Rome, 1953), Prefatory letter to Urban IV, p. 4.

37 A. Dondaine, 'Un commentaire scripturaire de Roland de Crémone, "Le livre de Job" ', *Arch. Frat. Pred.*, 11 (1941), 109–37.

38 Raynerius Sacconi, O.P., *Summa de Catharis*, *Arch. Frat. Pred.*, 44 (1974), 31–60.

39 Durand de Huesca, *Liber contra Manicheos*, ed. C. Thouzellier, *SSL*, 32 (1964), pp. 90–1.
40 *Ibid.*, p. 96.18–20. Durandus, as Miss Smalley comments, was perhaps sufficiently out of touch with the northern schools not to be aware of the new work on the extension of the literal sense to include at least something of the figurative. Smalley, 'William of Auvergne', p. 133, n. 36.
41 Durand, *op. cit.*, p. 98.23–4, p. 116.3, p. 116.4–5, p. 118.5–6.
42 *Ibid.*, p. 135.5–7: nos autem dicimus quod si predicta testimonia sanctarum Scripturarum bene intelliguntur et sane, sicut debent intelligi in veritate, multum obviant pravo intellectui catharorum.
43 *Ibid.*, pp. 122–35 and pp. 208–9.
44 William of Ockham, *Tractatus contra Benedictum*, iii, ed. H. S. Offler, *Guillielmi de Ockham, Opera Politica*, 3 (Manchester, 1956), p. 231 and see Smalley, *Friars*, p. 28.
45 Smalley, *Friars*, p. 186.
46 J. Loserth discusses Wyclif's emphasis on the preaching of the word of God as the most important duty of the priest in his introduction to the *Sermones*, I.v–vi. See *Sermones*, III.120 (Sermon 15), too.
47 Wyclif, *Sermones*, III.73 (Sermon 10).
48 Luther, *Table Talk*, no. 5177, pp. 394–5. Wyclif, *Sermones*, IV.264 (Sermon 31).
49 Wyclif, *Sermones*, III.88 (Sermon 12).
50 *Sermones*, II.277 (Sermon 38), cf. *De Veritate Sacrae Scripturae*, II.161 (Chapter 21).
51 Wyclif, *Sermones*, III.120 (Sermon 15).
52 Tyndale, *A Pathway into the Holy Scripture*, Prologue to his translation of the New Testament (Cambridge, 1848).
53 See A. Hudson, 'A Lollard Sermon-Cycle and its Implications', *Medium Aevum*, 40 (1971), 142–56; 'The Expurgation of a Lollard Sermon-Cycle', *Journal of Theological Studies*, 22 (1971), 451–66.
54 A. Hudson, *Selections*, p. 53.
55 *Ibid.*, p. 64.
56 *English Wycliffite Sermons*, ed. A. Hudson (Oxford, 1983), p. 223.
57 *Ibid.*, p. 474.
58 P. Auski, 'Wyclif's Sermons and the Plain Style', *Archiv für Reformationsgeschichte*, 64 (1973), p. 10 and 5–6, suggests that Tyndale owes something to Wyclif in his taste for a plain style in preaching.
59 J. Gerson, *Oeuvres Complètes*, ed. P. Glorieux (Paris, 1963), V.4, *Sermo in Coena Domini*.
60 *Six Sermons de Jean Gerson*, ed. L. Mourin (Paris, 1946), p. 71.
61 *Ibid.*, p. 164.
62 *Ibid.*, p. 263.
63 *Ibid.*, p. 278.
64 *Ibid.*, p. 418.757–8, cf. p. 427.951–7.
65 Luther, *Table Talk*, no. 5239, p. 402.
66 *Ibid.*, no. 3907, p. 291.

SELECT BIBLIOGRAPHY

Acta Capitulorum Generalium Ordinis Praedicatorum, ed. C. Douais, Toulouse, 1894.

Affeldt, W. *Die Weltliche Gewalt in der Paulus-Exegese*, Göttingen, 1969.

Ashworth, E. J. 'The Structure of Mental Language: Some Problems Discussed by Early Sixteenth Century Logicians', *Vivarium*, 20, 1982, 59–82.

Auerbach, E. *Typologische Motive in der Mittelalterlichen Literatur*, Schriften und Vorträge des Petrarca-Instituts Köln, Krefeld, 1964.

Auski, P. 'Wyclif's Sermons and the Plain Style', *Archiv für Reformationsgeschichte*, 64, 1971, 5–22.

Bentley, J. S. 'Erasmus' *Annotationes in Novum Testamentum* and the Textual Criticism of the Gospels', *Archiv für Reformationsgeschichte*, 67, 1976, 33–53.

Berger, S. *De l'histoire de la Vulgate en France*, Paris, 1887.

Boehner, P. 'The Mediaeval Crisis of Logic and the Author of the Colloquium attributed to Ockham', *Franciscan Studies*, 25, 1944, 151–70.

Boyle, M. O'Rourke, *Rhetoric and Reform: Erasmus' Civil Dispute with Luther*, Harvard, 1983.

Brod, M. *Johannes Reuchlin und sein Kampf*, Stuttgart, 1965.

Brown, M. A. 'The Role of the *Tractatus de Obligationibus* in Mediaeval Logic', *Franciscan Studies*, 25, 1966, 26–35.

Brown, R. E. *The Sensus Plenior of Sacred Scripture*, Baltimore, 1955.

Brown, S. F. 'Gerard Odon's *De Suppositionibus*', *Franciscan Studies*, 35, 1975.

Bühler, F. 'A Lollard Tract: On Translating the Bible into English', *Medium Aevum*, 7, 1938, 167–83.

Callus, D. A. (ed.), *Robert Grosseteste*, Oxford, 1955.

Cambridge History of Later Mediaeval Philosophy, ed. N. Kretzmann, A. Kenny and J. Pinborg, Cambridge, 1982.

Cambridge History of the Bible, ed. G. W. Lampe, Cambridge, 1963–70, 3 vols.

Caplan, H. 'A Late Mediaeval Tractate on Preaching', *Studies in Rhetoric and Public Speaking*, New York, 1925.

'The Four Senses of Scriptural Interpretation and the Mediaeval Theory of Preaching', *Speculum*, 4, 1929, 282–90.

'Henry of Hesse on the Art of Preaching', *Proceedings of the Modern Language Association*, 43, 1933, 347.

Charland, M. T. *Artes Praedicandi*, Paris, 1936.

Chenu, M. D. *Introduction à l'étude de S. Thomas d'Aquin*, Paris, 1950.

Chrisman, M. U. *Strasbourg and the Reform*, Yale, 1967.

Church, F. Forrester and George, Timothy, *Continuity and Discontinuity in Church History*, Leiden, 1979.

Colish, M. *The Mirror of Language*, revised edition, Nebraska, 1983.

Collins, A. B. *The Secular is Sacred: Platonism and Thomism in Marsilio Ficino's 'Platonic Theology'*, The Hague, 1974.
Courtenay, W. J. 'The Lost Matthew Commentary of Robert Holcot, O.P.', *Arch. Frat. Pred.*, 50, 1980, 103–12.
Curtius, E. *Europäische Literatur und Lateinisches Mittelalter*, Bern, 1948, and tr. W. R. Trask, London, 1953.
Dahlstrom, D. O. 'Signification and Logic: Scotus on Universals from a Logical Point of View', *Vivarium*, 18, 1980.
Deanesley, M. *The Lollard Bible*, Cambridge, 1920.
'The Gospel Harmony of John de Caulibus', *Coll. Franc.*, 2, ed. C. L. Kingsford *et al.*, Manchester, 1922, 10–20.
Dekkers, E. 'L'Eglise devant la Bible en langue vernaculaire', *The Bible and Mediaeval Culture*, ex. W. Lourdaux and D. Verhelst, Louvain, 1979, 1–15.
De Rijk, L. M. 'On Buridan's Doctrine of Connotation', in *The Logic of John Buridan*, ed. J. Pinborg, Copenhagen, 1976.
'Some Fourteenth Century Tracts on the *Probationes Terminorum*', *Artistarium*, 3, 1982.
Dondaine, A. 'Un commentaire scripturaire de Roland de Crémone, "Le livre de Job" ', *Arch. Frat. Pred.*, 11, 1941, 109–37.
Dondaine, H. F. 'Le *De 43 Quaestionibus* de Robert Kilwardby', *Arch. Frat. Pred.*, 47, 1977, 5–50.
Ebbesen, S. 'Paris 4720A, a Twelfth Century Compendium of Aristotle's *Sophistici Elenchi*', *Cahiers*, 10, 1973.
Ehrle, F. 'Der Kampf um die Lehre des hl. Thomas von Aquin in den ersten 50 Jahren nach seinem Tod', *Zeitschrift für Kathol. Theologie*, 37, 1913, 266–318.
Evans, G. R. 'Boethian and Euclidean Axiomatic Method in the Theology of the Later Twelfth Century', *Archives internationales d'histoire des sciences*, 30.105, 1980.
Alan of Lille, Cambridge, 1983.
The Language and Logic of the Bible: the Earlier Middle Ages, Cambridge, 1984.
Fierville, C. '*Une grammaire latine inédite du xiiie siècle*', Paris, 1886.
Fraenkel, P. '*Testimonia Patrum*: the Function of the Patristic Argument in the Theology of Philip Melanchthon', *Travaux d'humanisme et renaissance*, Geneva, 1961.
Franzesi, R. 'Dogmatic Theology in the Vernacular Sermons of St. Bernardine', *Franciscan Studies*, 25, 1944, 389–405.
Gál, G. 'Adam of Wodeham's Question on the *Complexe Significabile* as the Immediate Object of Scientific Knowledge', *Franciscan Studies*, 37, 1977, 66–102.
Gilson, J. P. 'Friar Alexander and his Historical Interpretation of the Apocalypse', *Coll. Franc.*, 2, ed. C. L. Kingsford *et al.*, Manchester, 1922.
Guisberti, F. 'A Treatise on Implicit Propositions from around the Turn of the Twelfth Century', *Cahiers*, 21, 1977, 45–115.
Gogan, B. *The Common Corps of Christendom*, Studies in the History of Christian Thought, 26, Leiden, 1982.
Grant, R. M. *The Letter and the Spirit*, London, 1957.
Green-Pedersen, N. J. 'Discussions about the Status of *Loci Dialectici* in Works from the Middle of the Thirteenth Century', *Cahiers*, 20, 1976, 27–78.
'Two Early Anonymous Tracts on Consequences', *Cahiers*, 35, 1980.

Guyot, B.-G. 'Questiones Guerrici, Alexandri et Aliorum Magistrorum Parisiensium', *Arch. Frat. Pred.*, 32, 1962, 5–125.

Gyekye, K. 'The Terms *Prima Intentio* and *Secunda Intentio* in Arabic Logic', *Speculum*, 46, 1971, 32–8.

Hagen, K. *A Theology of Testament in the Young Luther: The Lectures on the Hebrews*, Leiden, 1974.

Hargreaves, H. 'Popularising Biblical Scholarship: the Role of the Wycliffite *Glossed Gospels*', *The Bible and Mediaeval Culture*, ed. W. Lourdaux and D. Verhelst, Louvain, 1979, 171–89.

Heinimann, S. 'Zur Geschichte der grammatischen Terminologie im Mittelalter', *Zeitschrift für romanische Philologie*, 79, 1963, 23–37.

Henry, D. P. *The Logic of St. Anselm*, Oxford, 1967.

Henschel, M. 'Figuralbedeutung und Geschichtlichkeit', *Kerygma und Dogma*, 5, 1959, 306–17.

Hinnebusch, W. A. *The Early English Friars Preachers*, Rome, 1951.

Holeczek, H. *Humanistische Bibelphilologie als Reformproblem bei Erasmus von Rotterdam, Thomas More und William Tyndale*, Leiden, 1975.

Hudson, A. 'The Expurgation of a Lollard Sermon-Cycle', *Journal of Theological Studies*, 22, 1971, 451–66.

'A Lollard Sermon-Cycle and its Implications', *Medium Aevum*, 40, 1971, 142–56.

'A Lollard Mass', *Journal of Theological Studies*, 23, 1972, 407–19.

Hurley, M. '*Scriptura Sola*: Wyclif and his Critics', *Traditio*, 16, 1960, 275–352.

Iwakuma, Y. '*Instantiae* Revisited', *Cahiers*, 44, 1983, 61–80.

(with S. Ebbesen) '*Instantiae* and the Twelfth Century Schools', *Cahiers*, 44, 1983, 81–5.

Jayne, S. *John Colet and Marsilio Ficino*, Oxford, 1963.

Jeauneau, E. 'Nani gigantum humeris insidentes', *Vivarium*, 5, 1967.

Jones, W. R. 'Lollards and Images: the Defence of Religious Art in Later Mediaeval England', *Journal of the History of Ideas*, 34, 1973, 31.

Kaminsky, H. *A History of the Hussite Revolution*, Berkeley and Los Angeles, 1967.

Käppeli, T. 'La raccolta di discorsi e di alti scolastici di Simone da Cascina O.P. (d. c. 1420)', *Arch. Frat. Pred.*, 12, 1942, 185–246.

Kingdon, R. M. 'Peter Martyr Vermigli and the Marks of the True Church', in Church, F. Forrester *et al.* (ed.), *Continuity and Discontinuity*.

Klauch, H. F. 'Theorie der Exegese bei Bonaventura', *S. Bonaventura*, 4, Rome, 1974, 71–128.

Kneale, W. and M. *The Development of Logic*, Oxford, 1962.

Kneepkens, C. H. 'The *Relatio Simplex* in the Grammatical Tracts of the Late Twelfth and Early Thirteenth Century', *Vivarium* 15, 1977.

Knudsen, C. 'Ein Ockhamkritischer Text zu Signifikation und Supposition und zum Verhältnis von erster und zweiter Intention', *Cahiers*, 14, 1975, 1–26.

Krewitt, U. *Metaphor und tropische Rede in der Auffassung des Mittelalters*, Supplement to *Mittellateinisches Jahrbuch*, 7, Ratingen, 1971.

Kristeller, P. O. *Il Pensiero Filosofico di Marsilio Ficino*, Florence, 1953.

'Humanism and Scholasticism in the Italian Renaissance', *Studies in Renaissance Thought and Letters*, Rome, 1955, 553–84.

Landgraf, A. *Dogmengeschichte der Frühscholastik*, 3, 1, Regensberg, 1954.

Lares, M.-M. 'Types et optiques de traductions et "adaptations" de l'Ancien Testament en anglais du haut moyen âge', *The Bible and Mediaeval Culture*, ed. W. Lourdaux and D. Verhelst, Louvain, 1979, 70–88.

Law, V. 'Normative Grammar in the Thirteenth Century', *Proceedings of the Convegno Internazionale di Studi*: Aspetti della letteratura latina nel secolo 13, Perugia, forthcoming.

Leff, G. *Bradwardine and the Pelagians*, Cambridge, 1957.

The Universities of Oxford and Paris in the Thirteenth and Fourteenth Centuries, New York, 1968.

William of Ockham, Manchester, 1975.

The Dissolution of the Mediaeval Outlook, New York, 1976.

Little, A. G. (ed.), *Liber Exemplorum ad Usum Praedicantium*, Aberdeen, 1908.

Llinares, A. 'Théorie et practique de l'allégorie dans le *livre de contemplació* de Raymond Lulle', AHDLMA, 39, 1972, 190–36.

Lubac, H. de *Exégèse médiévale*, Paris, 1959, 2 vols.

McCord Adams, M. 'Ockham's Theory of Natural Signification', *The Monist*, 61, 1978.

Maierù, A. *Terminologia logica della Tarda Scholastica*, Rome, 1972.

Manselli, R. 'L'Apocalisse e l'interpretazione Francescana della storia', *The Bible and Mediaeval Culture*, ed. W. Lourdaux and D. Verhelst, Louvain, 1979, 157–70.

Matthews, G. B. 'Supposition and Quantification in Ockham', *Nous*, 7, 1973, 13–24.

Meersseman, G. 'La bibliothèque de la Minerve au XV siècle', *Mélanges A. Pelzer*, Louvain, 1947.

Miles, L. *John Colet and the Platonic Tradition*, London, 1962.

Mohrmann, C. *Etudes sur le latin des chrétiens*, Paris, 1961.

Murphy, J. J. (ed.), *Three Mediaeval Rhetorical Arts*, California, 1971.

Mediaeval Rhetoric, Toronto, 1972.

Mediaeval Eloquence, California, 1978.

Nappo, I. C. 'La Postilla in Marcum di Giovanni de Rupella – suoi riflessa nella Summa Halesiana', *Archivum Franciscana Historicum*, 50, 1957, 332–47.

Nielsen, O. L. 'Thomas Bradwardine's Treatise on *Incipit* and *Desinit*: Edition and Introduction', *Cahiers*, 42, 1982.

Oberman, H. A. *Forerunners of the Reformation*, London, 1967.

Masters of the Reformation, tr. D. Martin, Cambridge, 1981.

O'Carroll, M. 'The Educational Organisation of the Dominicans in England and Wales, 1221–1348', *Arch. Frat. Pred.*, 50, 1980, 23–61.

O'Carroll, M. R. *Thomas Stapleton and the Counter Reformation*, Yale, 1964.

Øhrstrøm, P. 'Richard Lavenham on Future Contingents', *Cahiers*, 44, 1983, 180–6.

Olin, J. C. *Christian Humanism in the Reformation: Selected Writings of Erasmus*, New York, 1965.

Østerrgaard-Nielsen, H. 'Scriptura sacra et viva vox', *Forschungen zur Geschichte und Lehre des Protestantismus*, 10, Munich, 1957.

Ottaviano, C. *Guglielmo d'Auxerre*, Biblioteca di Folosofia e Scienza, 12, Rome, 1950.

Ozment, S. *The Age of Reform, 1250–1550*, Yale, 1980.

Padley, G. A. *Grammatical Theory in Western Europe, 1500–1700*, Cambridge, 1976.

Payne, J. B. 'Erasmus and Lefèvre d'Etaples as Interpreters of Paul', *Archiv für Reformationsgeschichte*, 65, 1974, 54–83.

Pelster, A. 'An Oxford Collection of Sermons of the End of the Thirteenth Century', *Bodleian Quarterly Record*, 6, 67, 1930.

Pesch, C. *Praelectiones Dogmaticae*, Freiburg, 1924.

Pinborg, J. 'Die Entwicklung der Sprachtheorie im Mittelalter', *Beiträge zur Geschichte der Philosophie und Theologie des Mittelalters*, 42, 2, Munster, Copenhagen, 1967.

(ed.), *The Logic of John Buridan*, Copenhagen, 1976.

'Radulfus Brito on Universal', *Cahiers*, 35, 1980, 56–140.

Reeves, M. *The Influence of Prophecy in the Later Middle Ages*, Oxford, 1969.

Richter, M. 'Latina lingua: sacra seu vulgaris?', *The Bible and Mediaeval Culture*, ed. W. Lourdaux and D. Verhelst, Louvain, 1979, 16–57.

Riehle, W. *Studien zur englischen Mystik der Mittelalters unter besonderer Berücksichtigung ihrer Metaphorik*, Heidelberg, 1977, tr. B. Standring, London, 1981.

Ritter, G. *Studien zur Spätscholastik*, 2, Heidelberg, 1922, repr. 1975.

Robertson, D. W. 'Frequency of Preaching in Thirteenth Century England', *Speculum*, 24, 1949, 376–88.

Robson, J. A. *Wyclif and the Oxford Schools*, Cambridge, 1961.

Rouse, R. H. and M. A. 'Biblical *Distinctiones* in the Thirteenth Century', AHDLMA, 41, 1974, 27–37.

'The Verbal Concordance to the Scriptures', *Arch. Frat. Pred.*, 44, 1974, 5–30.

Schuessler, H. 'Sacred Doctrine and the Authority of Canonistic Thought on the Eve of the Reformation', *Reform and Authority in the Mediaeval and Reformation Church*, ed. G. F. Little, Washington, 1981.

Siekaniec, L. 'Duns Scotus and the English Reformation', *Franciscan Studies*, 23, 1942, 141–6.

Sirridge, M. 'Socrates' Hood. Lexical Meaning and Syntax in Jordanus and Kilwardby', *Cahiers*, 1944, 102–21.

Smalley, B. 'Andrew of St. Victor, a Twelfth Century Hebraist', RTAM, 10, 1938.

'The School of Andrew of St. Victor', RTAM, 11, 1939.

'Two Biblical Commentaries of Simon of Hinton', RTAM, 13, 1946, 57–85.

'Some Exegetical Works of Simon of Hinton', RTAM, 15, 1948, 97–106.

'The *Quaestiones* of Simon of Hinton', *Studies in Mediaeval History presented to F. M. Powicke*, ed. R. W. Hunt, W. A. Pantin and R. W. Southern, Oxford, 1948.

'William of Middleton and Guibert of Nogent', RTAM, 16, 1949, 281–91.

'A Commentary on the Hebraica by Herbert of Bosham', RTAM, 18, 1951, 29–66.

The Study of the Bible in the Middle Ages, 2nd ed., Oxford, 1952.

'A Commentary on the Hexameron by Henry of Ghent', RTAM, 20, 1953, 60–101.

'John Wyclif's *Postilla super Totam Bibliam*', *Bodleian Library Record*, 4, 1953, 186–205.

'Robert Holcot, O.P.', *Arch. Frat. Pred.*, 26, 1956, 5–97.

English Friars and Antiquity, Oxford, 1960.

'The Gospels in the Paris Schools in the Late Twelfth and Early Thirteenth Centuries', *Franciscan Studies*, 39, 1979, 230–55 and 40, 1980, 298–369.

Studies in Mediaeval Thought and Learning, Oxford, 1979.

Smith, G. Gregory (ed.), *Elizabethan Critical Essays*, Oxford, 1904.

Sneddon, C. R. 'The "Bible du xiii^c siècle": its Mediaeval Public in the Light of its Manuscript Tradition', *The Bible and Mediaeval Culture*, ed. W. Lourdaux and D. Verhelst, Louvain, 1979, 127–40.

Solomon, D. M. 'The Sentence Commentary of Richard Fishacre and the

Apocalypse Commentary of Hugh of St. Cher', *Arch. Frat. pred.*, 46, 1976, 367–77.

Southern, R. W. *Mediaeval Humanism*, Oxford, 1970.

Spade, P. V. *The Mediaeval Liar: a Catalogue of the Insolubilia-Literature*, Toronto, 1975.

'Ockham on Terms of First and Second Imposition and Intention, with Remarks on the Liar Paradox', *Vivarium*, 19, 1981, 47–55.

Spicq, C. *Esquisse d'une histoire de l'exégèse latine du moyen âge*, Paris, 1944.

Spinka, M. *John Hus at the Council of Constance*, New York, London, 1965.

Stegmuller, F. *Repertorium Biblicum Medii Aevi*, Madrid, 1940– .

Steinmetz, D. C. 'Hermeneutic and Old Testament Interpretation in Staupitz and the Young Martin Luther', *Archiv für Reformationsgeschichte*, 70, 1979, 24–58.

Strauss, G. *Luther's House of Learning*, Baltimore, 1978.

Tachau, K. 'Adam Wodeham on First and Second Intentions', *Cahiers*, 35, 1980, 29–55.

Théry, P. G. 'Thomas Gallus; aperçu biographique', AHDLMA, 12, 1939, 141–208.

Thompson, S. H. 'The Philosophical Basis of Wyclif's Theology', *Journal of Religion*, 11, 1931, 86–116.

Thouzellier, C. 'L'Emploi de la Bible par les Cathares au xiiie siècle', *The Bible and Mediaeval Culture*, ed. W. Lourdaux and D. Verhelst, Louvain, 1979, 141–56.

Torrell, J. P. 'Théorie de la prophétie et la connaissance aux environs de 1230', SSL, 40, 1977.

Trapp, D. 'Peter Ceffons of Clairvaux', RTAM, 24, 1957, 101–55.

Tugwell, S. *Early Dominicans*, London, 1982.

Ullman, B. L. *Studies in the Italian Renaissance*, Rome, 1955.

Van Dyk, J. 'Thirty years since Stegmüller', *Franciscan Studies*, 39, 1979, 255–315.

Vignaux, P. 'Luther, Commentateur des *Sentences*, Livre I, Distinction XVII', *Etudes de philosophie médiévale*, Paris, 1935.

Weisheipl, J. A. 'The Curriculum of the Faculty of Arts, at Oxford in the Early Fourteenth Century', *Mediaeval Studies*, 26, 1964, 142–85.

'Developments in the Arts Curriculum', *Mediaeval Studies*, 28, 1966, 151–75.

Friar Thomas d'Aquino, Oxford, 1974.

Welter, J. T. *L'Exemplum dans la littératur religieuse et didactique du moyen âge*, Paris, 1927.

Wickstead, P. H. and Gardner, E. G. *Dante and Giovanni de Vigilio*, London, 1902.

Zafarana, Z. 'La predicazione ai laici dal secolo xiii al xiv', *Studi Medievali*, 24, 1983, 265–74.

INDEX

190